The Secret to Maximizing Profitability

The Secret to Maximizing Profitability

A Business Novel on How to Successfully Combine the Theory of Constraints, Lean, and Six Sigma to Drive Profit Margins to New Levels

By
Bob Sproull

Routledge
Taylor & Francis Group

A PRODUCTIVITY PRESS BOOK

First edition published in 2020
by Routledge/Productivity Press
52 Vanderbilt Avenue, 11th Floor New York, NY 10017
2 Park Square, Milton Park, Abingdon, Oxon OX14 4RN, UK

Routledge/Productivity Press is an imprint of Taylor & Francis Group, an Informa business

No claim to original U.S. Government works

Printed on acid-free paper

International Standard Book Number-13: 978-0-367-41052-0 (Paperback)
International Standard Book Number-13: 978-0-367-41574-7 (Hardback)
International Standard Book Number-13: 978-0-367-81530-1 (eBook)

Library of Congress Cataloging-in-Publication Data

Names: Sproull, Robert, author.
Title: The secret to maximizing profitability : a business novel on how to
successfully combine the theory of constraints, lean, and six sigma to
drive profit margins to new levels / Bob Sproull.
Description: 1st Edition. | New York : Routledge, 2020. | Includes
bibliographical references and index.
Identifiers: LCCN 2019035216 (print) | LCCN 2019035217 (ebook) | ISBN
9780367410520 (paperback) | ISBN 9780367415747 (hardback) | ISBN
9780367815301 (ebook)
Subjects: LCSH: Lean manufacturing. | Production management. | Theory of
constraints (Management) | Six sigma (Quality control standard)
Classification: LCC HD58.9 .S687 2020 (print) | LCC HD58.9 (ebook) | DDC
658.4/013--dc23
LC record available at https://lccn.loc.gov/2019035216
LC ebook record available at https://lccn.loc.gov/2019035217

Visit the Taylor & Francis Web site at
http://www.taylorandfrancis.com

Contents

Author

Bob Sproull is an Independent Consultant and the owner of Focus and Leverage Consulting. Bob is a certified Lean Six Sigma Master Black Belt and a Theory of Constraints Jonah. Bob has served as a Vice President of Quality, Engineering, and Continuous Improvement for two different manufacturing companies, was General Manager for a manufacturing company, has an extensive consulting background in Healthcare, Manufacturing, and Maintenance, Repair, and Overhaul (MRO), and focuses on teaching companies how to maximize their profitability through an integrated Lean, Six Sigma, and Constraints Management improvement methodology. Bob is an internationally known speaker and author of numerous white papers and articles on continuous improvement. His background also includes nine years with the Presbyterian University Hospital complex in Pittsburgh, Pennsylvania, where he ran the Biochemistry Department at Children's Hospital, performed extensive research in breakthrough testing methods, and assisted with the development of organ transplant procedures. Bob completed his undergraduate work at the University of Pittsburgh and University of Rochester with a dual math/physics major. A results-driven Performance Improvement Professional with a diverse healthcare, manufacturing, MRO, and technical background, he has significant experience appraising under-performing companies, developing and executing highly successful improvement strategies based upon the integration of Lean, Six Sigma, and Constraints Management methodology. Bob is the author of four books, including *The Focus and Leverage Improvement Book* (CRC Press/ Taylor & Francis, 2018); *The Problem-Solving, Problem-Prevention, and Decision-Making Guide—Organized and Systematic Roadmaps for Managers* (CRC Press/Taylor & Francis, 2018); *The Ultimate Improvement Cycle: Maximizing Profits through the Integration of Lean, Six Sigma, and the Theory of Constraints* (Productivity Press, 2009); *Process Problem Solving: A Guide for Maintenance and Operation's Teams* (Productivity Press, 2001); and *Theory of Constraints, Lean, and Six Sigma Improvement Methodology: Making the Case for Integration* (Productivity Press, 2019). In addition, he is co-author of *Epiphanized: Integrating Theory of*

Constraints, Lean and Six Sigma (North River Press, 2012); *Epiphanized: A Novel on Unifying Theory of Constraints, Lean, and Six Sigma*, Second Edition; and *Focus and Leverage: The Critical Methodology for Theory of Constraints, Lean, and Six Sigma* (TLS).

Degrees, Certifications, and Memberships:

- Bachelor of Science Equivalent in Math and Physics, University of Rochester
- Certified Lean Six Sigma Master Black Belt, Kent State University
- Certified Six Sigma Black Belt, Sigma Breakthrough Technologies, Inc.
- TOCICO Strategic Thinking Process Program Certificate
- TOC Thinking Processes (Jonah Course) L-3 Communications
- Critical Chain Expert Certificate, Realization Technologies
- Lean MRO Operations Certificate, University of Tennessee

Bob resides in Prattville, Alabama.

Introduction

The underlying reason I decided to write this book was because of all the emails I have received asking me to please write another book, but this time please use a business novel format. Apparently, Bruce Nelson and my books, *Epiphanized* and its sequel, *Focus and Leverage* were very popular with our audience. And while this book is not a sequel to *Focus and Leverage*, it is written in the same style as both of its predecessors. So, I'm hoping that *The Secret to Maximizing Profitability* is an enjoyable read for everyone. Also, you will notice as you read this book that I have repeated the same key points in multiple chapters. I did this because these key points are imperative to learn for anyone attempting to improve their company's profitability. So, by repeating them in multiple settings, it is my belief that they will be learned faster by those not familiar with them, especially as they relate to improving profitability.

This book lays out, as the title suggests, the real secret to maximizing your company's profitability. While many companies have implemented improvement initiatives like Six Sigma and Lean Manufacturing, there is a missing link which when discovered and implemented, will take these same companies to profit levels not seen before. This missing link is the Theory of Constraints (TOC) and when it's combined with Lean and Six Sigma, amazing things will be sure to follow.

In this book, I walk you through the step-by-step method on how to combine these three methodologies with the result being significant improvements to flow, major improvements in variation, substantial reductions in waste, superior on-time delivery, and ultimately, maximized profitability. I have been using this integrated methodology for years, and each time, the results realized were well beyond what the leadership teams had experienced before.

In Chapter 1, I lay the foundation for a company struggling to be profitable enough to satisfy their Board of Directors. Their story begins with a man named Mark Roder, who has just left a meeting with the Board of Directors of a portfolio of companies, including his own company, Tires for All. Mark is the General Manager of Tires for All, a company that manufactures tires and rubber articles for the automotive and trucking industry. Mark's meeting with the Board did not go well as his reported profit margins were not high enough to satisfy the Board. Because of his low profit margins, Mark is given an ultimatum to either improve his profitability, or else! And the "or else" is the potential for Mark to lose his job.

In Chapter 2, I lay out the basics of Six Sigma in very simple terms. Mark has been reading about this improvement methodology and decides that he wants to try this method at Tires for All, to "right the ship" before drastic action is taken by the Board of Directors. Weeks of training take place at Tires for All to a plethora of employees on Six Sigma, and they even hire a Six Sigma Master Black Belt to help with their improvement efforts. Although improvements to their profit margins are the result of Six Sigma, the level of profitability is not enough to satisfy the Board of Directors. Although the Board recognizes that improvements have been made at Tires for All, Mark is given another ultimatum, so he begins looking elsewhere for another potential improvement methodology. What he finds is Lean Manufacturing.

In Chapter 3, I lay out the basics of Lean Manufacturing, again in simple terms. Mark is very excited about pursuing this as a way to realize much better improvements to his bottom line. He orders books, reads them, and then sends his Six Sigma Master Black Belt to a weeklong training session on Lean. He also arranges for Lean to be taught to all the employees at his plant. He's excited because he learned that Lean is all about identifying and removing excessive waste within his processes and he is convinced that this is the method that will significantly improve his bottom line. And again, as with Six Sigma, bottom-line improvements are realized using Lean, but they're not at the level he wanted to see. At the end of this chapter, Mark is at a restaurant and overhears a group celebrating their recent success using a different improvement initiative which took their profit levels very high. Upon discussions with them, he is given the name and a business card of the consultant that helped the company make their improvements.

Chapter 4 begins with a call to the consultant he learned about from the group celebrating their achievements. After a brief discussion with Bob Nelson, the improvement consultant, Mark invites him to come to Tires for All to have a discussion with him about his apparently different improvement methodology. Mark looked online and found Bob's website, Focus and Leverage Consulting, which stated, *I fix broken companies and make good companies great!* Mark continued reading and another comment caught his eye which read, *I change the way you think, so you can change the way you operate.* In this chapter, the concept of *focus and leverage* is learned and grasped by Mark as he learns about the Theory of Constraints. In any improvement initiative, knowing where to focus improvements is critical, and in this chapter, I will present the "how to" of this approach.

In Chapter 5, Mark learns about the Theory of Constraint's Five Focusing Steps and how they can be used to make dramatic improvements to manufacturing systems. In this chapter, Mark also becomes familiar with the various types of constraints that can exist within companies and within their systems. For those not familiar with the different types of constraints that can exist, this chapter provides a basic description of each type. After all that Bob Nelson taught Mark, Bob is offered a contract to come consult at Tires for All, which he accepts. And with this, Tires for All's improvement effort kicks off.

In Chapter 6, I present how by combining TOC with Lean and Six Sigma, major improvements will be achieved. This is the beginning of Tires for All's improvement journey where they learn about the absolute power of combining the Theory of Constraints with their already learned Six Sigma and Lean Manufacturing knowledge and experience. Tires for All also learns about a different type of Accounting that will change their course of history going forward. Their Director of Finance, Tom Mahanan, is one of the first to fully grasp and understand the potential future benefits of using Throughput Accounting to make real-time financial decisions. In this chapter, I will demonstrate how Throughput Accounting differs from traditional Cost Accounting and why it is the best method for making financial decisions.

As a result of his learning, Tom Mahanan becomes deeply involved in Tires for All's improvement journey. Tom realizes the problems associated with making financial decisions using traditional Cost Accounting as the basis for these decisions. Perhaps the most important learning in this chapter is that the real key to profitability should be based on how much money can be made, rather than how much money can be saved, and as you will see, the methodology for these two approaches are vastly different.

In Chapter 7, I present several key learnings for Tires for All, one of which is the importance of selecting and using the right performance metrics. They also learn that the performance metric efficiency, if measured in non-constraints and pushed higher, will do more harm than good. Tom Mahanan becomes even more involved in Tires for All's improvement effort and begins training the staff on the Theory of Constraints and the new accounting system. Chris Samuels, the head of the local union, is convinced that Tires for All's new direction will result in a better place for his fellow union employees and even volunteers to lead one of the improvement teams. In this chapter, I explain why it's so important to have the total involvement of all employees.

In Chapter 8, I present a Theory of Constraints parts replenishment solution that typically results in a 50 percent reduction in parts inventory while virtually eliminating stock-outs. Tires for All learns all about the Theory of Constraints Replenishment Solution, which is a much different way of ordering raw materials and parts necessary to produce their tires and rubber articles. Learning this replenishment method is a real eye-opener for Tires for All, but especially Tom. In this chapter, I present how this solution can be implemented in any type of manufacturing company.

In Chapter 9, I present a different type of planning and scheduling system that is based upon the teachings of the Theory of Constraints. If your company uses an Enterprise Resource Planning (ERP) system, you will see that this method can be integrated with it. Tires for All learns about a new methodology used to manage and use their existing planning and scheduling system. They learn that in a Theory of Constraints environment, production planning and scheduling is done with a tool known as the Drum Buffer Rope, coupled with Buffer Management. They learn that Drum Buffer Rope is designed to regulate the flow of work-in-process through a production line based upon the pace of the slowest resource, the constraint operation. Tires for All also learns that this method contains a shipping schedule, a constraint schedule, and a material release schedule which are all tied to the constraint schedule. Here you will learn how these components all work together to maximize your company's ability to ship products on time, while minimizing your work-in-process inventory.

In Chapter 10, Bob Nelson, Tires for All's improvement consultant, explains in detail, how to combine the best of Theory of Constraints, Lean Manufacturing, and Six Sigma. He first introduces what he has christened the Ultimate Improvement Cycle (UIC) as three, interactive concentric circles, one for TOC, one for Lean Manufacturing, and one for Six Sigma. Bob does a masterful job of presenting the first element of the UIC by presenting the basic requirements taken from each improvement method and how best to combine them into a single improvement methodology. He then presents the specific tools and techniques needed for success in implementing the Ultimate Improvement Cycle. In this chapter, I present the details of how these three methodologies can be combined and then present the basic tools to do so effectively.

In Chapter 11, I lay out all the deliverables you should end up with when you successfully implement the Ultimate Improvement Cycle. Bob Nelson continues his explanation of the Ultimate Improvement Cycle by presenting the expected deliverables when this integrated methodology is implemented at Tires for All.

In Chapter 12, I introduce the reader to another side of the Theory of Constraints known as Logical Thinking Processes (LTPs). I explain that the Theory of Constraints is systemic in nature and strives to identify those few constraints that limit the organization's success in terms of moving in the direction of its goal. I also let the audience know that it's very important to keep in mind that most organizations function as systems, rather than as a collection of processes. Tires for All is then presented the methodology used to create several of the LTPs.

In Chapter 13, I present a relatively new tool known as the Goal Tree. The Goal Tree is used to assess your organization's current state and then used to develop a strategic improvement plan. Tires for All learns about this new tool, which is used to create their own strategic improvement plan. This tool, above all others they have learned so far, is a true game changer for Tires for All because it lays the foundation for significant improvements to all areas of the company.

In Chapter 14, I explain the details of how to use the Goal Tree and then present how Tires for All creates their own Goal Tree and how they use it to assess their organization for strengths and weaknesses. This effort, which takes very little time, lays the foundation for the development of their very own strategic improvement plan.

In Chapter 15, the key learning is why the performance metric efficiency, if measured in non-constraints, will tie up cash needlessly and seriously erode on-time delivery, Mark is instructed to come to the Corporate Office to explain why his company's efficiency had declined so rapidly. Because, for the most part, Tom has led Tires for All's improvement effort, Mark convinces Tom to go with him and make a presentation to the Board. Tom had prepared a series of graphs that demonstrate what has happened to Tires for All's key performance metrics, including things like on-time delivery, efficiency, and profit margins. Tom does an excellent job of convincing the board that the direction and pathway Tires for All has taken is the right one. The Board is so impressed with what Tom has presented that the Chairman of the Board offers Tom a new role, which is to work directly for the Board of Directors and teach the rest of the other companies in their portfolio what he has done at Tires for All. Tom accepts the offer, but with one significant caveat.

In Chapter 16, Tom begins his new role, responsible for improvement efforts at all the portfolio of companies and he is very successful. The remainder of the book, Chapters 17 through 20, summarizes all the actions taken at the other companies in the Board's portfolio. Part of the agreement Tom made with the Board had to do with how he would be compensated, and if you're a fan of the TV show, *Shark Tank*, you will relate to his deal, especially if you are a fan of Kevin O'Leary.

The genesis behind the Ultimate Improvement Cycle is based upon my many years of analysis of both failures and successes using Lean, Six Sigma, and the Theory of Constraints as stand-alone improvement initiatives. My analysis revealed a common thread between successful initiatives no matter whether they were based on Lean, Six Sigma, or TOC models. The key to success is the leverage point or where the improvement efforts were focused. While eliminating waste, using Lean, and reducing variation using Six Sigma are both critical components of all successful improvement initiatives, where these efforts are focused will determine the ultimate impact on a company's bottom line. By integrating Lean, Six Sigma, and the Theory of Constraints into a single improvement cycle, I have developed a recipe that will maximize your return on investment, cash flow, and net profit.

I think you will find *The Secret to Maximizing Profitability* to be both stimulating and thought provoking, but more importantly, it will provide your organization with a roadmap for maximizing the use of your resources to achieve more bottom-line improvement than you ever imagined possible. I'm convinced that this book lays out the definitive improvement strategy going forward and I'm confident that, if you follow the guidelines I've developed, your company will not only survive in this new global economy, it will flourish, just like Tires for All did.

And as I finish all of my books, I wish you much luck in your improvement journey. But my definition of luck is <u>L</u>aboring <u>U</u>nder <u>C</u>orrect <u>K</u>nowledge … you make your own LUCK!

1

The Company Profile

"What a terrible meeting that was," he thought. Mark Roder was the General Manager of Tires for All, a manufacturing company that primarily produces tires for the transportation and auto industry. Mark had just attended a semi-annual board meeting where he had presented how the company was performing to Tires for All's Board of Directors located in Chicago. Although the company was making money, the numbers did not impress the Board of Directors. As a result, Mark was given an ultimatum to either improve the bottom line of the company or else! And the "or else" was that the board was threatening to send someone into his plant to make improvements to his profit levels or fire Mark and hire a new General Manager.

Tires for All had roughly 700 employees and had been in existence for thirty plus years. There were numerous types of tires produced at their manufacturing facility, located in Western Pennsylvania, including tires for cars and small trucks, but they also produced tires for large trucks as well. They were generally considered one of the "best in the business." Tires for All's innovative tire design had wide acceptance throughout the industry and demand had been increasing significantly, year over year. So much so, that additional manufacturing expansion was becoming necessary in order to meet this increasing demand. Because of this demand requirement, their first major expansion had just been planned and executed where they added a new 60,000 square-feet of additional manufacturing space within their Western Pennsylvania facility.

Tires for All continued their growth through both conventional product line development and significant product diversification. But because demand for their products continued to increase, Tires for All was now contemplating new manufacturing plants for Florida, Alabama, and Georgia. In addition to designing and manufacturing car and truck tires,

Tires for All also produced a variety of other rubber parts for automobiles and smaller trucks and it was these parts that prompted the expansion discussion. But even though their demand was increasing, Tires for All did have some negatives associated with them. Their on-time delivery percentage metric was not as good as it should be, as it was in the low seventies. In addition, their quality levels, which included metrics for scrap and rework, were 10 percent and 30 percent, respectively.

As Mark Roder drove back to his plant in Pennsylvania, he thought about the board meeting he had just attended. He had clearly been given an ultimatum to improve the financials of his plant and he had to do it relatively soon. As he drove, he thought about what might be done differently to turn his facility upward in terms of profitability. The demand for his products was at an all-time high and the cost of expansion would clearly be high, so he believed that the expansion would have a negative impact on their profitability. He thought about some of the areas that might reduce his cost of doing business. Things like the high cost associated with relatively high levels of scrap and repair, shipping costs, labor costs, and others. If he could just come up with a way to improve quality, he believed that would positively impact his bottom line.

One thing Mark knew for certain was that he had to have all his managers directly involved in reducing his plant's costs. He truly believed that by reducing the cost of goods produced, his margins would improve. As he continued driving, he planned a meeting of his managers and direct reports. He called his secretary, Margie Newsome, and asked her to set up a meeting with his direct reports for the next day. Many thoughts came into his mind as to how he could save more money. "I need to have Jim Fredo take a look at the quality of products being produced," he thought. Jim Fredo was his Director of Quality and had been in this role for the past fifteen years. "If Jim can come up with a way to reduce the levels of scrap and rework, this will surely have a positive impact on our bottom line." He continued thinking about how he could reduce costs.

His next thought centered on the Maintenance arena. Frank Delaney was his Director of Maintenance and he thought, "If Frank can come up with ways to reduce equipment downtime, that would surely have a positive impact on quality, and the company's bottom line." "Reducing downtime should improve the flow of products through our processes which should also translate into bottom line improvement," he reasoned. "What else can we do to improve our bottom line?" he thought. "What about Engineering?" he thought to himself.

"If we can reduce the number of steps in our processes, there would be less chance of mistakes, which should have a positive result in terms of the number of hourly workers we need to produce our tires," he thought. "And if we reduce our hourly headcount, that would absolutely improve our product costs!" he reasoned. Bill Simpson was his Director of Engineering, so he made a mental note to make sure that was part of their improvement effort. He continued thinking, "I will need to have Sam Plankton, my Human Resources Manager work closely with Bill as headcount is reduced," he concluded. He continued thinking, "I need to have my Finance Director, Tom Mahanan, involved in this effort as well, just to make sure we capitalize on all headcount reductions." He continued, "I think Sally Hodges, my Industrial Engineering Manager needs to be a part of this effort as well, just so our flow is not interrupted."

As Mark continued his drive home, he continued thinking about how he could improve things moving forward. "I need to get my Operations Manager, Cliff Hastings involved in all of this, just so that our Operations Supervisors understand the level of importance this effort must take on. And what about our Union Head, Chris Samuels?" he thought. "As soon as we start talking about reducing our headcount of hourly employees, Chris is going to be very upset!" He reasoned. "We need to have some kind of plan that will appease Chris," he believed. "Have I included everyone I need?" he thought.

As Mark continued driving, his thoughts moved to Marketing and Sales. "So, if we have streamlined our product flow, our capacity should increase. And if we increase our capacity, we need to bring in more work," he concluded. He decided, "I need to meet with Kathy Hendricks, my Sales Manager, and with Kristin James, my Marketing Manager, and have them work on a new sales and marketing plan. I think I've covered everything now."

Mark finally arrived home at two o'clock in the morning and needless to say, he was very tired from his long drive. But even though he was exhausted, Mark had trouble falling asleep, simply because he knew he didn't have much time to improve things at Tires for All. The Board of Director's message was very clear in that he had been mandated to fix things, or else! He finally fell asleep but continued tossing and turning throughout the night. Obviously, the state of his manufacturing plant was squarely on his mind.

THE MEETING

One by one, Mark's direct reports entered the conference room, not knowing exactly what the subject of this meeting would be. When everyone was seated, Mark began speaking. "Good morning everyone," he started. "As you know, yesterday I made a trip to Chicago to meet with our Board of Directors. The intent of that meeting was originally intended to be an update on our recent expansion, but as the meeting progressed, it took on an entirely different format. Yes, I presented the status of our expansion, but I was then asked to present, and defend, the financial state of our company. I did that and to my surprise, I was told that the Board was not happy with the profitability of our company. I explained that our profit margins were near 10 percent which did not sit well with the members of the Board. I was told by the Chairman of the Board that our bottom line had to improve significantly or else! And the 'or else' he was referring to was that the Board was ready to either send someone in to help us improve or they would simply hire a new General Manager! So, ladies and gentlemen, the purpose of this meeting is to begin our improvement journey! And this journey must come quickly, if we are to survive as a management team!"

Mark's last comment about survival seemed to peak everyone's interest! Mark continued speaking and said, "I have asked Tom Mahanan, our Director of Finance, to meet with each of you individually, so that everyone understands how your activities impact our profitability. We will then form a series of teams to focus efforts on how we intend to reduce costs, so that our profit margins will dramatically improve." He continued, "Does everyone understand the seriousness of what I just said?" Everyone in the room nodded their heads indicating that they did understand.

Before Mark could continue, Jim Fredo, the Director of Quality, raised his hand to ask a question that was probably on everyone's mind. Mark saw that Jim had a question and said, "Do you have a question Jim?" Jim nodded to indicate yes and asked a very simple question. "How much time do we have to make these improvements to our bottom line?" Mark looked him square in the eyes and responded, "My guess is that we probably have no more than three or four months." Jim responded, "So, if our current profit rate is near 10 percent, what is our targeted margins?" Mark replied, "I wasn't given a specific percentage, but I think if we shoot for 15 percent, we'll probably satisfy the Board." "Any other questions before I continue?" Mark asked. When there were no more questions, Mark continued.

"In the past week I have been reading about an improvement methodology known as Six Sigma," he explained. He held up a book and said, "This book, *Six Sigma—The Breakthrough Management Strategy Revolutionizing the World's Top Corporations*, by Mikel Harry and Richard Schroeder [1], lays out what Six Sigma is and how to go about implementing it. Basically, Six Sigma is an improvement methodology that is intended to continuously improve several different aspects of any business. Things like, reducing defects, streamlining the delivery of goods or services to customers, improving profitability, and contributing to the overall health of our company's culture. The good news is that Six Sigma can be applied to virtually all businesses. Very positive results can be expected as long as our management team and employees stay committed to improving operations and the experiences for our customer base." Mark looked around the room to see if all were engaged and they all seemed to be, so he continued.

"Six Sigma uses 'projects' to make improvements and these projects can be in any of the core processes, or support processes, or even external to the company. As I understand it, when Harry and Schroeder introduced their Six Sigma methodology, they laid out eight steps in their process," he explained. He continued, "The first step is to recognize functional problems that link to operational issues. The second step is intended to define the processes that contribute to these functional problems. The third step is that you should measure the capability of each process that offers operational leverage. Step four tells us that we should analyze the data to assess prevalent patterns and trends. Step five explains that we should improve the key product characteristics created by these key processes. In step six, we need to control the process variables that exert undue influence, while step seven tells us to standardize the methods and processes that produce best-in-class performance. And finally, in step eight we need to integrate standard methods and processes into the design cycle. I know that's a lot to digest, but it is my belief that if we follow these steps in order, our company is destined to improve and our profitability should move up," he explained. "And don't worry, we will bring someone in to provide training for everyone on Six Sigma," he stated.

Mark continued, "Somewhere along the way, these eight steps have been distilled into five steps which are Define (D), Measure (M), Analyze (A), Improve (I), and Control (C). So, going forward we will use this DMAIC methodology to improve our processes. Based on what I've read, I believe that there are six simple tools and one a bit more complicated that are critical to master, but more importantly they are critical for us to learn and use. The names of these tools are Run Charts, Pareto Charts, Cause-and-Effect Diagrams, Causal Chains, Control Charts, and Check Sheets. I know you must be wondering what these tools look like, but trust me, all of you will receive training on them in the very near future, but until then, I'll give you a brief description and purpose of all of them."

"Each of these basic tools plays a valuable role in the improvement process and, as such, each has a distinct purpose. The Run Chart serves several important purposes. First, it provides a history of where the process or product variable has been, where it is operating right now, and where it could likely be in the future. When changes are made to our processes, the Run Chart lets us know what the impact of changes were and from a problem-solving perspective, being able to relate changes to shifts in the response variables we are attempting to improve is priceless. By recording the changes that you are making, or have made, directly onto the Run Chart, you get a visual presentation of the impact of the change," Mark described.

"Pareto Charts serve a much different purpose than Run Charts in that they help us identify, focus on, and prioritize our defects and problems that offer the greatest opportunity for improvement. By seeing things in priority order, we have less of a tendency to waste our resources working on the wrong problem. Cause-and-Effect Diagrams help us organize potential causes of defects, problems, and so on, while Causal Chains facilitate the logical dissection of problems by continuing to ask why until we arrive at potential root causes of the problem we are attempting to solve," Mark explained.

"Control Charts provide us with the opportunity to identify sources and types of process variation. They also help us reduce process variation, let us know whether or not our processes are in a state of statistical control, and then allow us to predict what future results might be. And finally, Check Sheets help us pinpoint where on the object the problem or defect is occurring. There is one more tool that I haven't mentioned yet and it is called Design of Experiments or DOEs for short. DOEs are an important part of our improvement initiative and will help us identify which factors and interactions are most responsible for creating defects and excessive variation. DOEs also facilitate the optimization of our process and corresponding response variables. Every successful improvement tool kit must contain DOEs, but they are a bit complicated and I'm not sure how much we will be using them," Mark said as he completed his presentation on these tools.

Mark continued his Six Sigma sermon, "As I understand it, the Six Sigma methodology can be functional for any sized business, no matter whether you manufacture products or deliver a service. And when you use Six Sigma, your primary goal is to reduce defect rates from where they are, to 3.4 defects per million opportunities. But the ultimate objective of Six Sigma should be that your customers have picture-perfect experiences," he explained. He scanned the room and asked, "Are there any questions?"

Cliff Hastings, the Operations Manager asked, "So, what must we do to get started with this Six Sigma effort?" "Good question Cliff," Mark responded. "One of the first things is that we need to put together a leadership team that helps us identify opportunities for improvement, and that will include most of the people in this room," he explained. "We will then appoint a Six Sigma Deployment Leader, but as a management team we will drive our Six Sigma effort by doing some key things." He turned to the flip chart in the conference room and wrote the following:

- We will establish business objectives and the role of Six Sigma to achieve those objectives.
- We will create an environment which permits success including goals, measures, coaching, and communication, among others.
- We, as a group, must actively participate in all or our Six Sigma projects.

He turned to the group and said, "Success of our Six Sigma effort is very much dependent upon the relative interest and time that we as business leaders invest in it." He continued, "Our Six Sigma Deployment Leader will have several key deliverables," and he turned the page on the flip chart and wrote the deliverables as follows:

Deliverables of our Six Sigma Deployment Leader:

- Must develop our Six Sigma strategy and roll-out plan for the overall organization.
- Must provide training or hire a team that includes at least one Master Black Belt (MBB), several Black Belts (BB), a host of Green Belts (GB), and maybe even some Yellow and White Belts.

- Must work with the MBB to identify our organization's goal, vision, and mission.
- Must develop a strategic goal for our facility that will drive Six Sigma to all levels of our organization.

"It's important to understand that the person we designate as the Six Sigma Deployment Leader must help our plant develop the kind of Six Sigma culture that will help cultivate a culture of continuous process improvement," Mark explained. Again, Mark looked around the room and asked if there were questions and to his surprise, many hands went up. Mark pointed to Bill Simpson, his Director of Engineering, for his question. Bill replied, "I hate to sound stupid, but what the hell is a Master Black Belt and the other belts you mentioned?" Heads were nodding up and down indicating that many in the room had the same question.

The Leadership Team's response brought a smile to Mark's face. It wasn't surprising to him that this question had been asked. He began his explanation by saying, "Although Six Sigma training is a very popular term throughout the manufacturing and business world, it's not surprising to me that many people don't understand the difference between the various Six Sigma belts. "And although I'm no expert, I will tell you that the top level is a Master Black Belt, just like you might hear in a martial-arts setting. The Master Black Belt has the highest level of Six Sigma Training and experience and is typically responsible for training and mentoring the other belt levels," he explained as he scanned the room for understanding.

He continued, "At the project level, there are different levels of belts including Black Belts, Green Belts, Yellow Belts, and White Belts. These people all contribute at different levels to conduct projects and make improvements. After the Master Black Belt, the Black Belt is next in line and is responsible for leading problem-solving projects while training and coaching project teams. Next in line is the Green Belt, followed by the Yellow Belt, and, finally, the White Belt rounds off the list at the lowest level of training and experience. The Six Sigma belt system originated sometime in the 1980s, probably at General Electric, which is typically given credit for having initiated one of the first Six Sigma efforts. I'm pretty sure that each color belt represents certified levels of expertise," he explained. "Does this answer your question Bill?" he asked, and Bill indicated that he understood. "Any other questions?" Mark asked.

The Human Resources Manager, Sam Plankton, asked, "So, how are these certifications obtained for these belt categories?" Mark responded, "Great question Sam! Let's begin with the Green Belt Level. Certified Six Sigma Green Belts are part-time change agents and you may get this certification after finishing a Six Sigma Green Belt training program and then taking a certification exam. Six Sigma Black Belt certification is the second level in determining Six Sigma certification eligibility and they are intended to lead project teams and act as mentors to individual team members. Qualifications for a certified Six Sigma Black Belt generally include three to four years of relevant work experience and completion of two to three Six Sigma projects, plus passing a certification exam.

And finally, there is Master Black Belt certification, which is the highest level of Six Sigma certification. To become certified as an American Society for Quality (ASQ) MBB, a candidate must successfully meet all requirements. To be eligible to apply for the MBB examination, a candidate must hold a current ASQ Certified Six Sigma Black Belt (CSSBB) certificate. In addition, a candidate must have either of the following experience levels. At least five years of experience in the role of a Six Sigma BB or MBB or completion of ten Six Sigma Black Belt projects. And Sam, since you asked this question, I'd like you to coordinate all of this training and certifications," Mark explained. Sam responded by asking, "So, where do we get this training and who is going to get the training?" "We'll get to where and who later," said Mark.

"This meeting is now over, and I will be meeting with all of you individually to discuss our next steps," Mark said. "When you leave here today, I want you to think about who you might want to nominate for the Green Belt, Black Belt, Master Black Belt positions and the Six Sigma Deployment Leader that we discussed today. And don't make your choices based upon popularity, but rather who might be most qualified for each position," he explained. And with that, this meeting was adjourned.

REFERENCE

1. Mikel Harry and Richard Schroeder, 2000, *Six Sigma—The Breakthrough Management Strategy Revolutionizing the World's Top Corporations*, Doubleday, a division of Random House, Inc.

2

The Six Sigma Implementation

Meetings were held with Mark's staff and names were submitted for the Green Belt, Black Belt, and Master Black Belt positions, as well as the Six Sigma Deployment Leader. Mark approved all of the recommendations, except for the Master Black Belt. He then met with Sam Plankton, the HR Manager to discuss training requirements. The two decided to have a conference call with the American Society for Quality (ASQ) to discuss training options. The ASQ offered two different training alternatives with one being ASQ would send a trainer or trainers to their manufacturing plant and provide the necessary training for Green and Black Belts, or have the trainees come to their headquarters for training. Mark and Sam decided that they would do the training in-house. They also decided that because of the length of time required to become a Master Black Belt, they would attempt to hire one, hopefully with experience in the tire industry.

Mark held a meeting with his direct reports to get the final list of candidates for Green Belts and Black Belts with the list being as follows, Green Belt, Black Belt, and Master Black Belt candidates:

- Operations:
  - Green Belt: Sylvia Young
  - Green Belt: John Jansen
  - Black Belt: Billy Johnson
  - Black Belt: Tammy Sosa
- Quality:
  - Green Belt: Jim Hansen
  - Black Belt: Sally Denon
  - Master Black Belt: George Johnson

- Engineering:
  - Black Belt: Bobby Billingsley
- Industrial Engineering:
  - Black Belt: Tammy George
- Human Resources:
  - Black Belt: Buck Salinski
- Maintenance:
  - Black Belt: Carol Stone
- Union:
  - Green Belt: Chris Samuels

Mark approved the list of candidates except for the Master Black Belt candidate simply because he felt they couldn't wait for anyone to become a Master Black Belt, as time was a factor in terms of their improvement efforts.

Sam Plankton scheduled the necessary training to be held at their manufacturing facility in Western Pennsylvania. In addition to the belt training, Sam also scheduled a one-day training session for all of the staff members so they could learn about the basics of Six Sigma and what it might do for their plant in terms of improvement. The training sessions were scheduled for the same week, even though they had to pay more for it because of such short notice. Mark felt that time was a factor and he wanted to begin this training now rather than later.

After the one-day training was completed, Mark called another meeting of his staff to discuss potential projects that the Green Belts and Black Belts might work on. Prior to the meeting, Mark had instructed all of his direct reports to bring examples of the potential projects to the meeting, so they could be discussed as a team. In addition to the staff, Mark made sure that all of the future Green Belts and Black Belts were present to hear about the potential improvement projects. Frank Delaney was first to present his project which focused on reducing unplanned maintenance downtime. Frank made his presentation and it was very well received by everyone in attendance. His project called for first collecting downtime data and then analyzing it to determine which downtime cause should be selected as a project and then begin the project.

Next to present was Jim Fredo, and his project centered around collecting defect data as a function of time and then determining which defect was creating the most problems for the plant in terms of meeting delivery dates to their customers. Jim's project was also approved by Mark and everyone else. It was clear to Mark that this project could be one of the more important ones in terms of cost reduction, since scrap represents a significant portion of why the plant's profit levels were not good enough. One by one, each member of the management team presented their selections for projects and in all cases, they were approved.

The next week, representatives from ASQ arrived and spent the entire week training both the Green Belts and Black Belts on the key principles, tools, and methods of Six Sigma. In addition, the company also found and hired a Master Black Belt, so the stage was set for their improvement efforts to begin in earnest. The new Master Black Belt's name was Oscar Francis, and he had a very impressive resume. Oscar had been an MBB for five years for a company that supplied parts to the automobile industry. In the past, Oscar had seven Black Belts and numerous Green Belts reporting to him and came to Tires for All highly recommended.

When all the training was completed, Mark thought it would be a good idea to hold a general meeting of his staff and all of the new Six Sigma belts. Mark welcomed everyone and began. "I want to welcome everyone and congratulations to everyone who successfully completed our Six Sigma training. This marks the beginning of our company-wide improvement efforts and we are expecting major improvements going forward. Just so everyone understands, our Board of Directors is not happy with our profit margins, so as you work through your projects, cost reduction must be foremost on your minds. It is my belief that through the projects you will be a part of, we will be able to significantly reduce costs which should translate into improved profit margins for our company."

Mark continued, "For those of you who haven't yet met our new Master Black Belt, I want to introduce Oscar Francis. Oscar comes to Tires for All with a very impressive background, primarily from the automobile industry. Oscar has completed or has overseen numerous highly successful improvement projects and we look forward to his contribution to Tires for All's bottom line improvement. We have also designated that Oscar will be our Six Sigma Deployment Leader." After his introduction, Mark asked Oscar to address the group.

Oscar stood up and walked to the front of the room and began. "First I'd like to thank you Mark for your glowing introduction and thank you for hiring me. I have reviewed the processes here at Tires for All and I have reached a basic conclusion. Because the tire building process requires extruded material from our Preparation Department, it is my belief that we must start our effort there. If the extruded product has defects that aren't caught before the material is sent to our Assembly Department, then we'll end-up with mountains of tire carcasses that will either be scrapped or will need rework. Because of this, tomorrow, I will hold a meeting with the managers and supervisors from the Preparation Department to discuss possible Six Sigma projects. I will also include the trained Green Belts and Black Belts assigned to the Preparation Department."

Oscar continued, "I will also meet with the leadership and the Green and Black Belts of our Maintenance Department to discuss projects that are aimed at reducing unplanned downtime due to equipment breakdowns. I have looked at the unplanned downtime data and it does not look good. I believe we can make significant improvements in this area which should help improve the flow through our processes. This is especially true in our Assembly area with multiple product guide problems. We will start in these two areas and add more as we move along with our improvement efforts." And with Oscar's comments, the meeting ended.

Bright and early the next morning, Oscar held a meeting with the leadership of the Preparation Department to discuss the direction he wanted to take going forward. In addition to the leadership, Billy Johnson and Tammy Sosa, the two Operation's Blackbelts were in attendance along with the two Operation's Green Belts, Sylvia Young and John Jansen. Oscar began his meeting by first discussing his general approach to Six Sigma and then discussing probable projects in the department. As it turns out, his approach was to first collect real-time data, then analyze the data, and then decide on which projects his team would undertake. One thing that Oscar discovered, during his brief time at Tires for All, was that data collection was not something that had been undertaken seriously. So, because of this lack of existing data, a new, real-time data collection effort was a necessary first step.

Oscar assigned one Black Belt, Billy Johnson, and one Green Belt, Sylvia Young, to establish the data collection effort. The discussion next turned to deciding what characteristics within the Preparation Department on which the data would be collected. After much discussion, it was decided that this decision should be based upon which materials the Assembly Department had the most problems with. Oscar, Billy, and Sylvia decided to meet Cliff Hastings, the Operations Manager, to get his take on which materials gave this area the most problems. They met with Cliff and he thought that they should all go onto the Operations floor and talk with the equipment operators, since they were responsible for accepting or rejecting the incoming products from the Preparation Department. After speaking with five different Assembly machine operators, everyone concluded that there were two products that stood out from the rest in terms of problems. The operators indicated that the inner liner material and the sidewall material were the two biggest problems. When asked what the problems were, the operators indicated that both products had problems with their width, making them unable to be processed through the product guides when fabricating carcasses. (Note: carcasses are what is produced in the Assembly area and are then passed on to the finishing area where tread rubber is added.) So, with this information, the team decided to start their Six Sigma initiative with these two products in the Preparation Department.

During their meetings with the Assembly machine operators, Oscar also asked them if they had any maintenance problems. The operators indicated that they had problems with unexpected downtime on numerous occasions. When asked what those problems were, most indicated that they had electronic problems with the machine used to build their carcasses. In other words, because of these electronic problems, unexpected downtime occurred which delayed carcass completions. So, with this input, it was decided that John Jansen and Tammy Sosa would be assigned to oversee a Six Sigma project in this area.

Teams were formed in both the Preparation and Maintenance Departments with the first step being collection of relevant data on both problems. The teams then used a variety of Six Sigma tools and methods including Run Charts, Cause-and-Effect Diagrams, Scatter Plots, and so on, to analyze the data they had collected. Based upon the analysis of the data, both teams developed Control Charts and were able to identify root causes and then bring both problems under control, which resulted in improvement to the quality of the products being produced in the Preparation Department and significant reductions in unplanned downtime in the Assembly Department. Everyone was very happy with the results obtained so far.

For the next several months, Oscar and his team of belts identified numerous problems, established teams to correct them, and in all cases, improvements were being seen. Mark was very happy with what was happening in his facility and decided to go meet with his Director of

Finance, Tom Mahanan. "Hi Tom, hope all is going well with you?" he asked. "Everything is going well Mark," he responded. "Tom, it's been three months since we started our Six Sigma improvement initiative and I'd like to take a look at how much our profitability has improved," he said. "How long will it take you to update our financials?" asked Mark. Tom responded by saying, "I can have you something within a couple of days, if that's okay with you?" "That's fine Tom, just call me when you have completed the analysis," Mark said. "Why is it that you need this information Mark?" Tom asked. "This morning I received a call from the Chairman of the Board requesting another meeting in Chicago to review our profitability status," said Mark.

Two days later, Tom called Mark and told him that his analysis was ready to discuss with him. "I'll be there in thirty minutes Tom," Mark said. Mark arrived on schedule and was anxious to see the results. Tom presented his calculations and when his presentation seemed to be dragging on, Mark looked Tom in his eyes and said, "Tom, what is our new level of profit?" Tom responded, "Well, based upon the money we spent on Six Sigma training, and our hiring of our Master Black Belt, our margins have risen to about 13 percent." "Thirteen percent? That's all? Our Board of Directors won't be happy to hear that number!" exclaimed Mark. "What were you expecting our new margins to be Mark?" Tom asked. "I was hoping to be around 17 or 18 percent!" said Mark. Tom responded, "Mark, one of the major reasons we haven't seen our margins improve more was because of all the money we spent on training. Plus, we hired a Master Black Belt, which also cost us." "I have to go back to Chicago to present our financials to the Board of Directors in two weeks and I'm very worried about how the Board will react to our new profit margins." And, with that, Mark left and went back to his office.

It had been roughly three months since they had begun their Six Sigma improvement effort and Mark knew they had made improvements. His Six Sigma teams had made significant reductions in both scrap and rework levels on many of the products they produced, but the dollar savings just weren't there in high enough levels to move profitability to significantly higher levels. Based upon what he had read about Six Sigma, he had expected much higher levels of profitability, so he thought, "What are we doing wrong?" He decided to call in his Master Black Belt, Oscar Francis, and have a chat with him about their continuous improvement efforts.

Oscar arrived at Mark's office a short while later and Mark began the discussion, "So, Oscar, I hired you to lead our Six Sigma improvement effort about three months ago. I just met with Tom Mahanan to go over our financial results and to my surprise, our profit margins improved, but on to 13 percent. Based upon your experience with Six Sigma, wouldn't you have expected more of an improvement than that?" Oscar responded, "Mark, improvement takes time." "How much time?" asked Mark. "Most of the time Six Sigma projects take three to six months to complete, so I think if you give this effort a bit more time, we will see higher levels of profitability," Oscar said. "How much more time are you suggesting?" asked Mark. "I'm not sure about exactly how much more time we will need, but trust me, improvements will come, and they will come in a big way," Oscar replied. "Okay Oscar, if you need more time, you'll get it, but I hope we're not talking months?" said Mark.

Oscar then explained, "Mark, if you look at the reduction in scrap and rework, it's been significant over the past few months. In our Preparation Department alone, we've seen a 70 percent reduction in scrap. In our Assembly Department, we've seen a 50 percent reduction in unplanned downtime." "But Oscar, while these numbers are impressive, we're not seeing a significant improvement in the plant's profitability!" Mark replied. "We have fourteen other projects in the works right now and I suspect that if we see the same level of improvement in these, we'll see big improvements to our bottom line," Oscar responded.

Mark continued, "One other area that we're not seeing big improvements is in the area of on-time deliveries. When we started this effort, our on-time delivery was in the neighborhood of 70 percent and after reviewing our most current data, we are hovering around 75 percent." "Again, the improvements will come, but you have to be a bit more patient and let our projects run their course," Oscar replied. "Oscar, I am a very patient man, but even patience has a limit!" Mark replied.

There was one other result that really bothered Mark and that was the level of work-in-process (WIP) inventory that now existed in his facility. "Oscar, the other part that is bothering me is the level of WIP that has grown since we started our Six Sigma improvement initiative," said Mark. "Why has this grown so much?" he asked. Without hesitation, Oscar replied, "Mark, when you reduce the amount of downtime, rework, and scrap, the natural impact of these improvement is that more product flows through the system." "But Oscar, this new level of WIP is negatively impacting both our cash flow and on-time delivery!" replied Mark. "Mark, this too will improve as we complete more projects," Oscar replied. With that, Mark's meeting with Oscar ended.

The next week, Mark began preparing for his meeting with the Board of Directors and needless to say, he was worried about how they would respond to his company's new level of profitability. Increasing from roughly 10 percent to 13 percent was not what he had expected when he embarked on his Six Sigma journey. "Maybe Six Sigma was not the best option for his plant?" he thought. The good news was that every one of their Six Sigma projects had delivered improvements in variability reduction which resulted in much better control of their processes, but he believed the profitability improvement would not be good enough to impress the Board of Directors. "Maybe there's something else out there that would work?" he thought.

It was now time for Mark to travel to Chicago to meet with the Board of Directors, but this time he had decided to fly rather than drive. He arrived at his hotel, checked in and went to his room to review his presentation that he would deliver the next morning. Clearly, Mark was worried about the Board's reaction to his new profitability numbers. When he was finished reviewing his material, he went to dinner at a local restaurant and then returned to his hotel room. He decided to do an internet check to see what else he could find on process improvement. His thought was that if the Board wasn't happy with the results achieved since his last visit, he would have other ideas on how he could make additional improvements.

Mark searched the internet diligently and found what he thought was an interesting subject referred to as Lean Manufacturing. Mark really knew nothing about this improvement methodology but read that a couple of the key points associated with Lean were reduction of waste within the process and making value flow. He thought to himself, "Maybe this could be something that would work well in his factory?" Mark looked online and found several books on the subject and ordered them.

The next morning, Mark woke up early, feeling very anxious about his presentation later that morning. He got dressed, went to breakfast in his hotel, taking his presentation with him for review. On the cab ride to Corporate Headquarters, he thought more about his newly found subject, Lean Manufacturing, wondering just how this might work for him at his plant. He arrived at the Corporate Headquarters building and took the elevator to the twelfth floor and entered the Board's meeting room. To his surprise, all of the Board members were already there. The Chairman of the Board, Jonathan Briggs, welcomed him and took his seat at the end of the table. Mark walked to the front of the room, inserted his thumb drive with his presentation on it and began.

Mark started his presentation with a review of their Six Sigma initiative, explaining how they had gotten his people trained on Six Sigma and hired a Six Sigma Master Black Belt to oversee their improvement effort. One of his slides contained a list of projects they had worked on and gave a status update on each one. He then demonstrated the results they had obtained on the completed projects which were very impressive. In the middle of his presentation, the Board Chairman interrupted him and said, "Mark, while all of this is very impressive, and you and your team are to be congratulated for your efforts so far, our Board would like to hear about your new financials. What is your new level of profitability Mark?"

Mark skipped ahead in his PowerPoint presentation until he came to his slide that contained his plant's new financial results. Much of the slide had the typical Cost Accounting metrics, but at the bottom of the slide was his plant's new profit margin which now stood at 13 percent. A hush came over the conference room until Jonathan asked why the margins were so low? Mark sort of stuttered and simply said, "Improvement initiatives take time and Six Sigma is no different. Plus, we spent a lot of money training our workforce on Six Sigma. I am fully aware that 13 percent is not the profit level the Board was looking for, but I assure you on my next visit it should be significantly higher." "Should be?" asked Jonathan. "My mistake, I meant to say it will be," Mark replied.

There were numerous questions from the various board members and Mark answered them as best he could. Finally, the Chairman of the Board stood up and asked Mark, "When do you want to come back again and give us your new financials?" This question caught Mark completely off guard, but he said, "I think in three months we should see the benefit of our Six Sigma initiative." With that, the chairman ended the meeting and set a date three months from now for a follow-up meeting.

Mark left the board headquarters and took a cab to the airport. He was surprised by the reaction of the Board of Directors at his new profit margins. He was expecting a much more difficult meeting but was happy with the outcome. After all, he had been given an additional three months to improve his margins and he truly believed that in three months his facility would have significant improvements. While sitting in the terminal waiting for his flight, the subject of Lean Manufacturing entered his mind, so he logged on to the internet to see what else he could find on this improvement methodology. He found several case studies and downloaded them so he could read them on his flight home. He also ordered books on Lean and had them overnighted to his plant.

The first case study he read about involved a tire manufacturing facility which, like his own plant, had negative levels of quality and on-time delivery. As he read through this case study, he imagined what could happen at his plant if they could successfully implement their own Lean initiative. In this study, within eight months, profit levels improved by 20 percent due mostly to improvements in their quality levels and product flow. It seemed that the company in this case study had achieved a 50 percent reduction in rework, a 30 percent reduction in scrap levels, and their on-time delivery improved from 75 percent to 85 percent. The second case study involved a company that extruded rubber and they had achieved similar levels of improvement, but in this case, the results were achieved after a full year.

Mark knew that he had to achieve significant improvement in profitability, and he didn't have a year to wait. After all, his next meeting with the Board of Directors was scheduled for three short months from now. As his plane continued flying, Mark thought more and more about this thing called Lean Manufacturing. "Maybe we should pursue this methodology going forward?" he thought to himself.

The next morning after arriving at his plant, he was happy to see the books on Lean Manufacturing sitting on his desk that were delivered overnight and he immediately began reading one of them. He learned that while Six Sigma focused on variation reduction, from what he read, Lean focused on waste reduction. The more he read, the more excited he got as he imagined his processes with much less waste which surely would result in improved profit margins.

3

The Lean Initiative

Mark read the books he had purchased on Lean Manufacturing, and according to him, it was a real eye-opener. He learned all about the various types of waste that existed in virtually all processes. He learned that Lean manufacturing is a whole-systems approach that focuses on identifying and eliminating non-value-added activities within a process. He also learned that Lean attempts to involve everyone in the organization in the quest to eliminate any and all forms of waste everywhere in the process.

Mark also learned that Lean's objectives are to use less human effort, less inventory, less space, and less time to produce high-quality products as efficiently and economically as possible while being highly responsive to customer needs and demands. Lean thinking starts with a conscious effort to define value in very specific terms, through constant dialogue with customers. One other thing that the books on Lean kept mentioning was the concept of value. Mark asked himself the question, "So, just exactly what is value?"

Surprisingly, he also learned that value is not always an easy thing to define. One of the books he read by Womack and Jones [1], *Lean Thinking: Banish Waste and Create Wealth in Your Corporation*, explained that "part of the reason value is hard to define for most producers, is that most producers want to make what they are already making and partly because many customers only know how to ask for some variant of what they are already getting." Womack and Jones further explained that another reason why firms find it hard to get value right is, "that while value creation often flows through many firms, each one tends to define value in a different way to suit its own needs." Mark imagined value at his company as those things that his customers would be willing to pay for, while things like scrap and rework would be non-value-added.

As Mark continued reading, he kept learning new things and he was getting more and more excited about pursuing Lean. Mark thought to himself, "Lean's focus is on the complete elimination of waste everywhere within his company, with waste being defined as 'any activity that engages resources but creates no value.'" "Wow, I can think of many areas in our company where we engage our resources, but we aren't creating any value," he imagined.

Mark continued thinking more about this new concept. He thought, "This list kind of becomes really mind-boggling. Things like mistakes that require repairs or modification, production of parts that haven't been ordered, or that nobody wants; transportation of products within our plant that travel great distances to get from one process step to another; idle time of one process step created by downtime at another, or just differences in processing times; defective or scrap materials." "Hmm," he thought to himself, "If I were to create a list of the actual activities that create value in our plant, it probably wouldn't fill a single page!" With that thought, he began writing down those sources of waste that he knew existed within his plant.

"I know we have overproduction, because I know we produce material for which we don't have orders. And when we overproduce, we generate other waste like overstaffing, storage, and transportation costs because overproduction always results in excess inventory in our plant," he thought. "What else is there?" he thought. "I know we have extended waiting times. I have seen our Assembly workers standing around waiting for materials from our Preparation Department. I've also seen them waiting for tools and supplies that they need to process their own materials. Of course, I've seen them waiting because of equipment downtime. I've also seen them waiting for inspection results and even information," he continued thinking.

Another area Mark imagined was unnecessary transport of materials. He thought, "I know we have to transport raw material, work-in-process (WIP), and even finished goods long distances." "How about over-processing or even incorrect processing?" he thought. "I'm pretty sure we have unnecessary steps or extra effort within our processes that adds little or no value. Things like over-working or over-inspecting a part trying to make it 'perfect,' when perfection isn't required by our customers," he imagined. "Wow, we have tons of waste everywhere," he thought, but he wasn't finished.

"I know we have excess inventory in lots of places," he imagined. "This includes excess raw material, work-in-process, or finished goods that negatively impact our lead times and on-time delivery. And when we have excessive inventory, we have obsolescence, damaged parts, and transportation and storage costs. Excess inventory also hides other problems like defects, machine downtime, flow problems, and so on. We also have lots of unnecessary movement. Things like looking for parts or supplies, stacking and unstacking of parts, walking to get something, reaching, unnecessary twisting and turning, and so on." He continued thinking, "Production of products that result in repairs or scraps, replacement production, re-inspection, late deliveries, or those that require extra inspection, sorting, scrapping, downgrading, or replacement," Mark thought.

When he was finished with his list, he was amazed at how much waste existed in his facility. He thought to himself, "Imagine how removing these sources of waste would positively impact our plant's profitability?" And with that, he continued reading. Womack and Jones [1] say that implementing Lean typically follows five basic steps or principles.

1. Define value from the end customer's perspective with value being defined by the customer.
2. Identify the value stream which is all the actions required to bring products from a concept, through detailed design, to an order, to delivery of the products, to the customer. Womack and Jones state that "value stream analysis will almost always show that three types of actions are occurring along the value stream: (1) Many steps will be found to unambiguously create value; (2) Many other steps will be found to create no value, but to be unavoidable with current technologies and production assets; and (3) Many steps will be found to create no value and to be immediately avoidable." Translated, these three actions are (1) value-added; (2) non-value-added but necessary; and (3) non-value-added. For the non-value-added steps, Lean advocates eliminating them immediately.
3. Once value has been defined and precisely specified and the value stream analyzed with obvious non-value-added steps removed, make the remaining, value-creating steps flow. In this step, the focus is on maximizing value by producing only what's needed in the shortest time possible with the fewest resources needed.

4. Pull to customer demand by producing only at the rate of customer orders and no more. In other words, don't overproduce.
5. Pursue perfection by empowering employees with waste elimination tools to create a culture of continuous improvement.

"Wow," he thought, "That's a lot to digest! I hope as I keep reading, that these five points will be further explained in language I can understand." And with that thought, he continued reading about Lean. He read that in order to better understand how and why Lean works, it's a good idea to also understand the basic Lean building blocks. "Ah, great, here is what I was looking for," he thought as he read about the basic tools, techniques, and methods that are used during a Lean implementation. They included:

1. *5S*: A five-step procedure aimed at fashioning workplace organization and standardization with each step starting with the letter S. The five Ss originated in Japan and are (with the English translation) Seiri (Sort), Seiton (Set in Motion), Seison (Shine), Seiketsu (Standardize), and Shitsuke (Sustain).
2. *Visual Controls*: The assignment of all tools, parts, production procedures, performance metrics, orders, and so on in plain view so that the status of a process step can be understood in fewer than thirty seconds. Typically, one might expect to see things like lights or different colored flags that indicate at a glance the process status.
3. *Standardized Work*: A physical description (many times including photos) of exactly how to perform each job according to prescribed methods (developed with operator assistance), with the absolute minimum of waste.
4. *Cellular Layout*: The layout of a process (machines, materials, supplies, and people) performing different operations in a tight sequence (a manufacturing cell).
5. *One-Piece Flow*: The flow of product through a sequence of process steps that passes one piece at a time, with few interruptions, backflows, scrap, rework, or accumulated inventory.
6. *Quality at the Source*: Quality is the responsibility of the person producing the product with inspection and process control done at the source by the operator prior to passing the product onto the production step.

7. *Quick Changeover*: Being able to change from tooling set or fixtures to another rapidly, on a single machine, to permit the production of multiple products in small batches on the same equipment.

8. *Pull and Kanban*: A system of production and delivery instructions sent from downstream operations to upstream operations that is done so only after a signal, usually in the form of a small card.

9. *Total Productive Maintenance (TPM)*: A series of maintenance methods that assures process equipment will always be available when needed for as long as it is needed with minimal amounts of downtime.

"This is really great stuff," Mark thought as he continued reading. The next subject in the book discussed the tools used in Lean initiatives. The first tool Mark read about was a Value Stream Map (VSM), which is simply all those things we do to convert raw materials into a finished product that creates value. Value is defined as all of those things that a customer is willing to pay for. Mark learned that as a tool or technique, the VSM uses a variety of symbols, or a sort of shorthand notation to depict various elements within the process. For example, a triangle with a capital "I" inside of it represents inventory, with the amount of inventory entered directly beneath the triangle. He also learned that there are various material flow icons, general icons and information flow icons used to represent all of the specific elements within the process. The more he read, the more excited he was becoming. In the book he was reading, there was an example of a VSM (Figure 3.1).

As he was reading about VSMs he wondered, "Why is Value Stream Mapping such an essential tool?" In one of the books he was reading by Rother and Shook [2], he discovered eight different reasons that answered his question. First, it helps you visualize more than just the single process level, that is, Assembly, Finishing, and so on, in production. With the VSM, you can see the flow of the product and the information. The second reason is that mapping helps you see the sources of waste in your value stream that may not be obvious to you without visualizing it. The third reason he read about is that the VSM provides a common language for talking about manufacturing processes. "This is all so interesting," he thought as he kept reading.

The fourth reason listed was that it makes decisions about the flow apparent, so you can discuss them. "That makes perfect sense," he thought

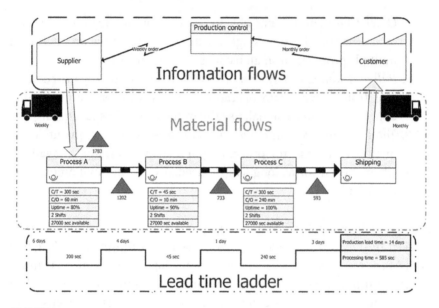

FIGURE 3.1
Example of a Value Stream Map.

to himself. "Otherwise, many details and decisions on your shop floor just happen by default," he thought and continued reading. The fifth reason given was that it ties together lean concepts and techniques, which help you avoid *cherry-picking*. "Cherry-picking is something I understand very well, and it exists within our plant," Mark understood. The sixth reason was that the VSM forms the basis of an implementation plan. By helping you design how the whole door-to-door flow should operate, which is a missing piece in so many Lean efforts, Value Stream Maps become a blueprint for lean implementation. Mark thought, "It's kind of like trying to build a house without a blueprint!"

The seventh reason is that a VSM will demonstrate the linkage between the information flow and the material flow and no other tool that Mark was familiar with does this. The eighth and final reason was that the VSM is much more useful than quantitative tools and layout diagrams that produce a tally of non-value-added steps, lead time, distance traveled, the amount of inventory, and so on. Mark thought, "It seems that value stream mapping is a qualitative tool by which you describe in detail how our plant should operate in order to create flow. It seems that numbers are good for creating a sense of urgency or as before/after measures. I can see that Value Stream Mapping is good for describing what you are actually planning to do to affect those numbers," he thought.

Mark continued reading and learned that you cannot create a Value Stream Map from your office, and you can't do it effectively in a vacuum, because it won't be accurate or even complete. For this reason, the book Mark was reading instructed him not to create a VSM by himself. Instead, other resources like his hourly operators, material handlers, and others should assist in creating the VSM just to make sure all facets of the flow of information and product are included. At this point, Mark thought, "Since we will probably lay off some of our employees to save enough money, this might be a good way to reduce the union's anxiety?"

"So just what should be included in our Value Stream Map?" he imagined. "Well, think about what you are trying to accomplish?" Mark thought, "What are all of the opportunities that could be used to reduce inventory and operating expense and improve our profitability? What about processing and cycle times? Cycle times certainly can have an impact on the rate of generation of inventory. How about delays, don't they negatively impact on-time deliveries? How about equipment downtime? And let's not forget inspection sites as well as defect rates and rework locations." Mark continued thinking, "We definitely want to identify the operations that are constraining our flow through the process and all of the other opportunities that could be used to reduce inventory and operating expense."

He continued reading about step-by-step value-added time, wait times, processing times, cycle times, and lead times and the more he read, the more excited he got! He learned about Value-Added Time (VAT) which was the average total time taken to transform the product into value and this does not include wait times. Wait Times represent the average time that a part waits within a process step before being able to move to the next process step. He imagined, "This might include any drying or curing times, waiting for an inspection to occur, and things like that. There's also Processing Time (PT) which is the average length of time it takes for a single part to be completed by a single process step which should equal wait times plus Processing Times. There's also Cycle Time (CT) which is the average length of time it takes from release of raw materials into the process to completion of finished goods ready to ship. And finally, there's Lead Time (LT) which is the average total elapsed time from receipt of the order from the customer to the receipt of the order by the customer." "Wow," Mark thought, "There certainly are a lot of different times to consider! In reality, many of these things could really be used as performance metrics to track. What other metrics might we consider?" Mark thought to himself. With this in mind, he made a list of things, and their definitions, that might be valuable to track.

1. *Inventory Levels*: The number of individual pieces or parts waiting to be processed in each step of the process.
2. *Capacity*: The average number of pieces or parts that a process step can produce in a given unit of time.
3. *Actual Demonstrated Capacity*: The average total pieces or parts produced/unit of time minus total average scrapped during the same time. This can be any unit of time depending upon the overall speed of the process.
4. *Percent Repaired*: The average number repaired compared with the average total reduced for any unit of time.
5. *Customer demand* or order rate.
6. *Actual rate* to be produced compared with order rate (i.e., takt time).
7. *Average defect rates* and the actual defects based upon inspection data for a given period of time (Pareto chart).
8. *Inspection points* and average inspection time required.
9. *The average downtime rates* and a description of actual downtime based upon maintenance history (Pareto chart).
10. *The number and location of operators* (i.e., how many and where they are).
11. *The average travel time and distance* traversed per any unit of time.
12. *The average percent Order On-Time Completion.*

Mark thought to himself, "While this is a good list of possible things to track, what about materials coming from our suppliers?" He continued thinking, "If I am frequently waiting for raw materials to begin production, or the quality of the incoming raw materials is poor, and I am confident that this supplier is restricting my output and on-time delivery, then these things need to be tracked. While most of the time I am concerned with what goes on inside the walls of my factory that limits our output, it doesn't mean that I should ignore our suppliers. I realize that most of the time the problems I see associated with limited output and less than optimal profit margins are related to internal issues and not external ones."

Mark continued reading and found something referred to as work cells. And while Mark was familiar with the positive effects of implementing Cellular Manufacturing (CM) in workplaces, such as the improved flow through the process, there can be overall cycle time reductions, throughput gains, as well as other benefits. But there is one other positive effect Mark didn't know about that can result from implementing Cellular Manufacturing and that is, they can work to reduce variation. He learned that it is not uncommon for products to travel great distances from machine to machine because of the equipment layout scheme. Because of the location of equipment, it is not uncommon for the parts to travel back and forth between different process steps as they make their way through the process sequence. Mark smiled when he read this because some of his processes are very disjointed, so Cellular Manufacturing could be really good for his plant. These long, drawn-out distances and inflated times can translate directly into routine delays throughout the process, with the ultimate consequence being late deliveries and missed shipment to customers. Mark concluded, "This could be the answer to our late deliveries!"

Mark concluded that Cellular Manufacturing and work cells lie at the heart of Lean Manufacturing with the general benefits being things like simplified flow, cycle time reductions, improved quality, improved intra-process communication, and so on. In cellular manufacturing, equipment and workstations are arranged in close proximity to each other in the normal process sequence. Once processing begins, products move directly from workstation to workstation with the result typically being significant improvements in overall cycle times and vastly improved teamwork and quality. Mark was getting very excited about pursuing Lean and couldn't wait until he met with his staff!

Mark imagined his plant with Cellular Manufacturing and realized its potential positive effects. He thought if we do this correctly, we could have smaller batch sizes, one-piece flow, flexible production, reduced travel time for parts, less equivalent manpower, improved quality, less damaged product, less required space, less obsolescence, immediate identification of problems, reduced walking time, and less lead time, all of which will translate to decreased cycle time, increased throughput, and reduced inventory and operating expense. "Wow!" he thought, "This could take us to the profitability promised land!"

The next day, Mark called a meeting with his staff to go over the results of the board meeting and to let them know that they had three short months to make more improvements to their bottom line. Oscar was in attendance, so Mark asked him to give him an update on recent progress in their Six Sigma initiative. Oscar stood up and said, "We have several projects that I think will deliver big improvements to our bottom line. One project involves improving the quality of our tread rubber coming off of our extruders and another one is aimed at improving the downtime of our carcass machines." Mark asked, "How much improvement do you expect from these two projects Oscar?" Oscar replied, "On the tread rubber one, I expect at least a 50 percent improvement in quality and on the downtime one, I'm estimating at least a 35 percent reduction in downtime on all of the carcass machines." "And how soon do you expect these improvements to be realized Oscar?" Mark asked. "Probably in another two months," Oscar replied. "What other projects are you working on Oscar?" Mark asked.

"We have ten other projects in progress Mark," Oscar said. "Two of the projects are in our tire curing area which are both aimed at reducing downtime on our curing presses, as well as improving quality levels. I fully expect that both of these projects will improve our output and significantly improve our on-time delivery. The other projects we have in place are scattered throughout our plant and are aimed at improving our rework and scrap levels." "How soon do you expect results in the two curing projects?" Mark asked. "I see them both being completed in another month," Oscar said. "Is there any way we can speed these projects up to get results sooner?" Mark asked. Oscar replied, "We will try our best, but results take time."

Mark knew that he had less than three months to make significant improvements to his bottom line, so he set up biweekly reviews of all of the Six Sigma projects. Weeks passed and while the reviews proved to be helpful, Mark was worried about the final outcome of these projects on their bottom line. A week before his next scheduled meeting with the Board of Directors, Mark arranged a meeting with his Finance Director, Tom Mahanan, to review their financials. Tom arrived for their scheduled meeting and took a seat. "Tom, what is our new level of profitability?" Mark asked. Tom replied, "Mark, although we have made progress, I'm sorry to say that our new profit margins are only 15 percent." Mark had a look of panic because he knew that the Board of Directors would not be happy with that number. "Are you sure that's our final number Tom?" Mark asked. "Yes Mark, and that is stretching it," Tom said.

The next week, Mark left for his board meeting and he anticipated that it would not go well. As it turned out, Mark was right. The Chairman of the Board, Jonathan Briggs, explained to Mark that he will give him one more chance to make his company's profit levels acceptable. Mark then asked the Board what levels would be acceptable to them and they told him that the margins must be at least 20 percent! Mark was worried that he would lose his job if he didn't come up with a plan to take profits to this new level. Mark left the meeting and headed to the airport for his flight home. As he was flying, he thought about what his next steps should be. "Lean Manufacturing might be our only hope," he thought.

The next morning, Mark set up a meeting with his staff aimed at accomplishing two things. First, he wanted to review his board meeting outcome and second, he wanted to lay out the basics of Lean Manufacturing. One by one, his staff entered the conference room and sat down, waiting for Mark to arrive. Mark came into the conference room and began. "Ladies and gentlemen, yesterday I met with the Board of Directors and like the last meeting, it did not go well. We have been given an ultimatum that we either improve our profit margins to 20 percent or drastic action would be taken by the Board." That statement got everyone's attention!

Cliff Hastings, the Operations Manager, raised his hand and Mark recognized him. "Mark, do we need to change our direction in order to improve our profit margins?" he asked. "I'm so glad you asked that question Cliff," Mark said. "I have been reading about a different improvement methodology known as Lean Manufacturing. Unlike Six Sigma, which focuses on variation reduction, Lean focuses on reducing waste. It is my belief that this could be the direction we need to take," Mark explained. Cliff responded, "Does this mean we abandon our Six Sigma efforts?" "Hell no, Cliff, we need to continue with it!" Mark exclaimed. "But having said this, it is my belief that Six Sigma is only part of the improvement puzzle," he continued. "Well, what do we need to do to jumpstart our Lean effort?" Cliff asked. "The first thing we need to do is to get some training on Lean for everyone in this plant," Mark responded. "For everyone?" Cliff asked. "Yes, I want everyone to receive some level of training because I want everyone to be active participants in our effort," Mark answered. "Sam and I will set up the training as soon as possible," Mark added. And with that, Mark adjourned the meeting.

Later that day, Sam and Mark met to plan their training strategy. The first thing they did was to search the internet for organizations equipped to deliver training in Lean. They checked the references for each of the candidates and decided to contact an organization known as The Lean Initiative Group. Based upon what they saw on their website, they were equipped to deliver training on all levels at Tires for All, so they contacted them and set up training for the following week.

Mark then called Oscar to his office to find out if he knew about Lean Manufacturing and as it turned out, he had worked for a company in the past that had implemented Lean. Mark told Oscar that he wanted him to "lead the charge" and make Lean part of his arsenal of tools. After much discussion, it was decided that Oscar would attend a week-long, off-site training session on Lean. Again, they contacted The Lean Initiative Group and it just so happened that they had scheduled a Lean Leadership training session for the following week in Pittsburgh. They had a couple of openings, so they were able to include Oscar to be a participant in the training.

The following week The Lean Initiative Group arrived and delivered all of the requested training. In addition, Oscar received his leadership training, so the stage was set for Tires for All to begin their Lean implementation. When the training was completed and Oscar was back from his off-site training session, Mark set up a "Lean Kick-off Meeting" on the shop floor so that everyone could attend. Mark opened the session by welcoming everyone and then he began his presentation. "I called this meeting to make sure everyone understands the significance of why we all went through Lean training. We have been given an ultimatum by our Board of Directors that we must raise our profit margins from where they are, which is about 15 percent, to at least 20 percent. I can't do this without everyone's help, so that is why you have all received the training this week," Mark stated. "Does anyone have any questions?" Mark asked.

Chris Samuels, the union leader at Tires for All, raised his hand. "Yes Chris, do you have a question for me?" asked Mark. Chris indicated that he did and said, "I can assure you that all members of our union will do everything we can to make our profits grow. But my one concern is that there will be layoffs, so is that in the plans?" Mark responded and said, "Good question, Chris. While I can't guarantee that we will not have lay-offs as a result of this effort, I can assure you that every effort will be made to raise our profit margins without layoffs. That would be a last resort." "Okay Mark, I will hold you to that," Chris responded. As there were no more questions, Mark adjourned the meeting.

Over the next several months, the team had implemented a variety of Lean tools and techniques including work cells, a Kanban system, and worked hard to remove much of the waste from the entire process. As a result, it appeared as though much progress was being made in terms of streamlining their processes. Mark was true to his word on no layoffs, but it was getting closer to his next meeting with the Board of Directors, so he needed to get a fresh look at his profit margins. He called a meeting with his staff.

He welcomed everyone to the meeting and asked Tom, his Director of Finance, to let everyone know what the new margins were. Tom had prepared an overhead of the financials and at the bottom of the slide was the new profit margin which was now 19 percent. In addition to the financials, Tom had also prepared a slide with some of their key performance metrics. Mark was very interested in their on-time delivery metric which now stood at 81 percent, which was well below what Mark had expected it to be. Everyone in the room could see that Mark was not a happy camper with these two metrics.

Mark began by saying, "I had hoped when we implemented our Six Sigma initiative that our margins and on-time delivery would be much higher. And now, after implementing our Lean initiative we still haven't hit the numbers that the Board wanted in terms of profitability." There was a murmur within the conference room with each member wondering what they now needed to do to make things better. Mark then said, "We need to understand why, after all of what we've done that our margins and on-time delivery are not what we expected them to be. I want everyone to give this some serious thought and we'll meet again next week."

That night, because Mark's wife was out of town visiting her mother, he decided to go out for dinner to his favorite restaurant. He arrived early and decided to go to the bar and have a glass of wine while he was waiting for the restaurant to open. As he sat at the bar drinking his favorite wine, Chianti Classico, he began thinking about the results his company had obtained in the past seven or eight months. He thought, "I know our quality and downtime have both improved because of their Six Sigma efforts. And I know we have much less waste in our processes because of our Lean efforts. Our profit margins have grown from 10 percent to nearly 20 percent, but our on-time delivery is still way below what I expected."

As he was sitting there, a group of men entered the bar and it was clear that they were celebrating something as they were all smiles and made a toast to their newfound success at their manufacturing facility. Mark ordered another glass of wine and continued listening. To his surprise, they were talking about how much they had improved their profit margins over the past year. In fact, one of the men stated that their margins had gone from negative to positive to the tune of 30 percent, which really caught his attention. He wondered what they had done to gain so much in their profit margins?

Mark decided that rather than guess what they had done, he was going to ask them more about it. He did this by buying them all a round of drinks. When the drinks arrived, the group invited Mark to come sit with them, which he did. He started the conversation by telling them he had heard what they were celebrating and that he was very impressed. He also asked them what kind of product they produced? One of the members of the group told him that at Metallic Management, their primary product was metal tools, but they also fabricated metal cans for the food industry.

Mark was very impressed with this company's improvement results and was full of questions. But before he could ask his questions, one member of the group asked him what kind of work he did. Mark explained that he was the General Manager of Tires for All. Mark then turned to the group and asked, "I overheard your toast to your new profit margins and I was wondering what you used to make such a leap in profits? Did you use things like Lean or Six Sigma?" he asked.

Mark could see a smile come over most of the group members until one member said, "We tried Lean and yes, we did get some improvements. We also tried Six Sigma, and again we did get improvements, but not what we were aiming for." Mark could relate to this as it sounded like what had happened in his company.

Mark continued listening as another member of the group said, "We discovered that we were missing something in that our focus was on how much money we could save, rather than how much money we could make." Mark didn't understand this comment and looked confused. He then asked, "What's the difference between saving money and making money? Aren't they one and the same?" Mark heard chuckles from most of the group until one of them said, "We used to think so, but we discovered that the actions intended to save money are totally different than the actions to make money." Mark was even more confused by this comment. "I don't understand?" Mark said. With a smile, one of the group members handed

Mark a business card and told Mark to call the name on the card and he will explain it all to him.

Mark looked at the card and read the man's name, Bob Nelson, owner of Focus and Leverage Consulting. The card also had written on it, "We fix broken companies." Mark thought to himself, "Tires for All isn't broken, but we could use some help." Since it was Friday night, Mark decided that he would call Bob Nelson on Monday and at least see what he had to offer.

REFERENCES

1. James P. Womack and Daniel T. Jones, 1996, *Lean Thinking: Banish Waste and Create Wealth in Your Corporation*, Free Press, New York, NY.
2. Mike Rother and John Shook, 1998, *Learning to See: Value Stream Mapping to Create Value and Eliminate Muda*, Lean Enterprise Institute, Boston, MA.

4

Focus and Leverage

Early Monday morning, Mark arrived at Tires for All, knowing that at the end of the week he had to travel to Corporate Headquarters to report on the financial status of his company. He wasn't as worried as he had been on previous trips, simply because his profit margins were only one point away from the magic number of 20 percent that the Board wanted. He was concerned that his on-time delivery metric was still too low, but he truly believed that it would improve with time. He decided to walk through his facility and look at things like the level of work-in-process (WIP) inventory, rework levels, and, of course, the scrap levels that currently existed. As he walked through his plant, he was pleased with the rework and scrap levels, but the WIP levels did not look good.

When he finished his walk through, he decided to make the call to Bob Nelson, the owner of Focus and Leverage Consulting. He dialed the number and after three rings, a voice on the other end said, "Focus and Leverage Consulting, this is Bob Nelson." Hi Bob, my name is Mark Roder and I am the General Manager of Tires for All located in Western Pennsylvania. "Hi Mark, what can I do for you?" Bob asked. Mark told him about his unplanned meeting with a group from Metallic Management and how impressed he was with their turnaround results. "I was wondering if it would be possible for you to come to our facility and have a discussion about how best to make improvements to this plant?" Mark asked. "Certainly, it is possible, when would you like me to come?" Bob asked. "Could you come this week?" Mark asked. "I think I could arrange that, what day would you like me to come?" he asked. Mark replied, "I have to meet with my Board of Directors in Chicago on Friday, so could you come either Tuesday or Wednesday?" "Which day works best for you Mark?" Bob asked. "How about Wednesday?" Mark replied. "Sounds good to me Mark," Bob responded. "I'll be there bright and early," Bob added.

Mark was excited about his upcoming meeting with Bob Nelson and decided to check out Focus and Leverage Consulting's website, so he logged in to it. The first thing that jumped out to Mark was the headline that read, *Focus and Leverage Consulting—I fix broken companies and make good companies great!* He continued reading and another comment caught his eye which read, *I change the way you think, so you can change the way you operate.* Both comments were profound and thought provoking, increasing Mark's anticipation of his meeting with Bob Nelson.

Mark continued reviewing the Focus and Leverage Consulting website and found a comment that excited Mark even more. The comment read, *"At Focus and Leverage Consulting we're passionate about helping companies maximize their profitability and we do so with our world-renowned improvement methodology named the Ultimate Improvement Cycle (UIC). Although we absolutely believe in Lean and Six Sigma, it is our belief that both can be significantly enhanced by integrating them with the Theory of Constraints."* "Could this be the answer to why we haven't achieved the results we wanted?" Mark thought. And with this, Mark logged out and decided to prepare for his meeting with the Board of Directors.

While Mark was preparing for his meeting on Friday, he kept thinking back to what he had read on Bob's website about this "thing" referred to as the Theory of Constraints. On Bob's website he remembered reading that both Lean and Six Sigma could be significantly enhanced by integrating them with this thing called the Theory of Constraints. He was getting more and more excited about his upcoming meeting with Bob Nelson. He kept thinking, "Could this be the answer to our on-time delivery problems and our profit enhancement?" And with that thought, he got back to his preparation for his board meeting on Friday.

Bright and early on Wednesday morning Mark arrived at his plant and was really looking forward to his meeting with Bob Nelson. Right on schedule, Bob Nelson arrived at Tires for All and Mark met him at the gate. They both walked to Mark's office, sat down and began a conversation. "So, Mark, what is it that you wanted to talk about?" Bob asked. Mark walked him through their improvement efforts. "We started our improvement journey with Six Sigma, trained lots of employees, but we only saw minimal improvements to our bottom line," Mark explained. "Next, we moved to Lean Manufacturing, but this time we trained our entire workforce," Mark continued. "And while we did see significant improvements to our bottom line, the improvements were less than I expected them to be," Mark explained.

Mark then talked about his impromptu meeting with the group from Metallic Management and how they had been celebrating their success. He told Bob that one member of the group had given him Bob's card and suggested that he call him. Bob responded, "Metallic Management did make substantial improvements to their business and it was a real pleasure working with them." "So what role did you play in their turnaround efforts Bob?" Mark asked. "Primarily, I just helped them see the world through a different lens," Bob replied. "What lens was that Bob?" Mark asked. "Before we get into the details, can you take me on a tour of your facility Mark?" Mark agreed and asked Bob, "Where would you like to start?" "Let's start at the beginning where you receive your raw materials," Bob said. And with that request, they both walked to the Receiving Department.

The first thing Bob noticed was seemingly mountains of raw materials used to make their tires. Bob's first question was, "So, Mark, why do you have so much raw material inventory?" Mark responded immediately, "So we never run out of products. In the past, as we were trying to limit the amount of raw materials we had on site, we ended up with shortages and stock-outs which negatively impacted our product output in our Preparation Department. This, in turn, hurt our Assembly Department, and ultimately had a negative impact on our on-time delivery." Bob made a note on his iPad.

They then walked through the Preparation Department and Mark explained how the extruders worked, where raw materials are fed into them and out comes the semi-finished products that are eventually sent to the Assembly Department where they assemble carcasses. Bob noticed again, that there was what appeared to be an excess of material waiting to be delivered to the Assembly Department. When asked why there appeared to be an excessive amount of materials waiting to be delivered to Assembly, Mark again told him that they were safety buffers aimed at reducing downtime in Assembly, plus it helps drive our performance metric efficiency upward. Again, Bob made a note on his iPad.

The two of them next walked to the Assembly Department where they had ten different assembly machines that produced carcasses. Once again, Bob made a note of the excessive number of carcasses waiting to be moved to the finishing department and when he asked Mark why they had so many carcasses, Mark told him they were trying to improve their efficiency metric by keeping everyone busy. Bob recorded Mark's response on his iPad.

They then moved to the Finishing Area and Mark explained this area as being where they mount the carcass onto their Finishing Machine, inflate it, and then apply the tire's tread rubber to the inflated carcass. This process creates what is referred to as a green tire. Nothing stood out to Bob on the Finishing machines, so they moved to the next department which was the Curing Department. Mark explained that curing is the process of applying pressure to the green tire in a mold in order to give the tire its final shape. He also explained that by applying heat energy, a chemical reaction takes place between the rubber and other materials. The green tire is inflated inside the curing press which forces the rubber to conform to the shape and contour of the mold. The cured tire is then moved to a trim post to remove any excess rubber before it moves to the final inspection area. Bob asked, "How is the finished tire transported from curing to the trim post and onto the inspection area?" Mark pointed upward and said, "We have a series of elevated conveyors with hooks that hold the cured tires to transfer all of the tires to the Inspection Department." Once again, Bob made a note in his iPad.

The two of them moved on to the trim area and then on to the Finished Product Inspection Department. Bob watched several tires being inspected and noticed that every tire had to be inspected and then run through a series of inspection machines to check for things like tire uniformity, balance, X-ray, and so on. In the final step, every tire was inspected to check for visual defects such as blisters, blemishes, incomplete mold fill, and a host of other possible defects. Bob did not make any notes, so they proceeded to the Warehouse and Shipping Department. Bob was amazed at the level of finished product stored in racks. He walked around and read many of the labels on the finished tires and found that many of them were over a year old. Again, he made a note in his iPad and then suggested that they go back to Mark's office.

When they got back to Mark's office, Bob took out his iPad and began explaining what he had observed. Foremost on his mind was that there was plenty of WIP inventory at many of the locations where they had stopped and reviewed. Bob then asked Mark a question, "Mark, why do you think you have so much WIP throughout your plant?" Mark looked surprised at Bob's question and said, "We have WIP as a safety buffer to make sure we always have work available for our processes." "Mark, you told me earlier that both your profit margins and on-time delivery were not where you wanted them to be, didn't you?" Bob asked. "Yes, I did, but what has excessive WIP have to do with either of those metrics?" Mark asked. "I think there are some basics about flow that we need to talk about," Bob replied. And with that, Bob pulled up a file on his iPad and began.

"The figure you see on my screen (Figure 4.1) is the cross section of a simple, gravity fed piping system used to transport water. As you can see, water enters into this system through Section A, then flows into Section B, then Section C, and so forth, until it exits Section I and is collected in a receptacle at the bottom of this system. So, here's my first question for you Mark," said Bob. "If you needed water to flow at a faster rate into the receptacle, what would you need to do to make this happen?" Bob asked. Mark studied the drawing and said, "Couldn't you just turn the pressure

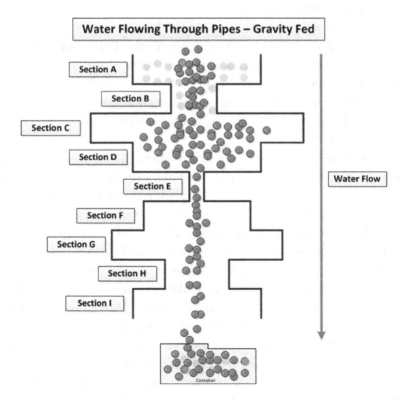

FIGURE 4.1
Cross section of a simple piping diagram.

up higher?" "No Mark, as I explained, this system is a gravity fed system," Bob replied. "Look closer Mark," he added.

Mark studied the drawing and said, "Well one way would be to increase the diameter of Section E." "And why would that work?" Bob asked. "Well, the water is being restricted at that point in the system," Mark replied. "That's correct Mark. Section E is referred to as this system's constraint, which is also known as a physical bottle neck," Bob responded. "Okay, that makes sense," Mark replied. "Now Mark, what do you think happens to this piping system after you've opened up Section E's diameter?" Bob asked. "What I mean by that is, from a physical perspective, how has the flow of water changed?" Bob added. Once again, Mark studied the drawing and said, "Well for one thing, water flow has increased." he stated. "Yes, it has Mark but what happens to the overall flow of water?" Bob asked.

Mark studied the drawing again and said, "I think that a new bottleneck or constraint forms in front of Section B." "Yes Mark, once you have identified the system constraint and took action to break the current constraint, a new constraint will immediately appear in the process," Bob replied and with that Bob put a new figure (Figure 4.2) on his screen. Bob then asked, "Mark, would increasing the diameter of any other section of this piping system, besides Section E, have resulted in more water flowing through this system?" Mark responded quickly and said, "No Bob, only increasing the diameter of Section E would have increased the flow of water through this system."

With that, Bob asked Mark another question. "Mark, based upon what you've learned so far, how would you know how much to increase the diameter of Section E?" Bob asked. "My guess is that it would depend upon how much more water was needed … the demand requirements?" Mark responded as a question. "That is absolutely correct!" Bob responded. "So, Mark, if you opened up Section E's diameter and the new constraint is Section B's diameter, what happens if you need still more water to flow?" Bob asked. Mark responded, "You would need to open up the diameter to meet the new demand." "Absolutely correct Mark!" Bob responded passionately. "Bob, what was the purpose of this piping diagram exercise?" Mark asked. "Be patient Mark, you'll see very soon," Bob replied and with that, he uploaded a new figure (Figure 4.3) onto his iPad screen.

"What you see on the screen is a very simple manufacturing process. Raw materials enter into Step 1 which takes five minutes to process and pass onto Step 2 which processes Step 1's output for thirty minutes. The

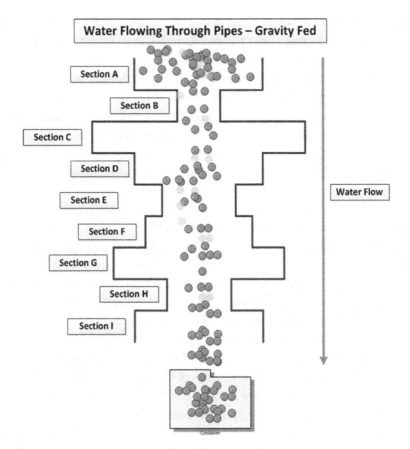

FIGURE 4.2
Piping diagram with new constraint.

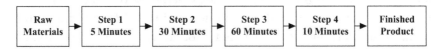

FIGURE 4.3
Manufacturing process.

semi-finished material is then passed onto Step 3 which takes sixty minutes to process before it passes it onto Step 4 which requires ten minutes to process. When completed, Step 4 passes the finished product onto shipping who then prepares the order and ships it to the end customer." Bob explained.

"If this was a new manufacturing process, just starting up, how long would it take to produce the first part?" Bob asked. Mark studied the drawing of the new process and said, "You would have to add the total of the individual cycle times to get the total time. In other words, five minutes plus thirty minutes plus sixty minutes plus ten minutes or a total of one hundred and five minutes for the first part," Mark replied. "That's correct," Bob said. "Now, assuming that this process has been running for a while, what is the production rate of this process?" Bob asked. "And please think about what you learned from the piping diagram," he added.

Mark studied the drawing and remembering the lessons from the piping diagram, said, "I guess it would be one part every sixty minutes?" "Correct Mark," Bob responded. "Okay, suppose someone comes up with an idea on how to shorten Step 2's cycle time from thirty minutes, down to twenty minutes. What is the new production rate?" Bob asked. "Based upon what I have learned today, I would say it would remain the same at sixty minutes?" he answered in a question format. "And why is that true?" Bob asked. "Because we haven't reduced the time of this system's constraint," Mark replied. "Very good Mark!" Bob exclaimed as he highlighted the system constraint on the process drawing (Figure 4.4).

"So, Mark, if you wanted to increase the flow or output of this process, what is the only way you could do this?" Bob asked. "Clearly, you would have to reduce the processing time of Step 3," Mark said with a smile. "Yes Mark, and you have just learned the concept of *focus and leverage!*" Bob said. "In other words, if you want to increase the throughput of any system, you must first locate the limiting factor and then focus your improvement efforts on it to leverage the full potential of the system in question," Bob explained. "This is exciting stuff Bob!" Mark exclaimed. "Please tell me more," Mark said to Bob. "Let's get back together next Monday Mark, as I have a conference call in thirty minutes and then I have to travel to a client in the morning," Bob suggested. "Sounds good Bob, I'll see you on Monday," Mark replied.

Mark was truly excited about what he had learned today. The basic concept of the system constraint, coupled with focus and leverage, had him thinking about why his company's Six Sigma and Lean efforts hadn't

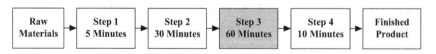

FIGURE 4.4
Manufacturing process with constraint highlighted.

delivered all that he had expected. For sure, both efforts had improved Tires for All's processes, but he now believed that by adding in these two new concepts, his company's results would improve at a much faster pace. Mark now turned his attention to his board meeting on Friday and decided to have a meeting with his Director of Finance, Tom Mahanan, to review the latest results.

Tom arrived at Mark's office and began the discussion by stating that the profit margin was the same, hovering around 19 percent. Tom was hoping that it would have edged up to 20 percent, but such was not the case. In fact, the margins came in at 18.5 percent and were rounded up to 19 percent. Tom also reported that the on-time delivery metric had ticked up to 86 percent, which was a bit better than his last report to the board. Mark hoped that this would be good enough for the Board, especially based upon what he had learned this week from Bob Nelson. On Friday, Mark traveled to Chicago to report the latest results. Surprisingly, the board did not say anything negative to Mark about the results, but he had this feeling that they still weren't happy.

Mark left the board meeting and drove to the airport. He pulled out his computer and did a search for information on system constraints. He found several books on the subject including *The Goal* by Goldratt and Cox and *Epiphanized* by Nelson and Sproull. He ordered both books and continued searching. He also found case study after case study on system constraints and downloaded several of them to read on his flight home. As he was reading these case studies, his thoughts turned to his meeting with Bob Nelson and what he had learned about constraints and focus and leverage. He wondered why, during his training on Six Sigma and Lean, he hadn't learned about the whole concept of system constraints?

5

More on the Theory of Constraints

Right on schedule, Bob Nelson arrived at Tires for All and went directly to Mark's office. Mark shook his hand and the conversation began. "Bob, what you taught me last week about constraints and focus and leverage, has changed my entire thought pattern on improvements to my plant," Mark explained. Mark looked forward to learning more from Bob, and asked, "What will we be talking about this morning?" Bob noticed the two new books on Mark's desk and asked if he had read them? Mark indicated that he had just received both books and that he hadn't yet read them. "You'll learn a lot from both books, so make sure you do read them, sooner rather than later," Bob instructed.

"Today, I want to begin with Goldratt and Cox's five focusing steps that you'll read about in your new books," Bob said. Goldratt and Cox identified the following five focusing steps, which appeared on Bob's iPad screen.

1. Identify the system constraint.
2. Decide how to exploit the system constraint.
3. Subordinate everything else to the system constraint.
4. If necessary, elevate the system constraint.
5. When the current constraint is broken, return to Step 1, but don't let inertia create a new system constraint.

"Let's now talk about each one of these steps in more detail," Bob said.

"Step 1, identify the system constraint, is the first step and I think you have a good idea of what that step means," Bob explained. "But having said that, it's important for you to understand that not all constraints are physical in nature," Bob continued. "There are other types of constraints that exist?" Mark asked. "There are a host of other type constraints but remember this basic definition. A constraint is anything that prevents the system from achieving its goal," Bob replied. "Also, constraints can be internal or external to the system," he added. "I'm getting confused Bob," Mark said.

"Okay, let's start over," Bob responded. "The first thing we have to do is find out what part of the system constitutes the weakest link," he added. "It's important to remember that most of the constraints we face in our systems actually originate from policies we have in place and not physical things. As you've seen from our example, physical constraints are relatively easy to both identify and ultimately break. On the other hand, policy constraints are much more difficult to both identify and break," Bob explained. "Can you give me an example of a policy constraint Bob?" Mark asked. "For example, you've already told me that one of your policies is to drive manpower efficiencies higher," Bob said. "Think about what happens when you drive efficiencies higher and higher. You end up with mountains worth of work-in-process (WIP) inventory which actually clogs the system," Bob explained. "Make sense Mark?" Bob asked and he could see Mark's head nodding in the affirmative. "Let's take another look at our process example," Bob suggested.

"Here we see that Step 3 (Figure 5.1) has been identified as the system constraint," Bob explained. "What happens to this process if you are measuring efficiencies and trying to drive this metric higher and higher?" Bob asked Mark. "I would guess that you would see WIP accumulating in front of Steps 2 and 3?" Mark responded. "That's exactly what would happen and what is the impact of the excessive levels of WIP in the process?" Bob asked. "As you said earlier, the excessive WIP tends to clog the system and, I might add, probably needlessly ties up cash that could be used for other things," Mark responded. "It looks something like this," Bob said as he flashed another drawing on his screen (Figure 5.2).

"So, here is a question for you, Mark. How fast should Steps 1 and 2 be running?" Bob asked. "Not sure I understand your question Bob, could you ask it a different way?" Mark said. "If you want to avoid this explosion

FIGURE 5.1
Process with the constraint highlighted.

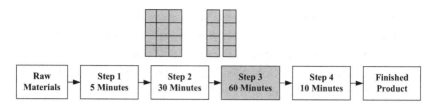

FIGURE 5.2
WIP levels in process.

of WIP in this process, then how fast should these two steps in front of the constraint be running?" Bob asked. "Okay, I see your point now. In order to prevent the system from being clogged with this excessive WIP, both Steps 1 and 2 should be running at the same speed as the system constraint. In other words, they should both be producing at a rate of one part every sixty minutes. Is that correct Bob?" Mark asked. "Yes Mark, that is spot on," Bob replied.

Mark had a worried look, so Bob stopped and asked him what was wrong. Mark explained that if he reduced the output of Steps 1 and 2, it would have a negative impact on one of their key metrics, manpower efficiency. Bob smiled and said, "And is that a bad thing to have happen?" Mark responded passionately, "Well yes, it would be a terrible thing!" "And why do you think it's a terrible thing?" Bob asked. "Bob, there's one thing you need to understand. At Tires for All, efficiency is a key metric that is tracked by our Board of Directors and if they see our numbers getting worse, they will take action!" Mark explained. Bob smiled again and asked, "So Mark, which is more important to you. Manpower efficiency or your profit margins?" "Obviously our margins are more important!" Mark exclaimed. He then added, "Do you think efficiency is a bad metric?" Bob responded, "The only place where efficiency matters is in the system constraint. In non-constraints, all it does is increase the amount of work-in-process inventory. And when your WIP increases, your customer on-time delivery deteriorates which ultimately negatively impacts you profit margins. Do you see my point Mark?" "Yes, I do Bob!" Mark responded.

"Let's get back to Goldratt and Cox's five focusing steps," Bob stated. "In Step 1, we said that you should identify the system constraint. In Step 2, you must decide how to exploit the system constraint. This means that you should focus your improvement efforts directly on the system constraint. Strengthening any link of a chain, other than the constraint, is usually a waste of time and resources. By the same token, the vast majority of improvement efforts in the organization fail to result in more profits for shareholders. This is because most initiatives are not focused on the constraint of the organization. Here's where you apply all that you have learned from your Six Sigma and Lean training, meaning that you should work to reduce and control variation and defects and eliminate waste, but you should do so primarily in the system constraint," Bob explained. "I have seen many companies over the years attempt to attack all steps in the process, when in reality you get the biggest bang for the buck if you do so only in the constraint. There are exceptions to this general rule, however. For example, if you have excessive rework or scrap occurring before or after the constraint, then these cannot be ignored," Bob continued to explain.

"In Step 3 of the five focusing steps we are instructed to *subordinate*. So, what does subordinate actually mean? Remember when you correctly answered the question about how fast Steps 1 and 2 should be running? By definition, any non-constraint has more capacity to produce than the constraint does. And if you attempt to drive efficiencies higher and higher, this will result in swollen WIP inventory, prolonged lead times, and frequent expediting or firefighting. It is absolutely critical to avoid outproducing the constraint. In any manufacturing environment this is accomplished by choking the release of raw material in line with the capacity of the constraint," Bob explained.

Bob continued, "Equally important is making sure that the rest of the system supports the work of the constraint at all times. This means that the constraint must never be starved for inputs or fed poor quality materials. This can easily be achieved by maintaining a practical buffer of safety stock. By the same token, other established policies can actually hinder productivity at the constraint and must be methodically aligned to achieve maximum performance," Bob continued. "The total output of the constraint controls the output of the total system. This is why it is so important that we work to squeeze as much as possible out of it. In terms of maximizing efficiency, as I explained, it only makes sense to do this in the constraint and not in the non-constraints," Bob explained.

Bob continued, "Step 4 of the five focusing steps tells us that it might be necessary to elevate the constraint. This means that rather than immediately rushing out to purchase more things that increase the output of the constraint, by doing things like buying more equipment or hiring more workers, or even increasing the advertising budget, we should first learn to better utilize the existing resources that we already have. Many times, I have seen companies spend excessive amounts of money needlessly because they haven't focused their improvement efforts on the system constraint to reduce waste and variation."

"Step 5 tells us that when the constraint is elevated, it will move to a new location within the system. And when it does move, we must be prepared to immediately move our improvement effort to the new constraint, if we are to keep the improvement effort moving in the right direction," Bob explained. "So, these are the five focusing steps that Goldratt and Cox wrote about in their book, *The Goal*," Bob said.

"Earlier, I mentioned that there were different types of system constraints, so let's talk about that for a minute. I said earlier that you must identify the physical constraints in a manufacturing process if you are to improve flow. But what if the constraint isn't located inside the process? What if the constraint is not physical in nature? Bill Dettmer [1], an expert in the Theory of Constraints, explains that, 'Identifying and breaking constraints becomes a little easier if there is an orderly way to classify them.' Dettmer also explains that there are seven basic types of constraints that are the following," he explained and flashed them on his screen.

1. Market constraint
2. Resource constraint
3. Material constraint
4. Supplier/Vendor constraint
5. Financial constraint
6. Knowledge/Competence constraint
7. Policy constraint

"Let's look at each of these constraint types in more detail and how we might be able to identify and overcome them. Market constraints exist when the demand for your product is less than your capacity to produce or deliver the product. That is, your company has not developed a competitive edge to realize enough orders for your product. Market constraints come about simply because your company is unable to differentiate itself from your competition. So how can your company differentiate itself? Quite simply, there are four primary factors associated with having or not having a competitive edge," Bob explained. "So, let's look at these four factors," Bob added.

"The first factor is quality. *Quality*, in its most basic form, is a measure of how well your product conforms to design standards. It's clear that Japanese manufacturers such as Toyota and Honda are the world's recognized leaders when it comes to producing the highest-quality products, but it is also clear that this was not always the case. You probably know the history here, when Dr. Deming went to Japan and taught the Japanese how to become competitive. The secret to becoming quality competitive is first, designing quality into the products; second, the complete eradication of special cause variation; and third, developing processes that are in control and capable. It is not rocket science, but so few companies focus on these three success elements for creating products and services that differentiate them in the marketplace. So, if you want more orders, the first step is to distinguish yourself from the competition from a quality perspective," Bob explained. "We've made significant improvements in our quality," Mark said.

Bob continued his explanation, "The second factor is *on-time delivery* and it requires that you produce products to the rate at which customers expect them. This means that you must have product flow within your facility that is better than that of your competition. The basics involve focusing on and improving the physical constraint that exists within your facility, removing wasted time within your processes, both physical and non-physical, eradicating things like downtime, quality problems, variation, and all the other things that cause your processes to be inconsistent. It also involves reducing unnecessary inventory that lengthens cycle times and hides defects. You must create consistent, reliable processes that do not hamper your ability to produce and ship your product on time." "This is one area that we are falling short, so we really need to work on this area," said Mark.

Bob continued, "The third factor is *customer service*. Customer service simply means that your company must be responsive to the needs of your customer base. Customers must feel comfortable that if their market changes, their supply base will be able to change right along with them. If the customer has an immediate need for more product, the supplier that separates itself in terms of response time will become the supplier of choice. This means that your manufacturing lead times must be short enough to respond to the ever-changing demands of the market. This only comes by creating processes with exceptional flow. It is important to remember that the greater the amount of work-in-process inventory, the longer the lead time to produce." Mark raised his eyebrows and said, "As you know Bob, we have way too much WIP in our processes."

Once again, Bob continued, "*Cost* is possibly the greatest differentiator of all, especially if you are in a down market. But having said this, low cost without the other three factors in place won't guarantee you more orders. Low costs are only achieved by removing waste and operating expense within the company. In order to be the lowest cost provider in the marketplace, your company must clearly manage all parts of the business. The quality of the products must be superior, with little scrap and rework. In addition, the quantity of raw materials must be low enough to minimize the carrying costs. The amount of labor required to produce the product must be optimal, with little or no overtime." "Wow, we need to work on every one of these factors!" Mark exclaimed.

"Let's get back to the types of constraints that can interfere with your company's ability to produce and ship products," Bob said. "The next type of constraint is called a *resource capacity constraint*. This type of constraint exists when the ability to produce or deliver your product is less than the demands of the marketplace. By that I mean that the orders are available, but your company has insufficient capacity to deliver them. Resource/capacity constraints are, quite simply, not enough operators, equipment, cash, knowledge, or reliable vendors to satisfy the demands of the marketplace. But do not be misled with this one. There is typically an irresistible urge to run off and either hire additional people or purchase additional machines, but quite often there is no need to do this. Many times, this problem is associated with not squeezing the maximum amount of throughput out of the physical constraint that exists within the operation." "Tell me more about this one Bob," Mark said.

Bob continued his explanation, "Quite simply, before you spend money, you must make every attempt to create more capacity. "But how?" you may be wondering. "Your process is full of waste and variation, so use the tools that you learned in your Six Sigma and Lean training and squeeze out more capacity before you try to buy your way out of it," Bob explained. Bob continued, "The cost of expedited shipments must be minimized. All these factors and more make up the cost of the product or service. If the costs are less than the competition's, cost can be a differentiator, but not without the other three factors, quality, on-time delivery, and customer service." "That makes perfect sense," Mark replied.

Bob continued, "The next type of constraint is referred to as a *material constraint*. This type of constraint occurs because the company is unable to obtain the critical materials in the quantity or quality needed to satisfy the demand of the marketplace. Material constraints are very real for your production managers, and I can't tell you how often I have heard managers lament that if they just had the materials, they could make the products. In fact, over the years this has been such a problem that material replenishment systems like MRP and ERP were invented to ensure material availability. However, as you know, even with MRP and ERP, and its various iterations, material shortages are still a common occurrence. Even MRP or ERP cannot predict scrap, or defects, or equipment downtime, or human-related causes like sickness," Bob explained.

"I once consulted for a company that produced buses that was always missing on-time delivery dates. And even though this company had many other problems, one of the biggest problems they experienced involved the excessive amount of time required to purchase and receive parts and materials. By creating a Value Stream Map (VSM), that you learned in your Lean training, this bus company was able to pinpoint the major source of material delays as the company's purchase order (PO) process. I helped them reconfigure their PO process and implemented a pull system and we were able to reduce the overall procurement time by 65 percent," Bob explained. "Wow, 65 percent is an amazing improvement!" Mark exclaimed. "This is so interesting Bob and I love it when you give actual examples," Mark added.

"The next type of constraint is a *supplier/vendor* constraint. Supplier/vendor constraints come about because of an inconsistent supplier or because of excessive lead times in responding to orders. This type of constraint is closely related to material constraints, and the net effect of this type of constraint is that because the raw materials are late arriving, products cannot be built and shipped on schedule. A supplier/vendor constraint is also a subset of a resource/capacity constraint. Let us look at an example," Bob said.

"I once worked in a company that designed, manufactured, and installed truck bodies. The company was losing market share, and I was asked to look into why this was happening. I created a VSM and identified the constraint as being the order entry system. All orders had to pass through Engineering to receive a build quote before the company would provide a quote to the customer. The VSM indicated that the average time spent in Engineering had increased to forty calendar days. As a result of this delay, customers were simply going elsewhere. Through value analysis and problem-solving techniques, we were able to reduce the Engineering lead time from forty days to an amazing average of forty-eight hours!" Bob explained.

"The good news was that because the quality of the bus company's products was superior and the cycle time through production was the best in the industry, we were able to increase market share to levels never before seen. All this by simply identifying one constraint. In reality then, there are two types of constraints that limit a company's ability to make money now or in the future: the marketplace, not enough orders, and the capacity to satisfy the marketplace, lack of capacity to deliver existing orders. Each of these two types of constraints are diametrically opposite and requires a completely different focus," Bob explained.

Bob continued, "The next type of constraint is referred to as a *financial constraint*. As you can probably guess, financial constraints occur when a company has insufficient cash flow. Financial constraints are not that common, but they are every bit as penalizing as the others when they exist. This type of constraint is often associated with a lack of available cash needed to purchase raw materials for future orders," he explained. And then he added, "And Mark, think about how much cash you're tying up with excessive amounts of inventory. Under this scenario, companies typically must wait to receive payment for an existing order before taking on any new orders. One common example of this type of constraint is an accounts receivable process. I was part of a team that transformed an accounts receivable process by reducing the billing process time by approximately sixty percent and in doing so, this company's cash flow rate improved by a proportional amount." Bob continued.

"The next type of constraint is referred to as a *knowledge or competence constraint*. Knowledge or competence constraints exist because the knowledge or skills needed to improve a company's business performance, or perform at a higher level, is not available within the company. A good example of this type of constraint is when a company purchases a new type of equipment but fails to develop the infrastructure and knowledge on the equipment itself. Things like the development of a preventive maintenance system and simple breakdown maintenance are needed to overcome this type of constraint. Without this knowledge or competence, the equipment remains down much longer than it should," Bob explained.

"The final type of constraint is actually the most common type, *policy constraints*. A policy constraint includes any written or unwritten policy, law, rule, or business practice that gets in the way of moving you closer to your goal of making more money now and in the future. In fact, my friend Bill Dettmer tells us that in most cases, a policy is most likely behind a constraint from any of the first six categories. For this reason, the Theory of Constraints assigns a very high importance to policy analysis. The most common example of policy constraints is one you are very familiar with and that is the use of operator efficiency or machine utilization or purchase price variance to measure and manage performance of all steps," Bob explained.

Bob continued, "When companies use operator efficiency as a performance metric, typically there is a push to maximize it in all steps of the process, like you do here at Tires for All. What typically happens as a result of this misguided focus, is the production floor becomes loaded with excess WIP inventory, lead times become lengthened, and throughput is encumbered. As I said earlier, measuring operator efficiency makes sense only in the constraint operation. In spite of this, many companies continue to use operator efficiency as a performance metric in each of the individual process steps."

"So, there you have the various types of constraints that could be negatively impacting your company's ability to ship your products on time which, of course, negatively impacts your company's profit margins," Bob stated. "I hope this has opened your eyes Mark in terms of some of the things you need to change to be more successful?" Bob asked. "Trust me Bob, what you've explained to me today is amazing and I know going forward, I have a whole new roadmap on what to change in my factory. One thing I would like to ask you is, would it be possible to hire you as a consultant to help us with our journey to our profitability promised land?" Mark asked. Bob smiled and said, "Of course you can." "Can you give me an idea of what your hourly or daily rate is?" Mark asked. Bob responded, "My rate is strictly based on how much your profits rise." Mark had a look on his face that indicated he did not understand.

Bob continued, "By that I mean, whatever your profit margins end up being as a result of my tenure here at your company, I'll take 10 percent of the total improvement, but not until you decide that you don't need me anymore." Mark had never heard an offer quite like that before and without hesitation he agreed. "Bob, I'll have my Director of Finance, Tom Mahanan, draw up a contract," Mark said. "One thing I want to make perfectly clear Mark is that what I tell you to do, you must do it without delay, even though you may not agree with me," Bob added. Mark agreed and with that, Tires for All began their new improvement journey. Mark and Bob had agreed that Bob would begin his consulting agreement the following week.

REFERENCE

1. Bill Dettmer, 1996, *Goldratt's Theory of Constraints: A System's Approach to Continuous Improvement*, Quality Press, Milwaukee, WI.

6

The New Improvement Journey

Mark arrived for work earlier than normal on Monday and was excited to start this new consulting agreement with Bob Nelson. When he looked back at what Bob had taught him, he was amazed that in such a short time, he had accumulated such a wealth of new information. He was excited to begin this new approach to improvement and felt confident that, with Bob Nelson's help, they could combine Six Sigma and Lean with the Theory of Constraints and great things were sure to happen within his company.

On schedule, Bob Nelson arrived at Tires for All, checked in through security and received his semi-permanent pass which permitted him to come and go without signing in each time. Mark thought this would be imperative as Bob had indicated that he would be working on any and all shifts during his consulting agreement. Once Bob was in, he walked directly to Mark's office. Once their greetings were completed, Bob began speaking, "Mark, one of the things I'd like to do is have you, your Finance Director, and myself have a closed-door meeting to discuss a different form of accounting that I want to begin using." Immediately, Mark pushed back and said, "We can't change our accounting system Bob, we're required by law to use it when we report out!" Mark exclaimed. "I'm not suggesting that we abandon your current Cost Accounting system Mark, but I do want to use a different system to make real-time financial decisions," Bob responded.

Mark called his Director of Finance into his office and Bob began his discussion. "In any improvement initiative, the person responsible for the financial well-being of your business plays a pivotal role in assuring that the initiative stays focused on the primary goal of most companies, which is to make money now and in the future. Within the confines of an improvement methodology known as the Theory of Constraints

(TOC), I'm going to present an alternate form of accounting, known as Throughput Accounting (TA), that is intended to be used for real-time financial decisions rather than basing decisions on what happened last month. Many businesses will emphatically state that the primary goal of their business is to make money and yet they spend the largest portion of their time trying to save money, which is what I have seen here at Tires for All," Bob said. Tom spoke up and asked, "Excuse me, but I have no idea what the Theory of Constraints is?" Bob replied, "Be patient Tom, I will explain it all to you. I want both of you to not only hear what I have to say, I want you both to be able to say it too. By that I mean, what I'm teaching you here today, I want you both to be able to teach others here at your plant."

Bob continued, "The key to profitability is by focusing on that part of the system that controls and drives revenue higher and higher, rather than cost-cutting. It matters not if you are a service provider, a small business owner, a distributor, or a manufacturer. What you need is a way to sell more product which increases revenue and, ultimately, profitability. In this meeting, I will systematically compare two accounting methods and demonstrate the superiority of Throughput Accounting in terms of profitability improvement. Much of what I'm going to explain in this meeting is taken from the book, *Reaching the Goal* by John Ricketts [1], and I highly recommend that both of you purchase and read this book!" Bob exclaimed. "But before we discuss these two accounting methods, I need to teach Tom something called the Theory of Constraints. I've already covered this with Mark, so Tom, this is intended to bring you up to speed," Bob said.

Bob continued, "Tom, I want you to consider this simple piping system (Figure 6.1) used to transport water. The system is gravity fed whereby water flows into Section A, then flows through Section B, then Section C, and so forth, until ultimately, the water collects in a receptacle immediately below Section I. It has been determined that the rate of water flow is insufficient to satisfy current demand and you have been called in to fix this problem. What would you do and why would you do it?" Tom looked at the drawing and said, "Well, it appears as though the only way to increase the flow of water through this system would be to open up the diameter of Section E's pipe?" he responded as a question. "Yes Tom, that is exactly what you need to do," Bob said. "Section E is referred to as this system's constraint and is also known as a bottleneck," Bob explained.

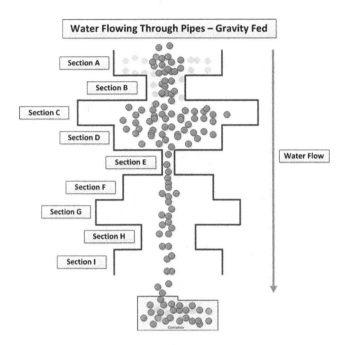

FIGURE 6.1
Piping diagram.

"And when you did open up Section E's diameter, can you tell me where the new system constraint would immediately appear?" Bob asked Tom. Tom studied the drawing and said, "Since the next smallest diameter is Section B, my guess is that this section would be the new system constraint." "Once again, you are exactly correct," Bob replied and flashed his next drawing on his iPad. Mark had a look of surprise on his face as Tom was able to answer both questions right away.

Bob continued, "In this figure (Figure 6.2), Section E's diameter has been changed and water flow has increased. If you selected your new diameter based upon the new demand requirements, you will have 'fixed' this problem. What if there is another surge in water demand?" Bob asked rhetorically. "What would you do? The correct answer would be to now enlarge Section B's diameter and again it is based upon the new demand requirement. Section E and now Section B are referred to as system constraints (a.k.a. bottlenecks). The inevitable conclusion in any business is that system constraints control the flow and throughput within any system. So how might this apply to your manufacturing business?" Bob asked and flashed Figure 6.3 on his iPad's screen.

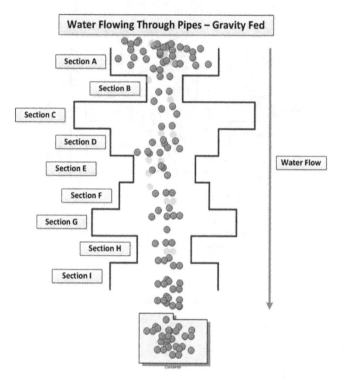

FIGURE 6.2
Piping diagram with new constraint.

FIGURE 6.3
Manufacturing process with cycle times.

"Okay, so what you see now is a simple four-step manufacturing process used to produce something. Raw materials enter the process at Step 1, are processed for five minutes and are then passed on to Step 2. Step 2 requires thirty minutes to process before passing the semi-finished material on to Step 3. Step 3 requires sixty minutes to complete its work and then passes it on to Step 4 which requires ten minutes to complete the finished product. My question for you Tom is, where is the constraint in this process?" he asked.

Tom reviewed the process in question and said, "Because Step 3 is the slowest process step at sixty minutes, it is just like Section E of the piping system, so it is the system constraint." "You are correct Tom," Bob said.

"So, if you wanted to increase the output rate of this process, what would you have to do?" Bob asked. "It's pretty clear to me that in order to speed up this process, you would need to reduce the cycle time of Step 3," Tom responded. "And what would this new cycle time be dependent upon Tom?" Bob asked. "I guess that would be based upon the demand for the product," Tom said. "Yes, you're right again Tom!" Bob responded.

"My next question is, based upon what you've heard so far, how fast should Steps 1 and 2 be running and why?" Bob asked Tom. "Well, based on what I've seen so far, Steps 1 and 2 should be running at the same speed as the system constraint. The reason being that if they continued running at their current capacity, all that would happen is that the system would be full of needless work-in-process inventory," Tom explained. Bob then said, "Tom, have you read about the Theory of Constraints before this meeting?" "No, why did you ask me that question?" Tom asked Bob. "I asked you that because you have answered every question correctly," Bob replied. "It's all just common sense Bob," Tom replied. With that, Bob flashed another figure on his iPad (Figure 6.4).

"So here is what the process would look like if Steps 1 and 2 continued running at their current capacities. With all this in mind, let's get back to our comparison of Cost Accounting and TOC's version referred to as Throughput Accounting," Bob said.

"Because traditional Cost Accounting is so complicated, in this discussion, and because both of you are familiar with Cost Accounting, I won't go into great detail, but I will cover the highlights of it so that a comparison with Throughput Accounting can be made. Before I start, have either of you ever heard of Throughput Accounting?" Bob asked them. Both of them shook their heads as if to say no, so he began his discussion. "If you have any questions as I present this, stop me and ask them," Bob said. "The figure (Figure 6.5) on my iPad illustrates selected elements of CA. When CA arose in the early 1900s, labor costs dominated manufacturing

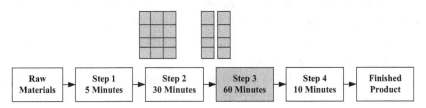

FIGURE 6.4
Process with WIP in it.

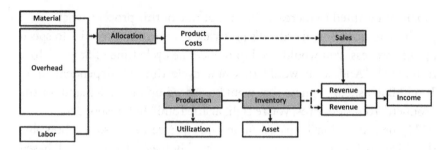

FIGURE 6.5
Basic elements of Cost Accounting.

and workers were paid by the piece. Back then, it was absolutely reasonable to allocate overhead expenses to products on the basis of direct labor costs for purposes of preparing financial statements. But since automation now dominates manufacturing, and workers are paid by the hour, allocation of large overhead expenses on the basis of small labor costs has created some real distortions," Bob explained.

"When re-aggregated at the enterprise level, product cost distortions do not affect financial statements very much. Yet, if prices are computed as product cost plus standard gross margin, the prevailing method in CA, product cost distortions carry into product pricing. The net effect is that some products appear to be profitable when they aren't and some products that appear unprofitable really are," Bob continued.

"A second problem with CA is that it encourages factories to produce excess inventory. This happens because of CA's push for higher levels of efficiency and utilization in non-constraints. Inventory accumulation can be driven by the counterintuitive effect it has on earnings. Rather than being expensed on the income statement in the period they were incurred, the cost of inventory goes on the balance sheet as an asset. Consequently, an inventory profit may be reported, which a business can use to smooth reported earnings, even though it has absolutely nothing to do with real income. If that inventory can't be sold, then inventory on the balance sheet turns into depreciation expense on the income statement and an inventory loss results," Bob explained. "Any questions?" he asked, but there weren't any.

"A third problem with CA concerns management priorities. Operating Expense tends to be managed closely because it is well-known and under direct control. Revenue, on the other hand, tends to be viewed as less controllable because the perception is that it is dependent upon the markets and customers. Inventory is a distant third in management priorities because reducing it has an adverse effect on reported income," Bob continued.

"Here is a very important point for both of you to consider. Even though most businesses practice it, the key to profitability is not through how much money you can save! The key to profitability is through how much money you can make! And these two approaches are drastically different! Let's now look at a different accounting method referred to as Throughput Accounting to answer this question," Bob said. "And again, if you have questions about the material I am presenting, stop me and ask away," Bob added.

"TA addresses all of the problems associated with CA that we just saw by not using product costs. Instead, Throughput Accounting eliminates incentives for excess inventory. It's important for both of you to understand that Throughput Accounting cannot be used in place of conventional financial reporting, simply because publicly traded companies are required by law to comply with GAAP requirements. But having said this, Throughput Accounting does provide a way to make 'real-time' financial decisions. Throughput Accounting will tell you which products combine to deliver the most profitable mix of products, and trust me, Throughput Accounting's mix will be different than what traditional Cost Accounting would give you," he explained. "Are you telling us that by using Throughput Accounting, the mix of products will change the level of profitability that is different than Cost Accounting?" Tom asked. "Yes, and I will give you an example of that shortly," Bob responded.

Bob began again, "Throughput Accounting uses three basic financial measures, which are, Throughput (T), Inventory or Investment (I), and Operating Expense (OE). So, let's look at each of these in more detail. Throughput (T) is the rate at which your system generates money through sales of products or services, or interest generated. If you produce something, but don't sell it, it's not Throughput, it's just Inventory. Throughput is obtained after subtracting the Totally Variable Costs (TVC). That is, the cost of raw materials, or those things that vary with the sale of a single unit of product or service from your revenue. Are you following me?" Bob asked and they both nodded their heads in agreement.

"The next basic financial measure is Inventory or Investment and it represents all of the money that the business has invested in things that it intends to sell. Primarily it includes the dollars tied up in WIP and finished product inventory. The third measure is Operating Expense and it represents all the money the system spends to turn Inventory into Throughput, and it includes all labor costs. It also includes rent, plus selling, general, and administrative (SG & A) costs. This point of including all labor costs is a huge departure from traditional Cost Accounting. Are you still with me?" he asked and again they both nodded in the affirmative.

Bob continued his explanation of Throughput Accounting, "Throughput is maximized by selling goods or services with the largest difference between price (revenue) and TVC, and by minimizing the elapsed time between spending money to produce product and receiving money from sales. It's important to understand that Throughput Accounting does not use labor costs to allocate Operating Expense. Unlike traditional Cost Accounting, direct labor is not treated as a variable cost." Tom immediately asked why, and Bob immediately responded, "Because just like Tires for All, businesses do not adjust their workforce every time demand varies," Bob replied.

Bob continued, "From these three basic elements of Throughput Accounting, namely T, I, and OE, we can calculate several other key metrics that he projected onto his iPad screen:

- Net Profit = Throughput – Operating Expense or NP = T – OE
- Return on Investment = Net Profit ÷ Inventory or ROI = NP/I
- Productivity = Throughput ÷ Operating Expense or P = T/OE
- Inventory Turns = Throughput ÷ Inventory or I = T/I

"In all of my years in Finance, I have never even heard of Throughput Accounting Bob," Tom said. "Me either," said Mark. "And the funny thing is, it all looks so simple," Tom added. "Okay, let's continue," Bob said.

"An ideal decision using Throughput Accounting would be one that increases T and decreases both I and OE while a good decision increases NP, ROI, P, and I. It's very important to remember that Net Profit is net operating profit before interest and taxes. Under Throughput Accounting, there are no product costs, but instead there are constraint measures that should also be tracked as follows," and he flashed another slide onto his iPad's screen.

- Throughput per Constraint Unit: T/CU = (Revenue – Totally Variable Cost)/units
- Constraint Utilization: U = time spent producing/time available to produce

Bob then explained, "The way to maximize T is to maximize these constraint measures. Constraint utilization is very important because every hour lost on the constraint is an hour lost for the entire business that you can't get back. On the other hand, utilization of non-constraints is not tracked simply because it encourages excess inventory." "Like our plant does," Mark added. Bob responded, "Yes, just like you guys have been doing."

"So, typical decisions based on the metric, T/CU include things like prioritizing use of the constraint, for example, choosing the best product mix; deciding whether to increase the constraint's capacity through investment; selecting products to introduce or discontinue and pricing products based on the opportunity cost of using the constraint," Bob explained. "Therefore, for normal product decisions, T/CU is used to determine the best mix that results in maximizing T. If, for example, producing less of one product in order to produce more of another product would increase T, then that is a good decision. But for major decisions that might shift the constraint or forfeit some Throughput on current products, then Throughput Accounting uses the following decision-support measures," and he displayed the following on his iPad screen.

- Change in Net Profit: $\Delta NP = \Delta T - \Delta OE$. In this case, the Δ symbol stands for the difference or change in or a comparison between alternatives. Likewise, to show the impact of these investment decisions, the metric Payback: $PB = \Delta NP / \Delta I$ should be used.
- To minimize unfavorable deviations from plans, Throughput Accounting advocates these control measures that should be minimized:
  - Throughput Dollar Days: TDD = Selling price of late order $\times$ days late
  - Inventory Dollar Days: IDD = Selling price of excess inventory $\times$ days unsold

Bob then explained, "Throughput Dollar Days measures something that should have been done but was not, like shipping orders on time while Inventory Dollar Days measures something that should not have been done but was, like creating unnecessary inventory. Are you guys still with me?" Bob asked and again, they both nodded their heads in the affirmative. "Let's take a little break for now," Bob suggested. And with that the three of them went to the break room to get some coffee.

"Bob, this is all starting to make perfect sense to me," Tom said. "And I really like the way you are presenting all of this," said Mark. "Well, most of what I presented today is from John Ricketts classic book, *Reaching the Goal: How Managers Improve a Services Business Using Goldratt's Theory of Constraints* [1], and, as I said earlier, I strongly encourage both of you to get this book and read it. Ironically, as you can see in the title, it was written to apply to service companies, but it equally applies to production-based companies like Tires for All. You guys ready to go back and hear some more?" Bob asked. "Yes!" both said in unison.

Once they were back in Mark's office, Bob began, "Throughput Accounting is used to identify constraints, monitor performance, control production, and determine the impact of your decisions," and with that, Bob presented a new table on his iPad screen (Table 6.1). "The table you see here is a manufacturing situation consisting of just three parts, with each part requiring the same three steps. Each product requires a different number of minutes per step, but the total time required for each part is the same. Labor costs per minute are the same across all steps," Bob explained.

Continuing, Bob explained, "As you can see, Part A clearly has the highest price and the lowest raw material cost per part while part C has the lowest price and highest raw material cost per part. Because the same workers will be used to produce any product mix, it would seem that the best mix would be to produce as much of part A as demanded, then B, then C. Following this priority order, the factory will produce 100 units of A, seventy-five of B, and none of C. Note that Step 2 limits enterprise production regardless of whether it's actually recognized as the constraint. Operating Expense includes rent, energy, and labor." "Let's look at an

TABLE 6.1

Manufacturing Requirements

| | Products | | | | |
	A	B	C	Have	Need
Demand	100	100	100		
Price	US$105	US$100	US$95		
Raw Material	US$45	US$50	US$55		
Step 1 Time	3	6	9	2,400 minutes	1,800 minutes
Step 2 Time	15	12	9	2,400 minutes	3,600 minutes
Step 3 Time	2	2	2	800 minutes	600 minutes
Total Time	20	20	20		

TABLE 6.2

Cost Accounting Product Mix

	Products				
	A	B	C	Have	Need
Demand	100	100	100		
Price	$105	$100	$95		
Raw Material	$45	$50	$55		
Step 1 Time	3	6	9	2,400	1,800 Minutes
Step 2 Time	15	12	9	2,400	3,600 Minutes
Step 3 Time	2	2	2	800	600 Minutes
Total Time	20	20	20		

Cost Accounting	Products			Total
	A	B	C	
Product Cost	$100	$111	0	
Mix	100	75	0	
Step 2 Used	1,500	900	0	2,400
Revenue	$10,500	$7,500	0	$18,000
Raw Material	$4,500	$3,750	0	$8,250
Gross Margin	$6,000	$3,750	0	$9,750
Operating Expense	$5,455	$4,545	0	$10,000
Net Profit	$545	($795)	0	($250)

example comparing Cost Accounting with Throughput Accounting's product mix decision," Bob said (Table 6.2).

Bob continued, "When Cost Accounting allocates Operating Expense to products based on their raw material costs, the resulting product costs confirm the expected priority: A has a lower product cost than B. Unfortunately, with this product mix, this business generates a net loss of US$250. Because Part A appears to be profitable while Part B generates a loss, it's tempting to conclude that producing none of B would stop the loss. However, the OE covered by B would then have to be covered entirely by A, which would yield an even larger loss. If additional work was started in an effort to keep the workers at Steps 1 and 3 fully utilized or to maximize their efficiency, Work-In-Process inventory would grow. The inevitable conclusion, using Cost Accounting, is that this business is not profitable!" Bob explained. "Let's now look at this same company using Throughput Accounting and see if the results tell us the same things or not," Bob said as he flashed a new table on his iPad screen (Table 6.3).

"As you can see in this table, Throughput Accounting provides an entirely different perspective when looking at this business and its potential product mix," Bob explained.

TABLE 6.3

Throughput Accounting Product Mix

	Products				
	A	B	C	Have	Need
Demand	100	100	100		
Price	$105	$100	$95		
Raw Material	$45	$50	$55		
Step 1 Time	3	6	9	2,400	1,800 Minutes
Step 2 Time	15	12	9	2,400	3,600 Minutes
Step 3 Time	2	2	2	800	600 Minutes
Total Time	20	20	20		

Throughput Accounting	Products			Total
	A	B	C	
T/CU	$60	$50	$40	
T/CUt	$4.00	$4.17	$4.44	
Mix	20	100	100	
Step 2 Used	300	1,200	900	2,400
Revenue	$2,100	$10,000	$9,500	$21,600
Raw Material (TVC)	$900	$5,000	$5,500	$11,400
Throughput (T)	$1,200	$5,000	$4,000	$10,200
Operating Expense (OE)				$10,000
Net Profit (NP)				$200

Bob then explained, "Throughput Accounting ranks product profitability according to Throughput on the constraint per minute (T/CU/t). And it does not allocate OE to products. So, based upon this, Product A yields $4 per minute on the constraint, B yields $4.17, and C yields $4.44. Throughput Accounting says the priority should be to produce as much of C as capacity will allow, then B, then A, which is the exact opposite priority of Cost Accounting. Because Step 2 is the constraint, producing 100 units of C, 100 of B, and twenty of A is all that can be done. But the good news is with this product mix from TA, instead of a $250 loss when using Cost Accounting, this business now generates a net profit of $200. The only difference being the product mix!" "Holy crap!" Mark exclaimed. "Could it be that we have been using the wrong product mix here in our plant?" Mark said. "It certainly appears that we might have been!" Tom added.

Bob continued, "Effective use of Throughput Accounting requires different information than from Cost Accounting, so new report formats must be developed and implemented. For example, a Throughput Accounting earnings statement shows T, I, and OE relative to the constraint, while conventional Cost Accounting reports are oblivious to the constraint. Just as Cost Accounting and Throughput Accounting rank product profitability differently, they may also rank customer profitability quite differently. Several Throughput Accounting outcomes are worth emphasizing," Bob explained as he flashed another slide on his iPad screen.

- Financial measures reverse management priorities from OE, T, and I for Cost Accounting to T, I, and OE for Throughput Accounting.
- Performance measures for Throughput Accounting are not distorted by cost allocations for Cost Accounting.
- Constraint measures eliminate conflict between local measures, like machine utilization or operator efficiency and global measures or performance of the business.
- Control measures remove the incentive to build excess inventory and replace it with the incentive to deliver products on time.

Bob began again, "Let's now review the primary components of Throughput Accounting, starting with Throughput. Throughput at your company is achieved by processing parts, selling or delivering them to customers, and receiving payment for all goods you sold. Again, inventory is not Throughput! Inventory or Investment is primarily the amount of

WIP and finished goods inventory, but it also includes all purchased parts for sales or the equipment, buildings, and other assets required to produce parts if you're a manufacturer. The real key to reducing 'I' is to stop the practice of pushing orders through your processes and replace it with pulling orders through your processes. Use the concept of nothing comes into your process until something exits the constraint or synchronizing flow. Too much WIP at one time leads to extending the productive cycle time of every part, causing late deliveries of parts and unhappy customers," Bob explained.

Bob continued, "And finally, Operating Expense is all the money the system spends in order to turn Inventory into Throughput including all labor costs. The key for your company to reduce labor costs is by improving Throughput at a much faster rate by removing waste and variation within the constraint. In doing so, this will reduce the dependence on overtime to play catch-up and reduce overall dollars spent on overtime. It will also improve the morale of the workforce because you have eliminated the fear of layoffs. Think about it, if you can generate additional Throughput with the same Operating Expense, you will return much more to your company's bottom line," Bob explained.

"So, there's your comparison of these two markedly different accounting methods. It should be clear to you that if you continue using traditional Cost Accounting to make your key decisions, like product mix, your company could be missing an opportunity to make more money. And since the goal of most companies is to make money now, and in the future, doesn't it make sense to use Throughput Accounting to make your real-time financial decisions?" Bob said as he finished his presentation on accounting methods. "So, what do you guys think?" Bob asked.

Tom was the first to comment, "I am truly amazed at what we heard today! I never dreamed that with such a simple set of metrics, profit numbers could be enhanced dramatically just by changing the mix!" Mark then added, "I have been searching for a way to dramatically increase profitability and thanks to the Theory of Constraints, we have found our way!" Tom then added, "I know I can speak for Mark when I say, thank you Bob for such an enlightening discussion." Bob then added, "Guys, there's a lot more to the Theory of Constraints and as we progress, you'll see new ways of doing business. Remember what I told you when I began this discussion, in that I want you two to present what you learned to other key members of your staff."

"I do have a question for you Bob," Mark said. "And what question is that Mark?" Bob asked. "When we first started our improvement journey, we began by implementing Six Sigma and we did see improvement in our profits and on-time delivery. We then implemented Lean Manufacturing and again, we saw another jump in both of these metrics," he added. "My question for you is this. Is there a way that we can combine both of these improvement methods with the Theory of Constraints?" Bob responded by asking a question, "What do you think Mark?" "I would think there would be, and I think the outcome would be major improvements in things like profits and on-time delivery," Mark said. Bob responded, "Well Mark, as they say, 'You ain't seen nothing yet!' And with that, Bob said goodbye to Tom and Mark and told them he would be back tomorrow morning.

REFERENCE

1. John Ricketts, 2008, *Reaching the Goal: How Managers Improve a Services Business Using Goldratt's Theory of Constraints*, IBM Press.

7

The New Beginning

After Bob left for the day, Tom and Mark decided to meet and strategize their next steps. Both were very excited about what they had learned from Bob and wanted to plan how they would get everyone involved in their new beginning. Both were very excited about the possibilities that could come about at their plant in terms of profitability. Mark was the first to speak and said, "Tom, I just want to tell you how impressed I am with you at how quickly you grasped the lessons Bob gave us today." "Well thank you Mark, but when you stop and think about it, it's all just common sense," Tom replied. "How do you think we should go about involving our employees with our new direction?" Mark asked Tom. "I think one of the first things we should do is present the basics of the Theory of Constraints to our Operation's Manager and the Supervisors," said Tom. "I also want my Finance employees to hear about it and our union leader," he added. "One thing that stood out for me in our discussion with Bob was that I don't think we have to be concerned with any layoffs," Mark said. "I agree," Tom said.

The two of them continued planning and decided to schedule a meeting to present the basics of TOC to their group of employees they just discussed. "Mark, do you think we should wait to discuss our plan with Bob?" Tom asked. Mark responded, "Bob was very clear that he wanted us to present this material to our team." Tom agreed, so they planned on making their presentation that afternoon. They decided that they would present the piping diagram and the simple four-step process using the slides that Bob had presented to them. Fortunately, Bob had given them a copy of his slides, so they wouldn't have to spend time making new ones.

One by one, the key employees entered the conference room, which included Jim Frego, the Director of Quality, Frank Delaney, the Director of Maintenance, Bill Simpson, the Director of Engineering, Sally Hodges, the Industrial Engineering Manager, Cliff Hastings, the Operations Manager, and his Supervisors, Chris Samuels, the Union Head, and Oscar Francis, the Master Black Belt. When everyone was seated, Mark began by welcoming everyone. Mark explained that the purpose of this meeting was to explain the company's new direction using something called the Theory of Constraints. And with that said, Mark turned the presentation over to Tom. One by one, Tom presented each of the slides containing the piping diagram and as he presented each one, he asked the same questions that Bob had asked. He then presented the slide of the simple four-step process that Bob had presented to them.

Upon completing his presentation, he asked the group if there were any questions, and to Tom and Mark's surprise, hands went up everywhere. Mark stood up and selected Chris Samuels to ask his question. "I must say, what you presented here was very interesting and informative," Chris began. "My question to you is a very simple one, in that I was wondering if the hourly employees would also hear this presentation?" Mark looked at Tom, indicating he should go ahead and answer that question. Tom responded by asking Chris a question. "After hearing this presentation, do you think our hourly employees should be given this presentation?" he asked. Chris, with a big smile, responded, "Absolutely yes! I think if you want this new approach to work, our front-line employees need to hear it. And, if it's alright with you guys, I'd like to be the one that delivers it." Mark was the first to respond and said, "Chris, I think that's a great idea! I think coming directly from you, it would be much more meaningful to them."

One by one, all of the questions the group had were answered to everyone's satisfaction and when the group left the conference room, it was clear that everyone had been energized by what they had heard. Only Chris remained and he approached Mark and Tom and told them that for the first time in a long time, he was very excited to be working at Tires for All, and that he believed their best days were ahead of them. Mark and Tom both thanked Chris for his comments and gave him a thumb drive with the slides on it. Chris thanked them and said that he was very excited to be able to present the material to his hourly workforce.

The next morning Bob arrived and went to Mark's office. He asked them how things were going, and Mark told him about the training session that he and Tom had delivered. Bob was both surprised and happy at the same time. He hadn't expected them to be this aggressive but thanked Mark for making it happen already. Bob asked Mark, "How do you think the training was received?" Mark let him know that it was well received and then he told him about what Chris was planning to do and Bob returned a big smile. Bob wanted to meet Chris, so they walked out onto the shop floor. Chris was one of the Assembly machine operators.

Mark introduced Chris to Bob and without hesitation, Chris let Bob know that he was very impressed with the Theory of Constraints and that he planned to deliver the same training to his fellow co-workers that afternoon. Chris had planned to have the sessions with small groups so not to negatively impact production. Mark told him that he thought it might be better to do it in groups such as all of the Assembly machine operators in one group, all of the Finishing machine operators in another, and so forth. When Chris told Bob he had arranged the training in this manner so as not to lose production, Mark told him that the training was more important than the production loss and that he could use the conference room whenever he needed it. And with this in mind, Chris agreed to change his training plans to match what Mark had recommended. Bob told Chris that he would like to come to several of his sessions in the event he needed help with any questions and Chris agreed.

Later that afternoon, Chris held his first training session using the slides Bob had prepared and, according to Bob, he did a masterful job of not only delivering the training, but also answering questions from the other Assembly operators. He repeated the same training with the Finishing operators, the extruder operators from the Preparation Department, the hourly Maintenance employees, and all of the other hourly operators in the plant. Bob was delighted with how the training was received by everyone and he let Chris know what a great job he had done. Bob then returned to Mark's office to let him know what a great job Chris had done with his training. With the training all completed, it was now time to get serious about their new improvement initiative.

Their next step was to create teams in the various departments made up of both salaried and hourly employees. And because Chris had delivered his training so well, Bob recommended that he be one of the team leaders. Mark agreed so they made him the team leader in the Carcass Assembly area. Chris agreed to be the team leader in his department and was asked to select his own teammates. He selected two Assembly machine operators, one Maintenance employee, one Quality employee, one of the trained

Six Sigma Blackbelts, one employee from the Curing Department, one Inspector, and one employee from the Preparation Department. Six other teams were formed in various parts of the plants including Preparation, Finishing, Curing, Maintenance, Final Inspection, and Shipping. With the formation of the teams, Tires for All was now ready to begin their new journey to hopefully improved profitability. One of the first assignments for all of the teams was to work together as a single team to create a company-wide, general process map. This would require that the full array of team members would work together to map the entire process.

The starting point for this process map would be the creation of raw materials, receipt of these raw materials from other company locations, and then all of the steps required to produce and ship tires to the customer. Because some of the team members had to travel to other company-owned factories to view the creation of raw materials, the team took three full days to complete the universal process map (Figure 7.1).

The purpose of the universal process map was for all of the teams to get a general idea of the entire tire build process, including the interactions between other factories, as well as each of the internal departments. Each of the individual teams then created their own process maps describing each of the individual process steps within Tires for All's tire production facility. Each team then developed and presented their own, more specific, process maps to the leadership team and Bob Nelson. When everyone was done, Bob spoke up and said, "Nice job everyone, but I want you to do one more thing. I want you to make a list of the performance metrics that are used in each step in the process." Chris Samuels asked, "Do you mean the measurements we make during the creation of our carcasses?" "No, not your measurements, but rather things like efficiency or utilization or on-time delivery of products," Bob responded. Having explained what he wanted, he dismissed everyone, but asked the leadership team to stay.

When everyone had left, Bob stood up and said, "I want to discuss a very important subject today and that subject is performance metrics. I know you are measuring efficiencies, but as of today, the only place I want that metric measured is in the system constraint." "What?" Mark exclaimed. "We have to report that back to Corporate every week Bob, so we can't stop measuring it," he explained. "I get that Mark, but what I'm telling you is that I want you to stop trying to drive it higher in your non-constraints," Bob responded. "But our board will be very upset if our efficiencies drop, Bob!" "Mark, remember when I agreed to come here and work with you, I

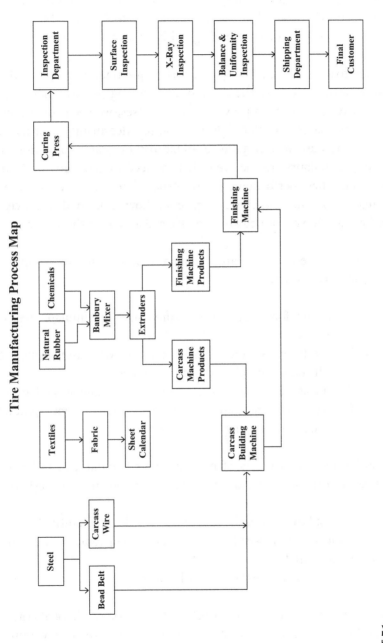

FIGURE 7.1
Universal process map.

told you that you have to do what I say?" Bob said. "Yes, I remember, but I wasn't expecting this to happen!" Mark responded with an angry tone in his voice. "Can you tell me why you want us to do this?" Mark asked. "Yes Mark," and with that, Bob began his presentation on performance metrics.

"I want to ask everyone a simple rhetorical question," Bob said, and that question was, "What are the right and the wrong performance metrics to track? When we are improving our processes, we need some type of feedback mechanism to tell us how we're doing. Measuring performance is important because we need a way to be able to know that the direction we're traveling is on course in the event that we need to make any midcourse corrections. These performance metrics should be system related, in that they tell us how the system is doing, versus how an individual process is functioning," Bob explained and then flashed a slide on the screen.

- Performance measures are intended to serve three very important functions or roles:

  - First, and foremost, the measures should stimulate the right behaviors.
  - The performance measures should reinforce and support the overall goals and objectives of the company.
  - The measures should be able to assess, evaluate, and provide feedback as to the status of the people, departments, products, and the total company.

"According to a good friend of mine, Charles Standard, in order to be effective, performance measures must have the following three criteria:

- They must be objective, be precisely defined, and quantifiable.
- They must be well within the control of the people or department being measured.
- They must encourage the right behaviors.

"And while I agree with Charles, I believe there is one additional criterion. The performance measure must be translatable to everyone within the organization. What I mean by that is each operator, manager, engineer, and so on, must understand how their individual actions impact the metric. Therefore, the metric should be presented as a hierarchy," Bob explained. "Performance metrics are intended to inform everyone, not just the managers!" Bob said, with an emphasis on everyone. "With this in mind, again I ask, 'What are the right and the wrong performance metrics to track? Let's look at financial metrics first,'" and flashed a PowerPoint slide on the screen.

Financial Metrics
- Throughput (T) is the rate at which the system generates money through sales.
- Inventory (I) is all of the money invested in things we intend to sell like raw materials or purchased parts, work-in-process, and finished goods.
- Operating Expense (OE) includes all fixed expenses including direct labor and overhead, office supplies, utility costs, interest expense, etc.
- Net Profit (NP) = T – OE
- Return on Investment (ROI) = (T – OE)/I

Bob then explained, "The key to using these metrics is simple. If Throughput (T) is increasing, while Operating Expense (OE) and Inventory (I) are decreasing or remaining the same, then you are doing well. These three metrics (T, I, and OE), and the two derivatives, Net Profit and Return on Investment, if used correctly, will tell you all you need to know regarding how well your business is running and whether or not your decisions are the right ones." Bob continued, "Now let's look at Operational Metrics," and flashed a new PowerPoint slide.

Bob explained, "For us, operational metrics should be all about flow. That is, the metrics need to let shop floor workers (i.e., Managers, Supervisors, Workers, etc.) know, in real time, how the operation is functioning. With this in mind, consider the following," Bob explained and posted a slide on his screen.

Operational Metrics
- I highly recommend that you abandon the metric efficiency in all places except the constraint.
- On-time delivery of control points and finished product points.
- Schedule compliance at your various control points.
- Quality levels and equipment uptime throughout the process.
- Safety levels of the entire organization.

"The point is, the operational part of the company needs to be focused on those things impacting flow, and not on cost reduction," Bob explained.

"Why not on cost reduction?" Mark asked. Without hesitation, Tom spoke up and said, "Mark, after Bob presented the comparison of Cost Accounting to Throughput Accounting the other day, it became clear to me that our focus needs to be on making money, rather than on saving money." Bob smiled and said, "I couldn't have said it better Tom!"

Bob then asked another question, "So what is your takeaway for the future from today's discussion on performance metrics?" Again, Tom responded and said, "We should remember that system improvement efforts are always better and more profitable than localized improvement. We should use the Theory of Constraints to identify the system constraint and focus our improvement efforts on it by using what we learned from our training in Lean and Six Sigma. We should move away from a cost-centric strategy to a flow-centric strategy that will result in maximum revenue. And we must answer five very important questions as they relate to our company, which are Why change? What to change? What to change to? How to cause the change? How to sustain the gains we make?" "Very good Tom," said Bob.

"With all due respect Bob, I'm not finished," Tom replied. "We must remember that tracking the performance metric efficiency and trying to drive it higher in non-constraints is not a good strategy. We should abandon the use of traditional Cost Accounting to make our real-time financial decisions and replace it with Throughput Accounting. And finally, we should apply Goldratt's five focusing steps which are first, identify the system constraint; second, decide how to exploit the system constraint; third, subordinate everything else to the exploitation decision; fourth, if necessary, elevate the constraint; and finally, when a constraint is broken, return to the first step, but avoid inertia," Tom stated. "Very well said Tom," Bob responded.

"I have another question for you?" Bob said. "How often do you run out of parts that you need to make your tires?" Bob asked. Mark was the first to answer Bob's question and said, "It happens too often to suit me Bob, but why do you ask this question?" "Sometime soon, I want to show you a method for ordering parts that will result in a 40 to 50 percent reduction in inventory, while virtually eliminating stock-outs." Bob responded. "Really?" Mark responded. "Yes, it is the Theory of Constraints Replenishment Solution," Bob said. "Can you tell us about it now?" Mark asked. "In due time Mark, in due time," Bob said.

Later that day, the team leaders presented the performance metrics that Bob had asked them to report to him. In every case, one metric stood out from all of the rest and that metric was manpower efficiency. Bob knew that this metric was the key factor that accounted for all of the work-in-process inventory that existed throughout the manufacturing plant and that if they were serious about improving the profitability, then this metric had to be stopped. That is, stopped in the non-constraint processes. In each case, Bob told the team leaders that they should stop the collection of data for this metrics in the non-constraints. He also told them that this metric should continue in the constraint process steps.

8

TOC's Parts Replenishment Solution

The next morning, Bob arranged a meeting with the leadership team to discuss how parts replenishment problems should be addressed. When everyone was seated, he began his presentation. "Most, if not all, businesses are linked one way or another to some kind of supply chain. They need parts or raw materials from somebody else in order to do what they do and pass it on to the next system in line until it finally arrives at the end consumer. Depending on what you make and how fast you make it, the supply chain can be your best friend or worst enemy. If it works well, it's your best friend. If it doesn't work well, it's your worst enemy."

Bob continued, "The fundamental problem with most supply-chain systems is that they have remained stagnant in their thinking through time, while business reality has flexed in a cycle of constant change, sometimes at an exponential rate. There are many new supply-chain software applications, each proposing that it will solve the problems associated with the supply chain. These new software applications have come about mostly because of advances in computer technology, but few have solved the real issues of the supply chain. While it is true that these systems can provide an enormous amount of information very fast, sometimes system speed is less important than having access to the correct information. What difference does it make how fast you get the information if it's the wrong information?"

"The new business reality has caused a need for change in supply-chain systems, but most systems simply have not changed. Businesses now are required to build products more cheaply, with higher quality, and faster delivery of products. These are the new rules of competition. You either play by the rules or get out of the way. The rules in business have changed, and yet many businesses insist on doing business the same 'old' way. How come?" he asked rhetorically. "Usually, the most common answer given is, 'Because that's the way we've always done it,'" he explained, and he noticed everyone moving their heads in agreement. Bob continued, "The old system and the old rules may have worked in the past, but times are changing. If your supply-chain system has not changed to align with the new rules, then the gap between supply-chain output and system needs will continue to grow. If the supply-chain system is not changed to meet future needs, then there is very little hope of getting different results, and such is the case at Tires for All," Bob explained.

Bob scanned the room to see if everyone was understanding what he had explained so far and then continued. "Many supply-chain systems were designed to solve a problem. And the problem they were trying to solve was the needed availability of parts, raw materials, or inventory. In other words, the right parts or material, in the right location, at the right time. These systems were designed to hold inventory in check. That is, don't buy too much, but also don't allow stock-out situations to occur. Then and now, managing the supply chain is a tough job and there are many variables that can require constant attention. You don't want to run out of parts, and yet, sometimes you still run out of parts. You don't want excess inventory, and yet sometimes you have too much inventory. This constant negative cycle of sometimes too much and sometimes too little has continued through time. The supply problems encountered years ago are still the problems being encountered today," Bob explained.

"For many companies the supply chain/inventory system of choice is one referred to as the minimum/maximum (Min/Max) system. Parts or inventory levels are evaluated based on need and usage, and some type of maximum and minimum levels are established for each item. The traditional rules and measures for these systems are usually quite simple," and with that Bob put a new slide on the screen:

- Rule 1: Determine the maximum and minimum levels for each item.
- Rule 2: Don't exceed the maximum level.
- Rule 3: Don't reorder until you go below the minimum level.

"Is this what rules you're using here at Tires for All?" Bob asked. Cliff Hastings, the Operations Manager responded, "Yes, pretty much so." Bob continued, "The foundational assumptions behind these rules and measures are primarily based in Cost Accounting and commonly referred to as cost-world thinking. In order to save money and minimize your expenditures for supply parts or inventory, you must reduce the amount of money you spend for these items. In order to reduce the amount of money you spend on these items you must never buy more than the maximum amount. In addition, in order to reduce the money spent on these items, you must not spend money until absolutely necessary which means you only order parts when they reach or go below the minimum level," Bob explained to a very captive audience.

Bob continued, "These assumptions seem valid, and if implemented correctly and monitored closely, they should deliver a supply system that controls dollars and maintains inventory within the minimum and maximum levels. However, most systems of this type, even in a perfect world, don't seem to generate the desired results that are required," and again, Bob could see most in attendance shaking their heads in agreement. "For some reason, there always seem to be situations of excess inventory for some items and of stock-out situations for others. There always seem to be constant gyrations between too much inventory and too little inventory. The whole operational concept behind the minimum/maximum systems was supposed to prevent these kinds of occurrences from happening, and yet they still do," Bob explained.

"Perhaps the best way to make this point is with a couple of examples," Bob said. "The first example deals with a company that measured and rewarded their procurement staff based on the amount of money they saved with parts purchases. For the procurement staff, their primary way to accomplish this objective was to buy in bulk, and for the most part this was usually quite easy to accomplish. Their suppliers preferred, and sometimes demanded, that their customers buy in bulk to receive the benefit of 'quantity discounts.' The more you bought, the less it cost per unit. The assumption being that the purchase price per part could be driven to the lowest possible level by buying in large quantities, and the company would save the maximum amount of money on their purchase. It seemed like a great idea and certainly a way to meet the objective of saving money. Sometimes these supply items were procured in amounts well in excess of the maximum, but the company got them at a great price!" Bob explained.

Bob continued, "The bottom line was that by using this cost-saving strategy, the company had a warehouse full of low-cost inventory that had used a large portion of their cash. The problem was, they didn't have the right mix of inventory to build even a single product. They had too many of some items and not enough of others. The bigger problem was they ran out of money to purchase any more parts, especially the parts they desperately needed!" Bob explained. "Do you suppose they wished they had at least some of the money back so they could buy the right parts, in the right quantity, at the right time, so they could produce products?" Bob asked the group. Without exception, everyone agreed with this question.

Bob continued, "The other cost-saving example is one I was involved in that was with a company who was a contractor to the federal government. In their contract with the government, the government had offered a very lucrative clause to save money. This company was given a budgeted amount to buy parts on a yearly basis, and based on this budgeted amount, the government offered to split fifty-fifty any amount the company could underrun their parts budget. The company took the total budgeted dollars and divided it by twelve to establish the monthly parts budget. They also held back a percentage of the budgeted amount each month so they could claim cost savings and split the difference. Any parts purchase that would have exceeded the targeted monthly budget was postponed until the next month, even if it was urgently needed. The ability of this company to make money slowed dramatically. They were literally jumping over dollars to pick up pennies. There were many jobs waiting for parts that couldn't finish until they had the parts to finish, but they had to wait, sometimes for several days or weeks, to get the parts, because of the cost-saving mentality."

Then Bob said, "In both of these examples, it's an issue of bad cost metrics driving the bad behavior. In both of these cases, cost savings were employed as the primary strategy. In the first example, the company ultimately went bankrupt and went out of business. They couldn't pay back the loans on the money they had borrowed to buy all of the low-cost parts because they couldn't make any products. In the second example, the company avoided bankruptcy because they provided a needed service for the government, they were ultimately spared by seeing the error of their ways, and they decided to spend the budgeted dollars to buy the needed parts."

Tom spoke up and commented on what he heard so far, "This is all so very interesting Bob!" Bob responded by saying, "I'm just getting started." Bob continued, "If the system as a whole isn't producing the desired results, then what segment of the system needs to be changed to produce the desired results? Perhaps the minimum and maximum levels are the wrong rules to engage, and saving money is the wrong financial measure to consider. In order to solve today's problems, we must think at an order of magnitude higher than we were thinking when we developed yesterday's solutions. In other words, yesterday's solutions are causing most of today's problems."

"One of the most important aspects of any manufacturing, production, or assembly operation system, like Tires for All, is to have and maintain the ability to supply raw materials or parts at a very predictable level. If the parts availability goes to zero, then your production activities will stop. The continual availability of parts, monitored accurately, implies a supply-chain system that contains all of the necessary and robust features to support the customer demand requirements," Bob explained. "Does everyone understand this basic comment?" Bob asked the group. Again, everyone in the audience nodded their heads in agreement.

Bob continued, "The minimum/maximum supply-chain system was developed years ago, and at the time it brought forward some favorable improvements. Then and now, the functional theory behind the supply-chain minimum/maximum concept is that supplies and materials should be distributed and stored at the lowest possible level of the user chain. In essence, this is a push system, one that pushes parts through the system to the lowest possible level. It seems to make some sense because parts must be available at the lowest level in order to be used. In this type of system, the parts are consumed until the minimum quantity is met or exceeded, and then an order is placed for more parts. The parts order goes up the chain from the point-of-use location back to some kind of central supply center. Or the necessary orders are placed directly back to the vendor, depending on the situation."

Bob continued, "When the orders are received at the central supply center, they are pushed back down the chain to the lowest point-of-use locations," Bob explained and then flashed a figure (Figure 8.1) on the screen.

"This drawing defines a simplified version of this parts-flow activity. This flow might not be applicable to all situations, but I believe it applies to Tires for All. Some companies, and smaller businesses, will have fewer steps, in that they order directly from a vendor and receive parts back into their business without the need for large, more complex, distribution systems. However, the thinking behind the minimum/maximum system will still apply, even to those smaller businesses," Bob explained.

"Larger companies, or those with numerous geographical locations, will most likely have developed some type of a central supply and/or distribution locations that feed the next level of the supply distribution system. Maybe a regional warehouse versus local distribution points. The

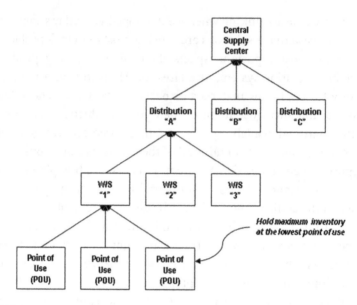

FIGURE 8.1
Supply chain parts-flow activity.

distribution points in turn feed the companies or business segments that use the raw material and parts at the final point-of-use location to build products. Some distribution systems may even be more complex than what is displayed here. But even with increased complexity, the results they are trying to achieve remain the same, which is to get the parts to where they need to be when they need to be there," he explained.

"The model of a central supply system versus a decentralized system has moved back and forth for many years. Some will say that the supply system should be centralized at the user location to make supply activities easier and more responsive. Others argue that the supply-chain activities should be decentralized to save money and reduce operating expense. Even with these different views, it seems that the current method is for the decentralized model of supply systems," Bob explained. Bob then suggested that they take a short break in order to digest what he had explained so far.

After the break, Bob continued his detailed explanation. "For all of its intent to save money and reduce operating expenses, this decentralized system can and usually does cause enormous hardships on the very systems it is designed to support. With all of the intended good this type of system is supposed to provide, there are some top-level rules that drive the system into chaos. Let's look at some of these rules and understand the

TABLE 8.1

Top-Level Rules for the Minimum/Maximum Supply System

1. The system reorder amount is the maximum amount no matter how many parts are currently in the bin box.
2. Most supply systems only allow for one order at a time to be present.
3. Orders for parts are triggered *only* after the minimum amount has been exceeded.
4. Total parts inventory is held at the lowest possible level of the distribution chain—the point-of-use (POU) location.
5. Parts are inventoried once or twice a month and orders placed, as required.

negative aspects that derive from them," as he flashed a table (Table 8.1) on the screen.

"This table provides a summary listing of the top-level rules for the Min/Max supply system," Bob explained. "Even though the minimum/maximum system appears to control the supply needs and cover the inventory demands, there are some significant negative effects caused by using this system. First and foremost, there is the problem of being reactive to an inventory or parts situation, rather than proactive. When minimum stock levels are used as the trigger to reorder parts, some supply-chain systems, as they are currently organized and used, will have a difficult time keeping up with the demands being placed upon them. And there is an increased probability that stock-outs will occur, possibly for long periods of time."

"Stock-outs occur most often when the lead time to replenish the part exceeds the minimum stock available. In other words, availability of the part between the minimum amount and zero is totally depleted before the part can be replenished from the vendor," Bob explained and flashed a new figure (Figure 8.2) on the screen. Bob then said, "This figure displays a graphical representation of this stock-out effect. The curved line shows the item usage through time and the possibility of a stock-out situation," he explained.

Bob added, "Of course, when parts are reordered, they are ordered at a level equal to the maximum amount, and the problem appears to quickly correct itself. However, there can be a significantly large segment of time between stock-out and correction, and if the part is urgently needed, its non-availability can cause havoc in the assembly sequence. Does everyone understand what this figure is actually saying?" Bob asked.

When everyone answered in the affirmative, Bob continued. "Some might argue that the solution to the problem is to simply increase the

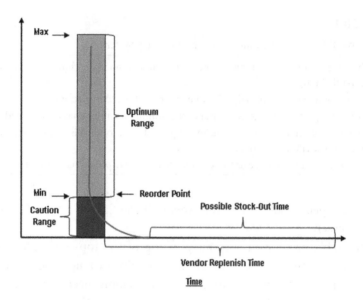

FIGURE 8.2
Graphical impact of the stock-out effect.

minimum amount to trigger a reorder sooner in the process and avoid the stock-out situation. While it is possible this solution could provide some short-term relief, in the long run, it causes inventory levels to increase, needlessly tying up cash and it continues at this elevated level. It is also possible that if you raise the minimum level, then the maximum level must be raised also. Many companies use a ratio variable to calculate the spread between minimum and maximum. If that's the case, then total inventory levels will go up, which costs more money to maintain, which is totally counter to Cost Accounting rules."

Once again Bob continued his presentation, "The minimum/maximum supply chain is based totally on being in a reactive mode waiting for the part to reach minimum stock level before a reorder request is activated. In many companies, the most used parts are managed using the minimum/maximum concepts and can frequently be out of stock. This Min/Max supply system also creates the disadvantage of having maybe several thousand dollars, or hundreds of thousands of dollars, tied up in inventory that may or may not get used before it becomes obsolete, modified, or dated because of expiration. If additional money is spent buying parts that might not be needed, at least in the quantity defined by the maximum limit, then you have effectively diverted money that could have been used to buy needed parts."

Just to reinforce the point he just made, Bob said, "As an example for purposes of discussion, suppose we pick a random part with a minimum/maximum level already established, and we track this part for a twenty-six-week period using the current system rules and follow the flow and cyclical events that take place. What happens at the end of the twenty-six weeks? For this example, we will assume that the maximum level is ninety items; the minimum reorder point is twenty items; and the lead time to replenish this part from the vendor averages four weeks. The average is based on the fact that there are times when this part can be delivered faster, say three weeks, and other times it is delivered slower, say five weeks. Let's also assume that usage of these parts varies by week, but on average is equal to about ten items per week," Bob explained.

Bob then flashed a new table (Table 8.2) on the screen and said, "This table shows the reorder trigger happening when current inventory drops below the minimum amount of twenty items. The first reorder would trigger between weeks six and seven, and again between weeks seventeen and eighteen, and again between weeks twenty-five and twenty-six. During this twenty-six-week period, there would be a total of about eight weeks of stock-out time. Remember, there is an average of four weeks of vendor lead time to replenish this part. This repeating cycle of maximum inventory and stock-outs becomes the norm, and the scenario is repeated time and time again." Bob explained. Bob followed this table with a new figure (Figure 8.3) that used data from the table.

"As I said, in this figure, we have used the data from our table to graphically display the results of the minimum/maximum system, and it demonstrates the potential negative consequences that can occur when using this system. If the vendor lead time is not considered as an important reorder variable, then stock-outs will continue to occur. Stock-outs can become a very predictable negative effect in this system.

In addition, Bob added that the graph shows the negative consequences of the supply system and demonstrates why supply-chain systems using the maximum/minimum concepts will periodically create excessive inventory and stock-out situations. The primary reason this happens is because part lead times are not properly considered. "This is amazing material Bob!" Tom said.

Bob continued, "In most cases, the most prominent measures for the minimum/maximum systems are focused in cost-world thinking, rather than what the system needs. If the lead times from the vendors are not

TABLE 8.2

Simulated Data for Minimum/Maximum Supply System

Week	Current Inventory	Actual Items Used	End of Week Inventory	Items Added (Replenish)
1	90	10	80	
2	80	15	65	
3	65	15	50	
4	50	15	35	
5	35	5	30	
6	30	15	15	
7	15	15	0	
8	0	0	0	
9	0	0	0	
10	0	0	0	90
11	90	15	75	
12	75	15	60	
13	60	8	52	
14	52	12	40	
15	40	10	30	
16	30	10	20	
17	20	15	5	
18	5	5	0	
19	0	0	0	
20	0	0	0	
21	90	15	75	90
22	75	18	57	
23	57	15	42	
24	42	12	30	
25	30	15	15	
26	15	15	0	

considered, then there remains a high probability that stock-outs will continue. The stock-out situation exacerbates itself even further when at the point-of-use a user has experienced a stock-out situation in the past. In that situation the users will often try to protect themselves against stock-outs by taking more than is needed." "Do we need another break?" Bob asked. Virtually everyone in the room indicated that they would rather continue.

Bob continued, "It is also possible that some companies will preorder inventory based on some type of forecast for the coming year, and this

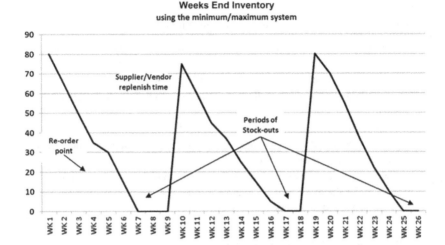

FIGURE 8.3
Consequences of the Min/Max supply system.

strategy only exacerbates the problem even more. At best, it is extremely difficult to forecast what a consumer may or may not buy. This problem is encountered at the manufacturing level and the retail level. Manufacturers will produce excess finished good inventory that must be stored at a great cost or sold to retailers at a discounted price. Because of the flaws in their forecast methods, some stores are left with large amounts of inventory when new models or products are released. This becomes most visible when stores offer 'year-end clearance sales' or 'inventory liquidation' events. They guessed wrong with the forecast and have much more inventory than they can sell. In many cases because stores couldn't get enough of the hot-selling product, they missed out on sales. Now they must sell any remaining inventory, sometimes at bargain prices, to generate enough cash to go buy more inventories for the coming year. This cycle of too much and too little repeats itself year after year." Bob then said, "What's the answer to this logistics dilemma?"

Bob began to answer his own question by saying, "One of the primary operating functions of the supply-chain system is to build and hold inventory at the lowest possible distribution level. This assumption is both correct and incorrect. The correct inventory should be held at the point-of-use location, but not based on minimum/maximum amounts. Instead, the necessary inventory should be based on the vendor lead times to replenish and maintain sufficient inventory to buffer the variations that exist in lead

TABLE 8.3

Criteria for the TOC Distribution and Replenishment Model

---

1. The system reorder amount needs to be based on daily or weekly usage and part lead time to replenish.
2. The system needs to allow for multiple replenish orders, if required.
3. Orders are triggered based on buffer requirements, with possible daily actions, as required.
4. *All* parts/inventory must be available when needed.
5. Parts inventory is held at a higher level, preferably at central supply locations or comes directly from the supplier /vendor.
6. Part buffer determined by usage rate and replenish supplier/vendor lead time. Baseline buffer should be equal to 1.5. If lead time is one week, buffer is set at 1.5 weeks. Adjust as required, based on historical data.

---

time. The Theory of Constraints Distribution and Replenishment Model is a robust parts replenishment system that allows the user to be proactive in managing the supply-chain system. It's also a system based on usage, either daily or weekly, but not the minimum amount. Some parts/inventory will require much more vigilance in day-to-day management." And with this comment, Bob flashed a new table on his screen and explained, "This table (Table 8.3) defines the suggested criteria required to implement a TOC Distribution and Replenishment Model in a supply-chain system."

Bob continued, "The TOC Distribution and Replenishment Model argues that the majority of the inventory should be held at a higher level in the distribution system and not at the lowest level. It is still important to keep what is needed at the lowest levels, but don't try to hold the total inventory at that location." Again, Bob checked for understanding and when he was comfortable that everyone was following what he had just said, he continued.

"The TOC model is based on the characteristics of a 'V' plant distribution model. The 'V' plant model assumes that distribution is fractal from a single location, which in this case is either a central supply location or a supplier/vendor location (the base of the 'V') and distribution is made to different locations which is the arms of the 'V.' The 'V' plant concept is not unlike any supply-chain distribution methodology. However, using a 'V' plant method has some negative consequences, especially when working under the minimum/maximum rules that I presented earlier. If one is not careful to understand these consequences, the system can suffer dramatically," Bob explained. He continued, "One of the major negative consequences of 'V' distribution is distributing items too early and sending them down the wrong path to the wrong location. In other words, inventory is released too early and possibly to the wrong destination. This is especially likely to happen when the same type of inventory or part is used in several locations."

Bob then asked the group a question, "Has it ever happened that at one location you have a stock-out situation, and one of the rapid response criteria for finding the part is to check another production line within Tires for All?" Mark answered his question by saying, "Yes, it happens often!" Bob responded, "If this is the case, then parts/inventory distribution has taken place too early in the system. Sometimes, it's not that the system does not have the right parts/inventory, but it's just that they are in the wrong location. Distribution from a higher level in the chain has been completed too quickly."

Bob continued his presentation, "The TOC Distribution and Replenishment Model also argues that the use of minimum/maximum amounts should be abolished. Instead the inventory should be monitored based on daily or weekly usage, with replenishment occurring, at a minimum weekly, and possibly daily for highly used items. The end result of these actions will be sufficient inventory in the right location at the right time, with zero or minimal stock-outs to support production activity. Instead of using the minimum amount to trigger the reorder process, it should be triggered by daily usage and vendor lead time to replenish and with that, Bob flashed another table onto the screen.

Bob then said, "As an example, suppose we apply the TOC Distribution and Replenishment Model rules to exactly the same criteria that we used for the minimum/maximum system we discussed earlier. We will use the same part simulation and the same period of time, with the same usage numbers. The difference will be in this simulation, we will change the rules to fit the TOC Distribution and Replenishment Model, based on usage amount and vendor lead time rather than minimum and maximum amount."

Bob explained, "This table (Table 8.4) represents the simulated data for a random reorder scenario using the TOC Distribution and Replenishment Model. In this example, we will assume that the maximum level is ninety items, which is the start point for the current inventory. We will also assume that there is no minimum reorder point, but rather reorder is based on usage and vendor lead time. We will also assume that the lead

TABLE 8.4

TOC Distribution and Replenishment Model

	Current Inventory	Actual Items Used	End of Week Inventory	Items Added (Replenish)
WK 1	90	10	80	
WK 2	80	15	65	
WK 3	65	15	50	
WK 4	50	15	35	10
WK 5	45	5	40	15
WK 6	55	15	40	15
WK 7	55	15	40	15
WK 8	55	10	45	5
WK 9	50	10	40	15
WK 10	55	15	40	15
WK 11	55	15	40	10
WK 12	50	15	35	10
WK 13	45	8	37	15
WK 14	52	12	40	15
WK 15	55	10	45	15
WK 16	60	10	50	8
WK 17	58	5	53	12
WK 18	65	10	55	10
WK 19	65	10	55	10
WK 20	65	10	55	5
WK 21	60	15	45	10
WK 22	55	18	37	10
WK 23	47	15	32	10
WK 24	42	12	30	15
WK 25	45	10	35	18
WK 26	53	15	38	15

time to replenish is still four weeks and that the average usage of the part is about ten per week." "Everyone understand?" Bob asked and again, it appeared that everyone did, so Bob continued with his example.

He began again, "The data in this table also assumes that no parts inventory is held at the next higher level and that the parts replenishment has to come from the vendor and consumes the allotted vendor lead time. However, if the parts/inventory were held at a higher level in the distribution chain, such as a central supply or a distribution point, and replenishment happened daily and/or weekly, then the total inventory required could go even lower than the data suggests. This could happen because distribution is completed weekly, rather than waiting the full four weeks for delivery. Is everyone still with me?" he asked and again, everyone was.

Bob continued, "The part usage rates are exactly the same as the previous run and the starting inventory is equal to ninety parts. This also assumes we have a weekly parts/inventory replenish after the initial four weeks of lead time has expired. In other words, every week we have delivered what was ordered four weeks ago. In the TOC scenario, the reorder point is at the end of each week based on usage. The total number of parts used is the same number of parts that should be reordered. Bob then flashed a new image on the screen (Figure 8.4).

Bob continued, "The figure on the screen demonstrates the effects of using the TOC Distribution and Replenishment Model. One of the most notable things you see in this graph is that total inventory required through time has decreased from ninety items to approximately forty-two items or roughly a 47 percent reduction. In essence, the required inventory has been cut in half. The other notable feature is that even though the inventory level has been cut in half, the number of stock-out situations has been reduced to zero!" Bob said with vigor. The group was somewhat flabbergasted in that by reducing the inventory by half, there were no stock-outs!

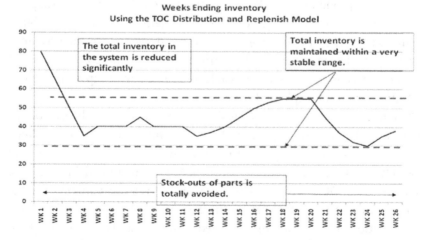

FIGURE 8.4
The overall effect of the TOC Replenishment method.

Bob continued, "When the TOC Distribution and Replenishment Model is used to manage the supply chain, there is always sufficient parts inventory to continue production work. The total inventory is also much more stable through time, without the large gaps and gyrations from zero inventories available to maximum inventory as noted on the minimum/maximum system."

With a smile, Bob then said, "Perhaps the best way to explain the TOC Distribution and Replenishment Model is with an easy example. Consider a soda vending machine. When the supplier, the soda vendor, opens the door on a vending machine, it is very easy to calculate the distribution of products sold. The soda person knows immediately which inventory has to be replaced and to what level to replace it. The soda person is holding the inventory at the next highest level, which in on the soda truck, so it's easy to make the required distribution when needed. He doesn't leave four cases of soda when only twenty cans are needed. If he were to do that, when he got to the next vending machine he might have run out of the necessary soda because he made distribution too early at the last stop." Bob could see by the expressions on everyone's face that they immediately related to this simple example.

"After completing the required daily distribution to the vending machines, the soda person returns to the warehouse or distribution point to replenish the supply on the soda truck and get ready for the next day's distribution. When the warehouse makes distribution to the soda truck, they move up one level in the chain and replenish from their supplier. This type of system does require discipline to gain the most benefits, but it assumes that regular and needed checks are taking place at the inventory locations to determine the replenishment needs. If these points are not checked on a regular basis, it is possible for the system to experience stock-out situations," Bob explained.

"So, let's summarize our conclusions from what you've heard today," Bob said. He continued, "The distinct contrast in results between simulated data runs using the minimum/maximum supply system and the TOC Distribution and Replenishment Model are undeniable. The true benefits of a TOC-based parts replenishment system are many, but the most significant impact is realized in these two areas. The first benefit is the reduction of total inventory required to manage and maintain the total supply-chain system by nearly 50 percent. This inventory reduction could lead to a significant dollar savings in total inventory required, perhaps thousands of dollars. And think about what would happen to your profit levels," Bob said.

"The second benefit is the elimination of stock-out situations. Without a doubt, not having parts available is an expensive situation because it slows throughput through the production system. Production lines sit idle, waiting for parts to become available. Or worse yet, they start making products that aren't really needed only because parts are available, and everyone needs to be kept busy to maintain efficiencies. Stock-out situations increase frustration, not only in not being able to complete the work, but also in the time spent waiting for parts to become available. When this happens, orders will be delivered late, and customers will be frustrated. So, think about what might happen to your on-time delivery metric," Bob suggested.

Bob completed his presentation by stating, "Looking for parts and experiencing part shortages are a continuing problem in most supply-chain systems. These problems are not caused by the production people, but by the negative effects of the supply-chain system and the way it is used. If your current Min/Max supply system is maintained, then the results from that system cannot be expected to change much, if at all. However, if new levels of output are required from the system, now and in the future, then new thinking must be applied to solve the parts supply-system issues. The concepts and methodologies of the TOC Distribution and Replenishment Model can positively impact the ability to produce products on time and in the correct quantity."

When Bob finished, he asked, "Are there any questions or comments?" Mark was the first to raise his hand and said, "I followed most of what you were explaining throughout most of your presentation, but I must say, when you finished with the soda vending machine example, it all fell into place." Cliff Hastings, then added, "I absolutely agree with Mark and going forward, I think we can make major improvements to our profit margins and on-time delivery!" Tom Mahanan then commented, "While I had never heard of the Theory of Constraints before you arrived, in the future I will be finding and reading everything I can. Do you have other elements of TOC that you'll be teaching us?" Bob just smiled and said, "As they say, you ain't seen nothing yet! In fact, I'd like to schedule another session to speak about another TOC tool referred to as Drum Buffer Rope." They scheduled the meeting for the next day and with that, the meeting ended.

9

Planning and Scheduling

Bright and early the next day, the leadership team assembled in the conference room for Bob's presentation on Drum Buffer Rope (DBR). When everyone was seated, Bob began, "Unlike yesterday's presentation on the Theory of Constraints Distribution and Replenishment Model, I want to keep today's discussion much simpler. In a Theory of Constraints environment, production planning and scheduling is done so with a tool known as the Drum Buffer Rope. Drum Buffer Rope is designed to regulate the flow of work-in-process through a production line based upon the pace of the slowest resource, the constraint operation, also known as the capacity constrained resource."

Bob continued, "In order to optimize the flow of product through the factory, material is released according to the capacity of the capacity constrained resource. The production rate of the capacity constrained resource is equated to the rhythm of a drum. The rope is the communication mechanism that connects the constraint to the material release to the first operation, in order to make certain that raw material is released in time to guarantee that the constraint always has material to work on. So, the first purpose of the rope is to assure that the constraint is never starved for work and not inundated with excess work-in-process inventory, sort of like you have here at Tires for All," Bob said jokingly.

Bob then explained, "Because of the existence of statistical fluctuations and disruptions in the upstream operations, a buffer is established to protect the constraint from being starved. By the same token, the rope assures that material is not introduced into the production process faster than the constraint can consume it. So DBR has three purposes, namely, first to protect the constraint from starvation; second, to ensure that excess material is not released into the system; and third, to protect the delivery due dates to the customer." Bob then flashed on a PowerPoint slide.

There are three main elements of the Drum Buffer Rope:

1. A shipping schedule which is based upon the rate that the constraint can produce parts. That is, use the throughput of the constraint for promised due dates.
2. A constraint schedule which is tied to the shipping schedule.
3. A material release schedule which is tied to the constraint schedule.

Bob then flashed a drawing of this system on the screen (Figure 9.1) and said, "Visually these three elements might look like this figure. Here we see the three elements of the Drum Buffer Rope system and the interconnectedness of each. The drum sets the pace of the production line and its capacity is hopefully greater than the number of orders in the system. In order to satisfy the shipping schedule, we must first fulfill the constraint schedule. In order to meet the constraint schedule, we must satisfy the material release schedule. Failure to release materials per the schedule will jeopardize the constraint schedule which will in turn jeopardize our shipping schedule. Because of this linkage of schedules, managing the buffers becomes critical!" Bob then asked the group if they had any questions.

Cliff Hastings, the Operations Manager, raised his hand and asked, "If we implement Drum Buffer Rope, what happens to our current scheduling system?" Bob responded, "That's a great question Cliff, and if you can hold on for a bit, I will answer it."

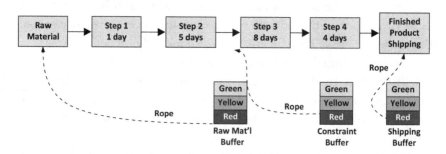

FIGURE 9.1
Visual display of a Drum Buffer Rope system.

Bob continued, "In this visual representation of a Drum Buffer Rope system, I have displayed three buffers, the raw material buffer, the constraint buffer, and the shipping buffer. And if you have an assembly operation that feeds parts into you process, you can place a buffer there as well. These buffers are comprised of two different dimensions which are both space and time. Now what do I mean by that? Since we don't want to have excess inventory in our process, the buffers contain some physical inventory and a liberal estimate of lead time from various points within our total process. In the case of the raw material buffer, we place an amount of needed raw materials at the beginning of the process as well as a time buffer to prevent material shortages at the beginning of the process. In the case of the constraint buffer, we place an amount of physical inventory in front of the constraint and a time buffer based upon the lead time from raw material release until the products arrive at the constraint operation. Likewise, if you have an assembly operation, the buffer would contain some amount of material and a time buffer based upon the lead time from the constraint operation to the assembly operation. The shipping buffer contains some amount of work-in-process inventory and a time buffer based upon the lead time from either the constraint operation (or assembly operation) to completion into finished product. So how much is 'some amount of material?'" Bob asked rhetorically.

Bob continued, "In order to size the buffer correctly, the arrival of parts to the buffer must be monitored and compared with the scheduled arrival time. By monitoring the buffer, we are essentially sending a signal to the plant as to when we need to expedite parts. You'll notice a section of the drawing of our Drum Buffer Rope system labeled as 'buffers.' When parts do not arrive into the buffer on schedule, it in essence creates what is referred to as a 'hole' in the buffer. If we divide the buffer into three zones, we will be able to successfully manage the buffer. So, what are these zones?" he asked.

Bob continued his explanation, "The first zone, which is the green zone in our drawing, means that everything is going according to the scheduled arrival date or time, so holes in the green zone are no cause for concern. The second zone, the yellow zone in our drawing, tells us that the parts are not arriving on schedule and that it is time to locate the missing parts and create an expediting plan in the event the parts need to be expedited. The third zone, the red zone in our drawing, means that the parts will definitely not be arriving into the buffer on schedule and that the jobs need to be expedited. Managing the constraint buffer focuses attention on late arrivals to the constraint and tells us when we need to expedite and when not to expedite. Any questions so far?" Bob asked and when there were none, he continued.

"How much physical inventory we need is a function of how stable or consistent our process is at producing product. That is, if we are never creating holes in our green zone, then our buffer is probably too high. By contrast, if we are constantly penetrating our red zone, then the buffer is clearly too low. If we have over-sized our buffer, then we are needlessly increasing operating expenses and cycle time, while at the same time decreasing inventory turns and cash flow. If we have undersized our buffer, then we run the risk of starving our constraint and losing valuable throughput. My advice to you is to err on the side of conservatism because losing valuable throughput is much more damaging to your plant than increasing operating expenses or reducing cash flow. Remember, according to the Theory of Constraints, Throughput is revenue minus Operating Expense, which is the key driver of your profitability," Bob explained.

Bob continued, "You may be wondering just how much of the buffer should be physical parts and how much should be time? Believe it or not, it depends upon the variability of our process. If we have a highly variable operation feeding the constraint, or one that has many disruptions, then most of our buffer will be in the form of physical materials. If, on the other hand, our feeder operation contains very little variability, then most of the buffer will be in the form of time. As you improve your process by reducing waste and variation using Lean and Six Sigma, rendering it more consistent and stable, then the ratio of physical inventory to time will change accordingly. Remember the purpose of these buffers is to protect our constraint from starvation and our delivery of product to customers." Bob looked directly at Cliff and said, "The Drum Buffer Rope system is a finite scheduling method that attempts to balance and control the optimum flow of materials through a plant in accordance with the demands of the market, while minimizing lead time, inventory and operating expenses." Again, Bob looked at Cliff and said, "Cliff, I'll get more into your question about what happens to your current scheduling system shortly."

Bob continued his Drum Buffer Rope explanation, "In addition to protecting the constraint from starvation and inundating the process with excess inventory, buffer management accomplishes another critical aspect. Buffer management provides you with a vehicle to systematically identify and quantify potential improvement opportunities in key non-constraint operations. By focusing improvements on the sources or causes of buffer holes, it provides you with the opportunity to improve throughput and reduce both cycle times and inventory. If you are continuously finding holes in your red zone, then you know that there are problems in one or more of the upstream processes. If you know this, then your improvement actions need to be focused on the operation creating the holes. As you continue to improve your process, these holes in your buffer will eventually disappear and provide you with the opportunity to safely reduce the size of your buffers and consistently improve throughput, reduce cycle times, and reduce inventory."

"As you analyze and prioritize the causes of the holes in your buffer, another important nuance occurs. You will be able to form a picture of protective capacity throughout your process. This is important for several very important reasons," and he posted another slide.

1. The non-constraint that has the least protective capacity will have the highest probability of becoming the next constraint when we break the current constraint.
2. It provides you with a way of estimating how much of the non-constraint capacity can be sold in a targeted market of the non-constraint products, if they are in a form that can be sold. However, you will only be able to exploit this market if it will not jeopardize the constraint buffer and the constraint throughput.
3. You are able to focus in on and prioritize improvement efforts in the right non-constraints.

"Okay, so let's now answer Cliff's question about how we use Drum Buffer Rope with your current scheduling system," Bob said. "The real question is, can Enterprise Resource Planning or ERP and TOC exist together in the same manufacturing facility? The short answer is a resounding yes! The Theory of Constraints is very often seen as an alternative to ERP, but it doesn't have to be. Scheduling in your ERP system begins by identifying a due date for an order and then attempts to start the order as late as possible, but still meet the date. Scheduling through a plant uses production rates and time to schedule each resource."

"The Theory of Constraints uses a much simpler approach. It begins by identifying the constraining operation and other resources are scheduled around the constraint. Remember, the rate of production that can pass through the constraint is the definitive rate that can pass through the entire plant and as I explained, that rate is the drum beat. So, with this in mind, you use ERP to schedule production in your plant around the beat of the drum. The next step is to set up buffers ahead of the constrained resource to ensure that it is never starved due to any unforeseen irregularity upstream. You then set up a buffer downstream of the constraint so that a downstream problem can never interfere with the constraints output." "Are you with me so far Cliff?" he asked, and Cliff indicated that he was.

Bob continued, "The buffer can be inventory or what ERP refers to as a safety stock. It can also be spare resources or whatever works in a particular environment, to never allow the constraint to move away from its drumbeat. Finally, a rope is tied to all the other resources so that they never fall behind or get too far ahead of the constraint. While falling slightly behind is not usually a problem, getting too far ahead is simply a waste which should be avoided. Together using the drum, the buffer, and the rope makes TOC a very simple system to implement and you use the ERP system to effectively manage the constraint. Simply schedule your upstream resources to keep the buffer full, and schedule downstream resources based on the output of the constraint. The bottom line is that ERP works on rules and the Theory of Constraints can easily be combined with it to give you a superior scheduling system." Bob then turned to Cliff and asked, "Did that answer your question?" Cliff responded and said, "I think so, but I may have questions for you in the future."

"Let me say a couple more things comparing Drum Buffer Rope and ERP," Bob said. "In their pure forms, ERP assumes infinite capacity and works to schedule all steps in the process. Drum Buffer Rope, on the other hand, assumes finite capacity and only schedules the constraint. Typically, ERP prohibits late release of materials, while Drum Buffer Rope prohibits early release, simply because early release only serves to drive up work-in-process inventory. Also, ERP drives material requirements all the way through the bill of materials, no matter how much stock is on hand, while Drum Buffer Rope takes existing stock and buffers into consideration. The bottom line is that ERP and Drum Buffer Rope are different solutions to scheduling, but they can co-exist. Simply use ERP to manage the constraint and schedule upstream resources to keep the buffer full and schedule downstream resources always forward from the output of the constraint. As I said earlier, ERP works on rules and those rules can be taken from TOC easily."

"Are there any questions or comments?" Bob asked. Mark raised his hand and said, "What you've presented in the last two days is a new way forward for us and I'm very excited to get moving on everything. I mean I can see clearly how our new replenishment solution and now, our new scheduling system will move us into new levels of profitability. My question is more of one on technique." "And what question are you referring to?" Bob asked. Mark responded with another question, "How do we combine our Lean and Six Sigma efforts with the Theory of Constraints?" "That's a great question Mark, so let's schedule an off-site meeting that will probably take two days to complete," Bob said. "I will have my secretary, Margie Newsome, set that up today," Mark replied. "Who would you like to be invited to this off-site session?" Mark asked. Bob replied, "Let's have our leadership team and Oscar Francis, our Master Black Belt." And with that, the meeting ended.

10

Combining TOC, Lean, and Six Sigma

Margie Newsome, Mark's assistant, had scheduled the off-site meeting at a local hotel and invited all members of the leadership team and Oscar Francis, Tires for All's Master Black Belt. Everyone arrived on time and took a seat in the hotel's conference room. Bob then started the meeting by welcoming everyone. "In the next two days we will be covering how we intend to combine our Lean, Six Sigma, and Theory of Constraints initiatives into a singular improvement method," Bob said. "And as we go, if you have questions or need clarification on any of the points I present, I want you to feel free to stop me," Bob said. And with that brief introduction, Bob began.

"When I first began my career in a manufacturing environment, I'll be the first to tell you that I knew nothing about the inner workings of a manufacturing facility. I knew that you had to process customer orders, order raw materials, create a production schedule, process them into a finished product, and then deliver them to a customer in a timely manner. What I was unaware of were the intricacies involved in doing all of this," Bob explained.

Bob continued, "In the years that followed I began to better understand the different roles of other groups within a typical company and how they impacted the success of the company. I learned that processes don't always produce product according to plan because of things like downtime and quality problems. I also began to realize the impact and influence that leadership can have on an organization and how performance metrics invariably influence the behaviors of the resources within the organization. I've been at it now for many years now and have come to several conclusions that I believe apply to all manufacturing companies. Some of these conclusions directly contradict what I had learned along the way from the various mentors and leaders that shaped and influenced my career."

"In hopes of not offending too many Cost Accountants, like you Tom, the first and perhaps the most important conclusion of all, is my belief that Cost Accounting influences the behaviors of many manufacturing organizations in very negative ways. I had always been taught that if you were able to minimize the cost of each individual operation, that the total system would operate at minimal cost. I had also been taught that the total cost of each operation is directly proportional to the cost of direct labor for each operation, and that the total cost for the system minus the raw material cost is proportional to the sum of direct labor costs," Bob explained.

Bob continued, "I had also been taught that if I maximized efficiencies and utilizations of each individual operation, like you do here at Tires for All, I would have maximized the efficiencies and utilization of the entire system. More succinctly, I was taught that the key to reaching global optimization was by achieving local optimums. I was taught that every operation was equal in value and that the key to increasing profits was to reduce the amount of money required to operate each individual process. In so doing, I was taught that manpower was expendable, so it was okay to lay off excess manpower."

"Finally, I was taught that inventory was needed to protect all of the steps in the process, so that if we had downtime on the previous step, we could use inventory to continue running. In essence, I was taught that inventory was a good thing because it was impossible to avoid downtime and defects that resulted in rework and scrap. And besides, inventory was viewed by Cost Accounting as an asset, so how could it possibly be bad?" he explained.

"As I continued learning, I began to realize that some of things I had taken as being the gospel were in fact, pretty much bogus! First, I realized that maximizing the efficiency and utilization of each operation did not result in optimization of the total system at all. In fact, I learned that maximizing the efficiency of all operations only served to create mountains of work-in-process inventory," he explained. "Sound familiar?" he asked with tongue in cheek. "I learned that inventory was not an asset at all because it actually had a carrying cost associated with it. But more importantly excess inventory increased the effective cycle time, which decreased an organization's ability to ship product on time. I also learned that inventory tends to hide other problems," Bob explained to a very captive audience.

"My first major conclusion was that cutting the cost of each individual operation did not result in the system cost being minimized. In fact, many times in an attempt to minimize the cost of individual operations, companies made drastic cuts in operating expense and labor that were too deep, causing motivational, quality, and delivery problems!" Bob stated.

"My second conclusion is that in every organization, there are only a few, and most of the time only one, operation that controls the rate of revenue generation and hence, the profits. All processes are comprised of constraining and non-constraining resources, and that the key improvement consideration is to always be focusing on the operation that is constraining throughput. Attempts to improve non-constraining resources usually result in very little improvement at all from a system perspective," Bob explained.

"My third conclusion is that variability is the root of all evil in a manufacturing process. Variability in product characteristics, or variability in process parameters, or variability in processing times, all degrade the performance of a process, an organization, and ultimately, the overall company. The presence of variability degrades our ability to effectively plan and execute our scheduled production, increases operational expense, and decreases our chances of producing and delivering products to our customers when they want them and at the cost they want to pay. Because variability is so devastating, every effort must be made to reduce it as much as possible," Bob stated.

"My fourth conclusion was that excessive waste exists in every process, and unless and until it is identified and removed, real process improvement will not happen. While there are many forms of waste, the most obvious, and perhaps the two most debilitating types, are the waste associated with waiting and over-producing. Waiting and over-production both work to lengthen the overall cycle time," Bob explained.

Bob continued, "My fifth conclusion is that how people and organizations are measured, significantly dictates their behavior. If, for example, a company like Tires for All measures operator efficiency, and values high efficiency in every step in the operation, then predictably the organization will have high levels of work-in-process inventory, low values of quality, and a high incidence of late or missed shipments. As a corollary to this, maximizing the efficiency of an operation that is limiting throughput is mandatory to maximizing revenue and profits!"

"My sixth conclusion is that most companies don't know how to focus and leverage their improvement efforts in the right area. Many companies, just like Tires for All, have embraced Lean or Six Sigma or a combination of the two, and in so doing, have attempted to effectively solve world hunger by struggling to improve every operation. When this happens, the efforts become diluted and improvements become protracted to the point of frustration. Both of these initiatives would have worked well, if they had only been focused in the right area of the organization!" Bob continued. Bob was very happy that everyone in the room was focused on his every word.

"My seventh conclusion is that organizations that fail to involve their workforce, typically do not succeed in the long run. Everyone in the organization needs to know the goals of the company and how they are doing relative to these goals. But even more importantly, everyone must be permitted to contribute to these goals. After all of these years, it is apparent to me that the shop floor workers have a vast array of information and ideas, both of which must be harvested," he explained while emphasizing this last point.

"Unfortunately, many of the companies that I have been involved with don't practice what I have learned. Many companies still use ineffective performance metrics and outdated accounting systems. Many companies fail to recognize and capitalize on the constraints that exist within their systems. Many companies still don't appreciate that waste and variability encumber their processes and that the general workforce is needed to make them successful," Bob stated.

Bob continued, "As a consultant, I have been able to study the inner workings of many companies, in many types of industries, and I have discovered a better way to make the most of your precious resources. Not only do I have an idea of why you might have failed to achieve an acceptable and sustainable return on your improvement investments, I have a solution for you as well. The solution isn't revolutionary, but it is innovative. What I have to offer you is a way to make certain that your improvement effort is focused in the right place, at the right time, using the right methods and tools, and the right amount of resources to deliver the maximum amount of return on your improvement investment. This method addresses the problems associated with Cost Accounting, variation, waste, and performance measurements. But most of all, it will focus your organization on the right area to optimize your throughput, operating expense, inventory, revenues, and margins," he explained in a passionate tone.

"I know, I know, you've heard it all before. You've heard the same declaration from experts in efforts like TQM, JIT, Six Sigma, Lean, and all of the others, but I believe once you see the simplicity and logic behind what I refer to as the Ultimate Improvement Cycle, you will be motivated and maybe even inspired to move forward with it. The Ultimate Improvement Cycle is based upon the basic principles associated with Lean, Six Sigma, and the Theory of Constraints, but it is unique in that it capitalizes on a time-released formula for use of the key tools, techniques, principles, and actions of all three initiatives focused on the right area. It doesn't require any more resources than you currently have available, but it does provide the focus needed to achieve maximum resource utilization which translates into maximum return on investment," Bob explained. "Using this method will provide you with a self-funded improvement effort that will sustain itself," he stated emphatically.

"The Theory of Constraints reveals interdependencies that exist within your operation and focuses your efforts on the constraining operation. While the Theory of Constraints provides the necessary focus, Lean works to simplify and free the constraint of unnecessary waste as well as increasing the throughput of your total system. While Lean is doing this, Six Sigma removes variation and defects while working to sustain the improvements," Bob continued.

"The genesis behind the Ultimate Improvement Cycle is based upon my many years of analysis of both failures and successes using Lean, Six Sigma, and the Theory of Constraints as stand-alone improvement initiatives. My analysis revealed a common thread between successful initiatives, no matter whether they were based on Lean, Six Sigma, or TOC models. The key to success is the leverage point, or where the improvement efforts were focused. While reducing or eliminating waste with Lean, and reducing variation with Six Sigma, are both critical components of all successful improvement initiatives, where these efforts are focused will determine the ultimate impact on a company's bottom line. By integrating Lean, Six Sigma, and the Theory of Constraints into a single improvement cycle, you will have a recipe that will maximize your return on investment, cash flow, on-time delivery, and net profit," Bob stated emphatically. He then said, "Before we get into the details of this integration, let's take a short break," Bob suggested.

It was clear to Bob that, based on all of the side conversations he witnessed, everyone was intrigued by what he had explained so far. When everyone was back in their seats, Bob began again. "For-profit organizations exist ostensibly for two purposes, to make money now and to make money in the future. Making money now requires organizations to relentlessly remove needless sources of waste and variation, so that their products and/ or services are not only profitable but are consistently delivered on time and at the right price. But in order to sustain these profits, organizations must continually reinvent themselves. What worked yesterday and today, probably won't work tomorrow or next year, so change is necessary. The good news is that it's much easier to manage change than it is to react to it. Because products or services have such short half-lives these days, change must not only be expected, it should be passionately pursued and embraced. But what is it that we should be changing is a question for the ages."

"Knowing what to change, what to change to, and how to implement change is usually the determining factor as to how successful an organization will be in the future. While change is necessary, unfortunately it isn't always so clear-cut. In fact, in an effort to reinvent themselves, just like Tires for All, many organizations have attempted improvement initiatives like Lean Manufacturing and Six Sigma but have failed to achieve the positive results they had expected or at least hoped for. Many times, these companies then become either disappointed or disillusioned and either abandon the initiative altogether or back-slide to their old, more comfortable way of doing business, or use bits and pieces of the improvement strategy," Bob explained.

He continued, "Based upon my many experiences, in a variety of organizations and industries, the disappointing results coming from Lean, and sometimes Six Sigma, are directly linked to failing to adequately answer the question, 'What to change?' or, worse yet, failing to ask it at all. Deciding what to change cannot be done in some happenstance or chance manner. It must be addressed logically at the strategic, tactical, and operational levels after careful deliberation and analysis. The roots of this disillusionment are manifested in ill-advised efforts wasted on local improvements that fail to achieve global or system improvement," Bob continued.

"But even if an organization successfully considered and visualized what to change, many times that same organization will fail to rightfully answer the question of 'What to change to?' It's one thing to change your way of doing business, but you had better make sure that what you are changing to makes sense strategically. So how do you know what to change to? In today's world there seems to be so many choices regarding improvement initiatives, so surely one of these will work, right? Not so fast!" Bob stated with emotion.

"Even if an organization is successful in determining what to change and what to change to, there's still the question of how to make the change happen. No matter how well-conceived an improvement initiative is planned, how the change is executed will play a huge role in the success or failure of the change. Establishing and implementing a sustainable improvement initiative requires selecting the right area to focus on, what the content of the improvement initiative should look like, carefully planning and developing a step-by-step execution plan, total support and buy-in from the leadership, and sincere collaboration with and involvement of the employees that make the product or deliver the service," Bob again stated emphatically.

"As you've just heard, many companies attempting either Lean or Six Sigma are having their problems, but it's not at all because Lean and Six Sigma aren't good improvement initiatives. It's really a question of planning, execution, *focus and leverage.* In recent years, we've also seen Lean and Six Sigma join forces to create a separate, supposedly more powerful improvement philosophy, known as Lean Six Sigma. Whether it's Lean, Six Sigma, or Lean Six Sigma, the hoped for, bottom line improvements have simply not materialized to the extent many companies had anticipated, or at least were led to believe," Bob explained. "So, why do you think these improvement initiatives have failed to deliver the expected results?" Bob asked the group. Tom raised his hand and said, "Based upon what I've heard so far this morning, I would say that the true improvement leverage point was missed." Bob responded and said, "Tell us more Tom and please come up front."

Tom began, "The question of why these stand-alone or integrated improvement initiatives have not lived up to their advanced billing, is in some ways not such a simple question to answer. It could be that the projects or processes selected to focus on were ill-conceived or it could be that their vision of the future was somewhat flawed. It could be that implementation plans were not well planned and executed or, worse yet, never developed. But again, as you explained, the reason for failure is not the initiative itself!"

Tom continued, "It's pretty clear to me that many of these initiatives fail for two primary reasons. First, the scope or size of the initiative is well beyond the capability of the available resources. The second reason is that companies generally fail to recognize their *leverage point.* Instead of developing a strategically focused and manageable plan, I would guess that many companies try to solve world hunger, instead of focusing on the areas of greatest payback! Many companies probably attempt to use these improvement initiatives across the board and end up making very few sustainable improvements. While many Lean initiatives attempt to drive waste out of the entire system, they are probably disappointed that the predicted waste reduction didn't impact their bottom line to the extent that they had hoped. That happened to us here at Tires for All with both our Lean and Six Sigma initiatives." "Tom, that was an excellent summary!" Bob stated.

Bob continued his presentation by posting a table (Table 10.1) onto the screen and said, "The table you see on the screen is a summary comparison of Lean and Six Sigma and there are clear differences. While Lean seeks to eliminate or eradicate waste in all forms, Six Sigma seeks variation and defect reduction everywhere. But even if Lean and Six Sigma are different, it certainly doesn't mean they aren't or can't be complementary. Both Lean and Six Sigma are excellent improvement initiatives, but neither of them guarantees that the organization's financial goal will be met, even if they are relentlessly pursued."

"Part of the problem with failed Lean and Six Sigma initiatives is that many companies simply have too many ongoing projects that drain valuable resources needed for the day-to-day issues facing many companies. It can also be confusing to managers that have reached the saturation point and aren't able to distinguish which projects are vital or important and which aren't. The economic reality that supersedes and overrides everything else is that companies have always wanted the most improvement for the

TABLE 10.1

Six Sigma vs. Lean

	Six Sigma	Lean
Principle Activity	Reduction of variation and defects	Elimination of waste
Defined Method	1. Define	1. Define value
	2. Measure	2. Identify the value stream
	3. Analyze	3. Make value flow
	4. Improve	4. Pull to customer demand
	5. Control	5. Pursue perfection
Primary Focus	Defining and solving problems	Improving processes
Primary Objective	Improve reliability and predictability	Simplify processes

least amount of investment. Attacking all of the processes and problems simultaneously, as part of an enterprise-wide Lean Six Sigma initiative, quite simply overloads the organization and does not deliver an acceptable return on investment in many cases," Bob explained. "So, with all this being said, let's get to the real reason we all came here today, how do we combine Lean, Six Sigma, and the Theory of Constraints?" he said.

And so, Bob began his explanation. "So just what would happen if we were to combine the best of all three improvement initiatives into a single improvement process? Just what might this amalgamation look like? Logic would tell us that we would have an improvement process that reduces waste and variation, but primarily focusing on the operation that is constraining throughput." And with that, Bob loaded a new figure (Figure 10.1).

FIGURE 10.1
The Ultimate Improvement Cycle.

"The figure you see on the screen is what I refer to as the Ultimate Improvement Cycle that combines the power of Lean, Six Sigma, and Theory of Constraints improvement cycles to form a more powerful and profitable improvement strategy. This improvement cycle weaves together the DNA of Lean and Six Sigma with the focusing power of the Theory of Constraints to deliver a powerful and compelling improvement methodology. All of the strategies, principles, tools, techniques, and methods contained within all three improvement initiatives are synergistically blended and then time released to yield improvements that far exceed those obtained from doing these three initiatives in isolation from each other," Bob explained.

He continued, "You will notice that I used three different shades of gray to designate each of the components of the individual initiatives. By combining Lean, Six Sigma, and the Theory of Constraints we are attempting to, first, identify, define, measure, and analyze the process. The actions in Steps 1a, 1b, and 1c serve to characterize the process value stream by identifying which step is limiting the full potential of the process, pinpointing the potential sources of waste, and locating and measuring potential sources of defects and variation. There will be a compelling urge to make changes during this phase, but my advice is to resist this temptation. In this phase of the improvement cycle, we are simply trying to define, analyze, and understand what is currently happening in our process."

Continuing, Bob then explained, "By the same token, we are also looking for sources of variation within the process. What are the things we see that are preventing our process from being consistent and stable? Keep in mind that the next phase deals with stabilizing the process, by reducing both waste and variation in the constraining operation so it's important, for now, to remember that we are simply trying to understand what is happening in our current process and more specifically our constraint operation." "Any questions so far?" he asked the group.

When there were no questions, he continued his presentation. "Although we will be focusing our attention primarily on the operation that is limiting our throughput, since the upstream and downstream process steps could be contributing to this limitation, they must be observed as well. For example, if an upstream process consistently stops the flow of product to the constraint, then we can't ignore it. Conversely, if a downstream operation is consistently losing constraint output to scrap or rework, then it can't be ignored either. In both cases, the result would be less than optimal throughput."

"In the next series of steps, we are attempting to create stability. Before any process can be improved, there must be a focused plan developed or improvement efforts will be disjointed. In Steps 2a, 2b, and 2c we are attempting to simultaneously stabilize and improve our process. What does stabilize actually mean? Quite simply, stabilizing means that we are attempting to make our process more predictable, reliable, and consistent. In this sense, the actions in Steps 2a, 2b, and 2c serve primarily to reduce waste and variation within the constraint operation so that a new level of consistency and reliability are achieved. What we observed in the analysis phase will form the basis for our plan to achieve stability. It's important to remember that true and lasting improvement will never occur unless and until the process is consistent and stable over time. We will use a variety of tools and techniques during this phase of the Ultimate Improvement Cycle to accomplish this end. In order to achieve improved process flow, you must be patient and deliberate when reducing waste and variation," Bob explained. "Please, if you have any questions, stop me and I will answer them as we move along," Bob said.

Bob continued, "In the next series of steps, we are trying to create both flow and pull. Specifically, the actions in Steps 3a, 3b, and 3c are intended to optimize flow. Flow in this phase includes the flow of materials, information, and products through the process. Although we are seeking to create flow, creating it will also surface any problem that inhibits it! So, in order to sustain flow, we must stop and solve these problems. Because of your past experiences you might be tempted to fix these problems on the fly, but don't do it! You must begin to view problems as opportunities for long-term improvement and not as a failure, so by stopping and fixing problems, it is actually a sign of strength in an organization."

"In the last series of steps, we want to control the process so that we can sustain the gains we have made. The actions in Steps 4a, 4b, and 4c serve to both increase constraint capacity, if we need to, and to assure that all of the changes made, and improvements realized, won't be wasted effort. What a shame it would be to make big improvements that we can't sustain. Sustaining the gains is a hallmark of great organizations!" Bob emphasized. "So again, the four phases of the Ultimate Improvement Cycle are, analyze, stabilize, flow, and control. Each phase is critical to the optimization of revenue and profits. Don't jump from one to the other, simply follow them in sequential order," Bob said as he scanned the audience for questions or comments, but again there weren't any, so he continued. Bob then flashed a new slide on the screen.

The Ultimate Improvement Cycle accomplishes five primary objectives that serve as a springboard to maximizing revenue and profits:

1. It guarantees that we are focusing on the correct area of the process or system, the constraint operation, to maximize throughput and minimize inventory and operating expense.
2. It provides a roadmap for improvement to ensure a systematic, structured, and orderly approach to assure the maximize utilization of resources to realize optimum revenue and profits.
3. It integrates the best of Lean, Six Sigma, and the Theory of Constraints strategies, tools, techniques, and philosophies, to maximize your organization's full improvement potential.
4. It assures that the necessary, up-front planning is completed in advance of changes to the process or organization so as to avoid the "Fire, Ready, Aim!" mindset.
5. Provides the synergy and involvement of the total organization needed to maximize your return on investment.

Bob finished this part of his presentation by saying, "If Tires for All is seriously committed to following the steps of the Ultimate Improvement Cycle, in the sequence illustrated in the figure I had on the screen, then I am convinced that you will see bottom line improvements that far exceed what you've experienced using stand-alone initiatives. Just like any new initiative, it requires the entire organization's focus, discipline, determination, and a little bit of patience. This is new territory for Tires for All, so follow the path of least resistance that I have provided for you ... it truly does work!" He then recommended another break.

When everyone returned from the break, Bob flashed a new figure (Figure 10.2) on the screen and began speaking, "So just how do we accomplish each of the steps in the Ultimate Improvement Cycle, you may be wondering? We do so by using all of the tools and actions that we would use if we were implementing Lean and Six Sigma as stand-alone improvement initiatives, but this time we focus most, if not all, of our efforts primarily on the constraint operation. The figure on the screen lays out the tools and actions we will use and perform at each step of the Ultimate Improvement Cycle and as you can see there are no new or exotic tools that I am introducing. In creating the Ultimate Improvement Cycle one of my objectives was to keep things simple and I think you'll agree

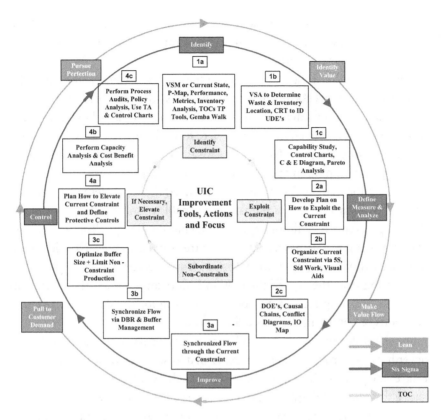

FIGURE 10.2
Improvement tools, actions, and focus.

that the tools I've laid out to use are all of the basic and time-tested tools that have been around for years."

"For example, in Step 1a we will be creating a simple current state Value Stream Map to analyze things like where the excess inventory is, what the individual processing times are, cycle times, and the overall lead time within the process. We will use this tool to identify both the current and next constraint. We will also be looking at the current process and information flow and performance metrics to make certain that the metrics stimulate the right behaviors and that they will in fact track the true impact of our improvement efforts," he explained.

He continued, "Likewise in Steps 1b and 1c, we will be analyzing our process by using simple tools like Pareto Charts, Run Charts, Spaghetti Diagrams, Time and Motion Studies, Cause and Effect Diagrams, Causal Chains, and so on. Keep in mind that these are by no means the only tools you can utilize, just some of the more common ones. In each phase of the Ultimate Improvement Cycle, I have recommended simple tools used to perform the tasks at hand."

"One last point I need to make. One of the primary reasons why companies have excess inventory on hand is to compensate for hidden problems, a kind of safety net if you will. Some people believe that there should be a radical inventory reduction to force the problems to the surface, but I adamantly disagree. The reason I disagree with this strategy is because most organizations aren't prepared to tackle these problems that have been covered up for so long. As inventory is reduced these problems will surface and if the organization isn't prepared or capable of solving these problems, then improvements will not happen, and chaos will reign. There are many good books on problem-solving, so prepare yourselves now. Now let's look more closely at each step in the Ultimate Improvement Cycle," Bob said. It was getting near the end of the day, so Bob recommended that they stop now and finish up tomorrow. "Before we leave for the day, are there any questions or comments?" he asked the group.

Oscar raised his hand and said, "In all my years of doing this, I have never heard improvement efforts explained in so much detail, and for sure, I have never been given a roadmap with such detail. I am so very excited to use this methodology and can't wait to see the results we achieve." Cliff Hastings then raised his hand and said, "Bob, I too am excited about using this method, but I do have one question for you." "And your question is?" Bob asked. "What are the expected deliverables we should be expected to deliver?" Cliff asked. Without hesitation, Bob responded and said, "It's ironic that you would ask that question Cliff, because tomorrow's presentation will be focused on the expected deliverables from the Ultimate Improvement Cycle." And with that comment, this day's session ended.

11

The Deliverables of the Ultimate Improvement Cycle

Bright and early the next morning, everyone arrived at the hotel conference room and took their seats. Bob welcomed everyone and began his presentation. "In today's session, I'm going to lay out each of the basic steps in the Ultimate Improvement Cycle." And with that, Bob flashed onto a new figure (Figure 11.1). "In this figure I have laid out the expected deliverables for each step of the Ultimate Improvement Cycle that Cliff asked about yesterday. I'm sure you will have questions as we progress around this figure, so speak up when you do," Bob encouraged everyone.

Bob then began his presentation on deliverables. "As I said yesterday, when I created this methodology, I wanted to keep everything simple, so as you can see, the wording is very descriptive and simple. In Step 1a, using things like Value Steam Maps, or simple Process Maps, or even Gemba walks, you should come away with a complete picture of the system you're attempting to improve in terms of flow and predicted people behaviors. In addition, you need to make sure that efficiency is now only measured in the step that is constraining system throughput. This, of course, assumes that you have correctly identified the system constraint."

Bob continued, "In Step 1b, you are attempting to gain knowledge of both the location and type of waste within your system, plus the location of inventory, plus any potential core problems that exist within the system you're attempting to improve. These problems could be a variety of different types of problems including things like high levels of work-in-process inventory, high levels of waste, or even excessive amounts of equipment downtime."

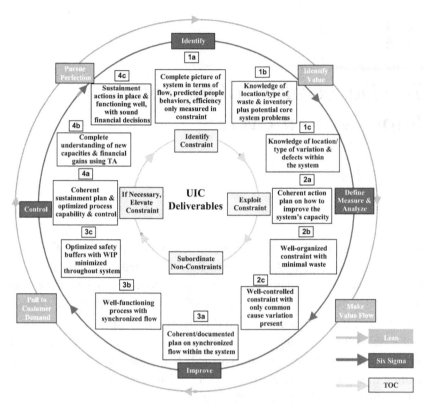

FIGURE 11.1
Deliverables of the Ultimate Improvement Cycle.

Continuing, Bob said, "In Step 1c, we are interested in understanding both the location and type of variation we are experiencing, as well as any recurring defects that exist within the system being improved. Here, you will be running Process Capability studies, performing Pareto Analyses, creating Cause and Effect Diagrams, and maybe even creating Control Charts. This is a very important step, simply because recurring defects that result in either scrap or rework can seriously impede the flow of products through your production system. We are concerned with defects ahead of the constraint that might starve the constraints, but equally important are defects that occur after the constraint as they leave the system constraint. In both cases, these defects could significantly reduce the throughput of the total system which could result in missed shipments and late deliveries of products to the end customer," Bob explained. "Are there any questions on what you've heard so far?" Bob asked the group.

Once again, Cliff raised his hand and said, "This make perfect sense to me, but if I remember what you said earlier, we aren't supposed to take action on things just yet. Is that correct?" he asked. "Great question, Cliff," Bob responded. "The answer is, yes and no," Bob said with a smile. "What we are attempting to do is only collect information so that we can develop a coherent improvement plan. But having said that, it would make no sense at all if you found a problem that was fixable immediately, and then wait for a plan to be generated before taking action," Bob explained. "Does that make sense to you Cliff?" Bob asked, and Cliff responded, nodding up and down indicating that it did. "Are there any other questions?" he asked that group, and when there weren't any, he continued his presentation on deliverables.

"In Step 2a, we will use all of the information collected in Steps 1a, 1b, and 1c to develop a coherent system action plan on how we intend to improve the quality and capacity of the system being improved. In effect, we will be using Goldratt's second step, 'exploiting' the system constraint. You should now know where the system constraint is located, the performance metrics that are in place which stimulate the expected people behaviors, the location of excessive waste and variation, and you should no longer be measuring efficiencies in non-constraints. Here we are applying Goldratt's third step, 'subordination.' My recommendation is that this plan should be developed as a team and not just by a single person. The plan should clearly identify specific actions to be taken," he explained. Bob continued, "In Steps 2b and 2c your deliverable should be a well-organized constraint with minimal amounts of waste. You will be effectively executing both your waste and variation reduction plan focused on the system constraint. In addition, after implementing your improvement plan, you should only have common cause variation with the system being controlled using things like Control Charts to maintain control."

"Continuing, Step 3a's deliverable is a coherent, well documented plan on synchronizing flow throughout and within the system. Here your plan will be focused on how to subordinate non-constraints to the current system constraint. When implemented, this plan will result in a well-functioning process with synchronized flow, using both Drum Buffer Rope coupled with Buffer Management which is the hallmark of Step 3b. In Step 3c, you will have also optimized your buffer size and will have limited your non-constraint production by never out-pacing the drum or system constraint. I can't emphasize enough how important this step is! Any questions here?" he asked.

Sally Hodges, the Industrial Engineering Manager, raised her hand and asked, "How long should it have taken to get this far along on the Ultimate Improvement Cycle?" Bob thought to himself, "Being an Industrial Engineer, a question related to time doesn't surprise me at all, Sally. While there isn't a specific amount of time expected to complete these first three steps, I would tell you not to apply a time limit. Think about what you're attempting to do here. Obviously, if your process is already functioning well, then you might expect to complete this rotation fairly quickly. On the other hand, if your current system is delivering poor results, then it will take much longer. The key point here is, don't rush through this process!" Bob explained.

"Having completed the first three major steps of the Ultimate Improvement Cycle, you will have significantly improved your production system. In fact, if you've done your work correctly, you may have already 'broken' your current constraint, but if you haven't, then you must develop a plan on how to 'elevate' the constraint. Remember back in Step 1a, I told you to identify both the current and next constraint? I did this in anticipation that the current constraint would eventually be broken and a new one would immediately appear, so be ready to move to it," Bob explained.

Bob continued, "In addition, we want to make sure that all of our improvements will remain in effect, so I instruct you to define protective controls to guard against this happening. Having said this, your other deliverable in Step 3a is the development of a coherent sustainment plan which will include protective control devices such as Control Charts. Wouldn't it be a shame that after all of your hard work to bring your process under control that you might take actions that remove your control?"

"So, the deliverables for Steps 4a, 4b, and 4c would all be aimed at sustaining the gains you have already made. Your actions would include actions like performing routine process audits and maintaining Process Control Charts. Another important deliverable in this step is at least a basic understanding of Throughput Accounting by the shop floor employees so that sound financial decisions can be made in real time. In addition, it is very important that the operators running the machines understand how Control Charts are maintained so that process control can be a way of life on the shop floor," Bob explained.

"This completes the first rotation of the Ultimate Improvement Cycle, but we're not finished yet. We must make sure that everyone is prepared for the next constraint which will appear almost immediately when the current constraint is broken, and it will be. By preparation, I mean that all of the sustainment tools we developed as we progressed around the Ultimate Improvement Cycle must be maintained if our improvements are to be sustained. This completes my presentation, so I want to open the floor for questions, comments, and concerns," Bob stated.

Mark was the first one to comment, "I have been involved in manufacturing for most of my career and I've been to many training sessions on a variety of subjects. Having said that, I have never been in a training session that was as complete as this one. So, Bob, I just want to say thank you for the last two days. As I look into the future, I see very positive things happening at Tires for All! I truly believe that my next visit to the Board of Directors will be a very positive event. Why do I say that? I say that because I know that, if we follow the steps outline in the Ultimate Improvement Cycle, we will have record profit margins and a plethora of satisfied customers. I see our on-time delivery becoming one of the best in the business!"

Tom was the next one to speak and said, "I too have a positive outlook for the future of Tires for All! One of the keys to our success will be how well we embrace the concepts of Throughput Accounting. By using this method, I can see a vast improvement in our real time financial decisions. I also believe that by implementing the Theory of Constraints Replenishment Solution, our cash on hand will be significantly improved, simply because we won't be tying up our cash on excessive amounts of inventory. This includes raw materials, work-in-process, and finished goods inventory."

Cliff Hastings, Tires for All's Operations Manager, then spoke up and said, "I'm excited for a variety of reasons. First, I always worry about having to lay people off, but with the Theory of Constraints in place, our future growth will mean that we need all of our hourly workers to satisfy our future demand. I can also see our equipment downtime improving dramatically and our flow improving intensely! I can honestly say, I have never been this excited about the future of Tires for All!" "Any other comments, questions, or concerns?" Bob asked.

Oscar Francis, the company's Master Black Belt was the next to speak, "I am so happy that our path to improvement took the route that it did. Think about it, we first tried Six Sigma and learned valuable tools and techniques. We then employed Lean Manufacturing and learned all about waste and value. But as good as these two methods are, their full potential won't be realized until we combine them both with the Theory of Constraints! Using the Ultimate Improvement Cycle is the key to improvement and I'm excited to get all of the Green Belts and Black Belts leading the charge to our future. I can absolutely say that Tires for All will be the leader in the tire industry!"

Frank Delaney, Tires for All's Director of Maintenance, was next to speak, "I can honestly say that I now realize what a key role maintenance will play in our future. I guess I knew it before but knowing where to focus our maintenance efforts is a turning point for me and my guys! The system constraint is our leverage point and we must make sure that reducing equipment downtime there will be our primary focus. I just want to thank you Bob for teaching all of us about the Theory of Constraints and how to combine it with our maintenance efforts."

When there were no more comments, Bob addressed the group. "I appreciate all of your glowing comments about what you heard the last two days, but I want to tell you that there is a completely different side of the Theory of Constraints that you haven't heard about yet. This other side is referred to as the Logical Thinking Processes or LTP for short. LTPs are a series of logic diagrams that do things like resolve conflicts and dissect problems so that solutions can be achieved. One of the key tools in the LTP arsenal is something referred to as The Goal Tree and I will be scheduling a session on this tool in the near future. The Goal Tree is a tool we can use to plan our future strategically and I think when you see it, you'll fall in love with it. I think it's time to call it a day, so thank you again for taking the time to listen to what I had to say the past two days."

12

The Logical Thinking Processes

As planned, Bob Nelson scheduled another training session for the leadership team and other select employees from Tires for All. This training session was on another side of the Theory of Constraints (TOC) referred to as the Logical Thinking Processes, which are a series of problem-solving tools. As usual, Bob welcomed everyone and began speaking. "When we study organizations, we find that there are three basic types of problems that must be dealt with. Problems can be chronic, change-related, or a hybrid of the two. Chronic problems are those problems that have seemingly been around forever and have defied all previous attempts at resolution. Chronic problems are very often associated with things like product defects, equipment downtime, and so on. Change-related problems, on the other hand, are characterized by their sudden onset and can usually be traced to a change made somewhere within the organization or process. Solving this type of problem is done so by first locating the change and either changing it back or coming up with a different solution. Hybrid problems are a combination of chronic and change-related problems, in that a chronic problem suddenly becomes worse. All three of these problems are typically associated with the physical world or physical processes and require a very systematic approach for resolution."

Bob continued, "While physical world problems can be solved using a systematic process, what about more complex problems related to systems and organizations or the policies within them? How do we determine that these type problems exist and then how do you go about solving them? Although it's been said that a well-defined problem is already half-solved, the problem must surely be identified first. Bill Dettmer, in his ground-breaking book, *Breaking the Constraints to World-Class Performance* [1], explains, 'Before we can effectively solve a complex system problem, we must thoroughly understand the cause and effect behind the reality of our current situation.'"

Bob continued, "In recent years, there has been much written about the Theory of Constraints, and although it is not my intention to go into a detailed explanation of this subject, it certainly deserves some level of discussion simply because of its usefulness as related to complex system type problems. It's relatively easy to identify or locate physical constraints, but constraints related to systems and policies can be somewhat difficult or even frustrating. It's difficult because there are three things that conspire to work against breaking it. First, most people have trouble identifying exactly what policy might be causing the constraint, and secondly, many times policy constraints are located outside your own area and typically require someone else to change the policy. It's probably normal for this last reason simply because nobody likes to admit that something they are doing is the cause of poor performance. Because of this, the person responsible seems to be in denial and always requires some form of proof as to the need to change the constraining policy. The final barrier is normal human resistance to change. Changing the status quo is difficult, unless a strong and compelling case is made where the conclusion is obvious. Is everyone with me so far?" Bob asked and they were.

"The Theory of Constraints is systemic in nature and strives to identify those few constraints that limit the organization's success in terms of moving in the direction of its goal. It's important to keep in mind that most organizations function as systems, rather than as a collection of processes. Goldratt introduced his five focusing steps, that I discussed earlier, plus what he calls a Logical Thinking Process. Goldratt then teaches us that good managers must answer three important questions in order to be successful," he explained and put up a simple PowerPoint slide that contained three questions.

1. What to change?
2. What to change to?
3. How to make the change happen.

"As part of the Logical Thinking Process, Goldratt introduced a set of tools used to identify the root causes of negative symptoms, or Undesirable Effects or UDEs pronounced oodees, that exist within organizations. Goldratt believed that there are generally only a few core problems that create most of the UDEs, and if we can identify these core problems, or what to change, and find their root causes and eliminate them, then most of the UDEs will disappear. Let's talk a bit more about these things called Undesirable Effects and how we can identify and understand them," Bob explained.

Bob continued, "In order to understand what UDEs are, we must first understand that they must be considered in the context of an organization's goals, necessary conditions, and performance metrics. For example, suppose the organization's goal is to make money now and in the future, and its necessary conditions are things like keeping its employees happy and secure, keeping customer satisfaction high, achieving superior quality, on-time delivery, and so on. Further suppose that the organization measures its performance by things like on-time delivery, some kind of productivity measurement like efficiency, the cost to produce products, a customer satisfaction index, and quality through parts per million defective. Any organizational effect that moves the organization away from its goal, or violates one of the necessary conditions, or drives a performance metric in a negative direction, with respect to its target, is considered undesirable. So, think for a minute about what UDEs might exist within Tires for All."

Bob then explained, "The tool Goldratt developed to expose system type problems, or policy constraints, is referred to as the Current Reality Tree. The Current Reality Tree is used to discover organizational problems, or UDEs, and then works backward to identify at least one root cause that leads to most of the UDEs. Dettmer [1] defines a root cause as, 'the lowest cause in a chain of cause and effect at which we have some capability to cause the break.' His point being that the cause and effect chain could continue on indefinitely, but unless the cause lies within the scope and control of the organization, it will not be solved. I happen to believe Dettmer's definition of a root cause is the finest characterization I have ever observed. Dettmer further explains that two characteristics apply to root causes," as he flashed to another slide.

1. It's the lowest point at which human intervention can change or break the cause.
2. It's within our capability to unilaterally control or to influence changes to the cause.

He continued, "The Current Reality Tree begins with identifying undesirable effects, or those negative symptoms existing within an organization that let us know that a core problem exists. Core problems are unique in that if the root cause or causes can be found, they can usually be traced to an exceptionally large percentage of the undesirable effects. Actually, Dettmer suggests that this percentage could be as high as 70 percent and sometimes higher. Dettmer refers to a Current Reality Tree as a 'snapshot of reality as it exists at a particular moment in time.' Dettmer further explains, 'As with a photograph, it's not really reality itself, just a picture of reality, and like a photo, it encloses only what we choose to aim at through the camera's viewfinder.'"

"By aiming our 'logical camera' at the undesirable effects and their root causes, we're essentially eliminating all of the details that don't relate to them. In other words, the Current Reality Tree helps us focus in on and pinpoint core problems. There are several different versions of the Current Reality Tree available in the literature on the subject, but they all provide the same end product, at least one actionable core problem. Some Current Reality Trees are very detailed, while some are more general in nature," Bob explained. He then said to the group, "Remember, if you have any questions, stop me and ask away."

"The example I will present today is a company that was having a problem generating enough throughput, which is interpreted as a capacity constraint. Like Tires for All, they had plenty of orders, but were unable to produce enough parts to satisfy the market demand. It is clear to me that many of the problems organizations encounter on a daily basis are really interconnected systems-related problems. It is further clear to me that by focusing on these core problems, organizations can essentially kill multiple birds with a few stones!" he explained. "Any questions before I present this example?" he asked, but there were none, so he began.

"I said earlier that it was not my intention to present an in-depth discussion of either the Theory of Constraints or Current Reality Trees, or the remaining Logical thinking Process tools, but since I have presented how to utilize the Current Reality Tree, it seems appropriate to discuss the basics of how to prepare one."

Bob continued, "The company involved here produces flexible tanks used to hold and transport volatile organic liquids. This company had serious problems generating enough throughput to satisfy the volume and delivery requirements of their customers. By creating a Current Reality Tree, this company was able to pinpoint specific system problems that were constraining their throughput and then take actions to alleviate the problem. And by the way, I seriously recommend that you go buy Bill Dettmer's [1] book for future reference. The following are the steps used to create this Current Reality Tree, or CRT, as developed by Dettmer," and with that, Bob loaded a series of PowerPoint slides that summarized how to create a CRT.

1. *Define the system boundaries, goals, necessary conditions, and performance measures*

"Because we are talking about a system, it is important that we avoid sub-optimization. That is, we must always avoid trying to optimize individual processes and assume that if we do so, we will have optimized the system. This assumption or belief that the sum of individual process step optimizations will result in optimization of the total system is completely invalid," Bob explained.

"All organizations exist for some purpose or goal which is simply the end toward which effort is being directed. Usually, this goal is to make money now and in the future. The necessary conditions, on the other hand, are vital success factors that must be satisfied if we are to achieve our goal. The performance measurements are simply those organizational metrics that tell us how the organization is performing as it pursues its goal. The following are the actual boundaries, goals, necessary conditions, and performance measures from our example." And with that said, a new set of slides appeared on the screen.

a. Boundary: Manufacturing and Assembly Area.
b. Goal: Make money now and in the future.
c. Necessary conditions:
  • Minimize customer returns and complaints.
  • Achieve at least 95% on-time delivery to all customers.
  • Provide a safe, comfortable, and secure work environment for all employees.
  • Meet budget P & L expectations for the Board of Directors.
  • Performance measures:
    – On-time delivery.
    – Rework hours per tank.
    – Sales $s per labor hour.
    – Accident rate.

- Workstation efficiency.
- Throughput/revenue.
- Operating expense.

2. State the System Problem

Bob explained, "In order to develop a meaningful problem statement, we should always formulate it as a 'why?' question. Whatever the biggest issue that you don't like about your system's performance, simply state it as a why question. The problem statement created by this company was: 'Why is our throughput/revenue so low?'"

3. Create a Causes, Negatives, and Whys Table

"This is done by first creating three columns and then listing, in the Negatives column, the center column, the things you don't like about the way your system is currently performing, which includes all of the things that make your job more difficult to perform. My clear advice to you is, don't try to solve world hunger. List no more than five to eight Negatives, otherwise the Current Reality Tree will become unmanageable. Table 12.1 is from our example and as you can see, there are eight entries listed as 'Negatives' in the center column. It is important to remember that each of the negatives should be considered in the context of our problem statement," Bob explained.

"As I just stated, it's important that you don't try to solve world hunger by creating an unnecessary number of Negatives because you will have difficulty managing your finished Current Reality Tree. I cannot emphasize this point enough!" Bob added.

4. Next, sequentially number all of the negatives and then explain why you believe the negative is considered a negative

"This is done so by asking the question, 'Why is this negative a bad thing in light of our goal, necessary conditions or performance measurements?' Although Dettmer [1] suggests that if you have multiple whys, then you should add a lower-case letter to the appropriate number. I have always added a lower-case letter to the number, even if I had only one why. I find that it helps me distinguish the negatives, whys, and causes as we construct

TABLE 12.1

Listing of Causes and Negatives

Causes (What Is Causing This Negative?)	Negatives (What I Don't Like about the Current Situation)	Why Is This Negative Bad for Our Goal, Necessary Condition, or Measurement?
	1. Absenteeism is high and unstable.	
	2. Processes are not stable and predictable.	
	3. Operators don't/won't follow specifications.	
	4. Product build cycle times are excessively long.	
	5. Equipment breaks down frequently.	
	6. Incoming materials are frequently non-conforming.	
	7. QA inspections are inconsistent between inspectors.	
	8. Problems are never really solved.	

the Current Reality Tree. One thing I have always told people in my life as a consultant, learn a tool and then make it your own. By this I mean, just because you learned a new tool, doesn't mean that the way you learned it is the only way it can be used. The Current Reality Tree is this kind of tool," Bob explained (Table 12.2).

5. *Once the Why column of the table has been completed, move to the "Cause" column, and for each negative ask the following question, "What is causing this negative?" or "Why does this negative exist?"*

Bob continued, "It's important to remember that there could very well be more than one cause responsible for creating this negative, and if there are, make sure you list them. The next table (Table 12.3) includes the Negatives, Whys, and Causes. For each Cause, place an upper-case letter beside the appropriate number, again, to distinguish between negatives, causes, and whys. When this table is complete, you are now ready to construct your

TABLE 12.2

Table with Whys Added

Causes (What Is Causing This Negative?)	Negatives (What I Don't Like about the Current Situation)	Why Is This Negative Bad for Our Goal, Necessary Condition, or Measurement?
	1. Absenteeism is high and unstable.	1a. P & A is forced to overstaff operations which drives up operating expenses.
	2. Processes are not stable and predictable.	2a. Wet cement and grout drive cycle times higher.
	3. Operators don't/won't follow specifications.	3a. Excessive rework causes higher operating expense.
	4. Product build cycle times are excessively long.	4a. Throughput rates are too low causing late P & A deliveries to customers.
	5. Equipment breaks down frequently.	5a. Cycle times are extended causing late deliveries to P & A customers.
	6. Incoming materials are frequently non-conforming.	6a. Product cycle times are extended causing late deliveries to customers.
	7. QA inspections are inconsistent between inspectors.	7a. Excess repairs drive up operating expenses and delay shipments.
	8. Problems are never really solved.	8a. Repetitive defects occur which result in excessive repair time which drives up OE.

current reality tree. All of the Causes, Negatives, and Whys will serve as your initial building blocks for your CRT."

6. *Convert All Negatives, Whys, and Causes to CRT Entities (Graphic Blocks)*

"Using the alpha-numeric entries from Table 12.3, word your Negatives, Whys, and Causes in such a way that they will fit neatly inside the graphic blocks or boxes. The information inside the block should be complete statements and should leave no ambiguity as to its meaning. The following figure (Figure 12.1) is an example of what your graphic blocks should resemble. Note that the information is a complete statement and its content leaves no doubt about what is negative," he explained.

TABLE 12.3

Completed Table of Negatives, Whys, and Causes

Causes (What Is Causing This Negative?)	Negatives (What I Don't Like about the Current Situation)	Why Is This Negative Bad for Our Goal, Necessary Condition, or Measurement?
A1. Attendance policy is not enforced by HR and/or operations.	1. Absenteeism is high and unstable.	1a. P & A is forced to overstaff operations which drives up operating expenses.
A2. Effective process control system does not exist.	2. Processes are not stable and predictable.	2a. Wet adhesives drive cycle times higher.
A3. Specifications are vague, not current, and difficult to understand.	3. Operators don't or won't follow specifications.	3a. Excessive rework causes higher operating expense.
A4. Material dry/cure times are excessively long.	4. Product build cycle times are excessively long.	4a. Throughput rates are too low causing late P & A deliveries to customers.
A5. Preventive maintenance on key equipment is inconsistent or ineffective.	5. Equipment breaks down frequently.	5a. Cycle times are extended causing late deliveries to P & A customers.
A6. Suppliers are not always held accountable to produce in-spec mat'l.	6. Incoming materials are frequently non-conforming.	6a. Product cycle times are extended causing late deliveries to customers.
A7. Clear and concise acceptance stds do not exist.	7. QA inspections are inconsistent between inspectors.	7a. Excess repairs drive up operating expenses and delay shipments.
A8. Most problem-solving efforts focused on treating the symptoms instead of the root cause(s).	8. Problems are never really solved.	8a. Repetitive defects occur which result in excessive repair time which drives up OE.

7. Identify and Designate the Undesirable Effects

Bob continued, "After you have converted all of the Negatives, Whys, and Causes into graphic blocks, it's time to determine which of the negatives and whys are Undesirable Effects, or UDEs. UDEs are those whys and negatives that are negative in relation to the organization's goal or necessary conditions or the key measures of progress toward achievement

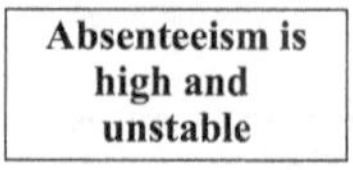

> Absenteeism is
> high and
> unstable

FIGURE 12.1
CRT graphic block.

of the goal. Normally, all of the whys will be considered UDEs and probably some of the negatives will as well. In some cases, even some of the root causes could be considered UDEs."

Bob stopped for a moment to let this point resonate, "The key point to remember is whether or not the contents of the graphic block would be considered negative at face value or detrimental to achievement of the system's goal. If they are, then designate them as a UDE. Once they are designated as a UDE, assuming you are using a drawing software such as Visio, mark the UDE in some fashion, so as to make it visual. In my example, I have changed the wall thickness of the graphic block to designate which of them are UDEs."

8. Group the Graphic Blocks into Clusters

Bob quoted Dettmer [1], "From this point on, building the CRT is going to be very much like assembling a jigsaw puzzle with the graphic blocks being the puzzle pieces. Grouping is done by aligning the Whys (now a UDE) at the top of the page, appropriate Cause directly beneath the corresponding Negative as shown in Figure 12.2."

9. Connect the Causes, Negatives, and Undesirable Effects

Bob continued, "Using dotted or dashed lines, connect the negatives individually to each of the UDEs and then connect the causes to the negatives as demonstrated in Figure 12.3."

"Figure 12.4 contains all of the connected clusters, with a cluster defined as the connected UDEs, Negatives, and Causes from our example. Note that the UDEs are designated by thicker walls on the graphic blocks. Table 12.3 permits us to group together related graphic blocks. Actually, constructing the Current Reality Tree is very similar to constructing an affinity diagram for those of you familiar with this tool," Bob explained.

FIGURE 12.2
Interconnected graphic blocks.

10. *Group Related Clusters Together*

Bob continued, "In this step, we need to search for clusters that appear to be related in some way and then place them in close proximity to each other. From our example, we see that UDE 7a states that 'excess repairs drive up operating expenses and delay shipments.' That is closely related to UDE 8a, 'Repetitive defects occur which result in excessive overtime and OE.' We then look for connection points between the two clusters. In this particular example, the connection point appears to be at the UDE level, so we place a dotted or hashed line to connect the two clusters at the connection point as shown in Figure 12.5."

"In a similar fashion, we search for other related clusters and connection points, and then connect them. This activity is not as simple as it may sound, simply because much thought must go into how the clusters are related and where the connection point is located," Bob explained.

"My recommendation is that if you aren't sure, seek out other opinions or do more research. Figure 12.6 displays how the clusters are related from our example. Don't worry about how pretty your grouped cluster arrangement is, just try to connect them in a way that is legitimate and makes sense.

FIGURE 12.3
Cluster of graphic blocks.

It's always a good idea to seek out an objective opinion to make sure what you've constructed makes sense," Bob stated.

Bob then stopped his presentation and asked for questions relative to the creation of the Current Reality Tree. When he didn't get any, he decided to do a quick overview of what he had presented so far. "I want to review some of the things we've discussed so far, just to make sure you're getting it." And with that, he began, "According to Bill Dettmer [1], a Current Reality Tree is a logical structure designed to depict the state of reality as it currently exists in a given system. It reflects the most probable chain of cause and effect, given a specific, fixed set of circumstances. The CRT seeks cause-and-effect connections between visible indications of a system's condition and the originating causes that produce them. The objective of the CRT is to help you isolate the things that you aren't currently satisfied with and by tracing those 'gripes' back to one or more basic causes. Keep

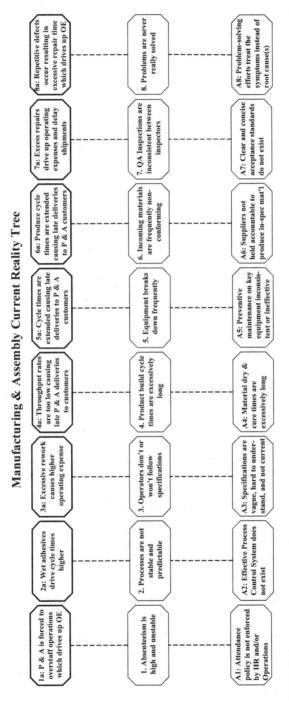

FIGURE 12.4

CRT connected clusters.

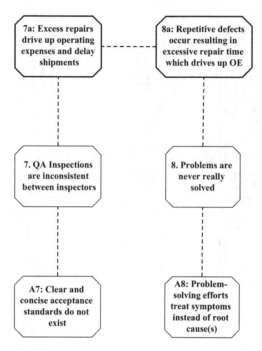

FIGURE 12.5
Group-related clusters.

this in mind as we continue working on creating our Current Reality Tree for our example."

11. *Scrutinize and Finalize the Connections*

Bob continued, "I mentioned earlier that I had no intentions of providing detailed instructions of how to construct Current Reality Trees, so I highly recommend Dettmer's book, *Breaking the Constraints to World-Class Performance* [1], for a detailed description of how to construct Current Reality Trees. This is especially true from this step forward as we construct the Current Reality Tree. Dettmer emphasizes the need to use the Categories of Legitimate Reservation (CLR) to solidify the logic of each causal connection. CLRs help us construct our own logical relationships and they enable us to evaluate the logic of others. That is, CLRs help us avoid errors in logic as we construct our Current Reality Tree." Bob then inserted a new slide.

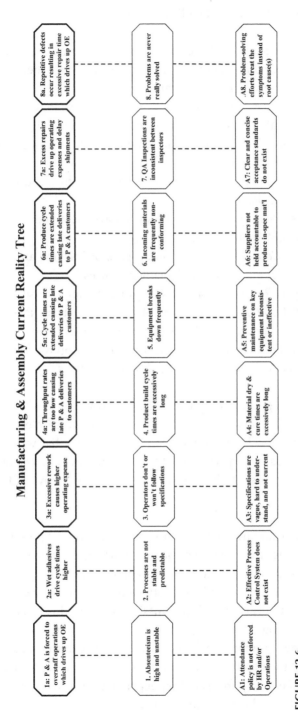

Manufacturing & Assembly Current Reality Tree

FIGURE 12.6
Grouped clusters.

Dettmer lists eight different CLRs as follows:

a. *Clarity*: Be certain that the individual words used are understood, that there is comprehension of the idea, and that there is a clear connection between the cause and the effect.

b. *Entity Existence*: When constructing the graphic blocks (entities) we must be certain that the text is a complete grammatical sentence, that we have not created a compound sentence, and the idea contained in the sentence is valid.

c. *Causality Existence*: Cause and effect relationships must be direct and unavoidable.

d. *Cause Insufficiency*: Be certain that you have identified and included all major contributing causes.

e. *Additional Cause*: Each time you observe or imagine an effect, you must consider all possible independent causes.

f. *Cause-Effect Reversal*: Don't mistake an effect for a cause.

g. *Predicted Effect Existence*: Most of the time causes have multiple effects, so make certain all effects are considered.

h. *Tautology*: Don't take the effect as unequivocal proof alone that the cause exists without considering other alternatives.

"These eight categories of legitimate reservation act as the 'rules-of-engagement' as we construct our Current Reality Trees, so be certain to use them as you check your logic. Dettmer explains that we must pick a cluster and, beginning with the cause at the bottom, ask ourselves three basic questions," Bob explained and flashed a new slide on the screen.

1. Could this cause by itself create that effect or would it need help from another cause that we haven't yet acknowledged? If there is another contributing cause, place it in a graphic block beside the original cause, add an ellipse, and pass both causes through the ellipse.

2. Is there a step (graphic block) missing between this cause and that effect that would better explain what is happening? If there is, then create a new graphic block and insert it between the cause and the effect and then recheck both connections for cause sufficiency. That is, does it need help from another dependent cause to create the effect or is it a stand-alone, independent cause?

3. Is there another independent cause that could produce the same effect, without any assistance from the one already listed? If there is, then create another graphic block and insert it beside the original cause and connect it to the effect.

Bob continued, "Dettmer recommends the use of ellipses to show cause sufficiency or bow ties to show magnitudinal effects when they're needed. Magnitudinal effects are similar in nature to interactions in designed experiments (DOEs). That is, there may be several independent causes creating an effect, but when more than one is present at the same time, the effect is actually amplified. Once you are satisfied that a connection is logically sound enough to survive the criticism of someone else, make them permanent by changing the dotted lines to solid lines. Continue in this manner until all connections are considered to be solid and incontrovertible."

12. *Look for Additional Causes*

"As additional causes and connections are determined, add them to the CRT and solidify the logical connection as demonstrated in Figure 12.7. You are able to distinguish the additional causes added as the graphic blocks without numbers or letters assigned to them," he explained.

Bob then added, "Figure 12.8 is the completed version of the Current Reality Tree with highlighted Undesirable Effects, ellipses, and connecting errors. The clusters in the Current Reality Tree have been tested according to the categories of legitimate reservation so we are now ready for the next step."

13. *Redesignate Undesirable Effects*

"Now that all of the clusters are joined into a tree and new causes have been added, it is time to review everything you've done starting with your UDEs. It's entirely possible that some of the UDEs that you considered to be UDEs might not seem undesirable any longer. Or, as you've added new graphic blocks to the tree, there could be new effects that are considered undesirable. Dettmer advises us to ask two basic questions as we're revisiting the CRT," and flashed onto a new slide.

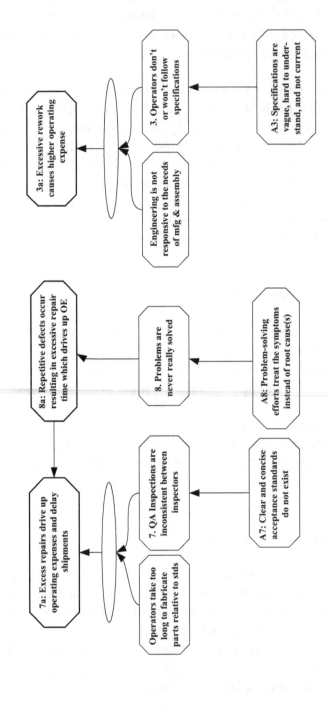

FIGURE 12.7
Additional causes.

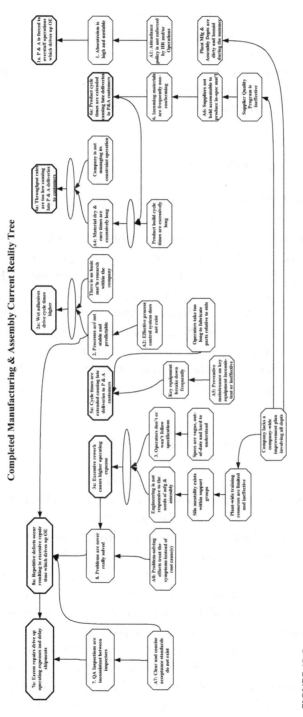

FIGURE 12.8
Completed Current Reality Tree.

a. Are all of my original UDEs bad enough to still be considered undesirable? If they are, don't change their designation. If they aren't, then remove them.
b. Have I added any new effects that might now qualify as undesirable effects using the same guidelines that we used to identify the original ones? If there are, then incorporate them into the tree.

14. *Look for Negative Reinforcing Loops (NRLs)*

Bob explained, "A negative reinforcing loop is a scenario where a negative effect of some cause reinforces the cause. For example, suppose an inspector records a defect, based upon his or her interpretation of an ambiguous acceptance standard, and he or she is praised for doing so. Since the inspector was praised, the expected behavior one might expect to see from this inspector is interpreting other ambiguous acceptance standards so as to find a new defect. It could be that this condition has been acceptable for years, but because of the first event (i.e., finding the first defect) was positively reinforced, the apparent defect might now be looked at differently. Although not common, a good place to look for these are situations are where effects seem to be disproportionately magnified."

15. *Identify All Root Causes and a Core Problem(s)*

"In this step, we are interested in identifying the root causes upon which we can take action and, hopefully, identify a single core problem. Remember Dettmer's [1] definition of root causes? A root cause is the lowest cause in a chain of cause and effect at which we have some capability to cause the break. This means that it's the lowest point at which human intervention can change or break a cause that is within our capability to control or influence. That is to say, we have no control over things like the weather because it's outside our capability to control or influence it," Bob explained.

He continued his presentation, "A core problem, on the other hand, is a unique kind of root cause because it can be traced to an extraordinarily large number of undesirable effects, maybe as high as 70 percent. If we are fortunate enough to have located a core problem, just imagine what would happen to our system's problems if we were to resolve it? In one fell swoop we could eliminate most of our UDEs, so it's important to be methodical in the development of our Current Reality Tree. But having said this, what if the core problem is beyond our scope of influence or control? If it is, then elevate it! I haven't met many leaders that wouldn't be interested in solving a core problem when the potential results are so enormous!"

"In our example (see Figure 12.8), there are actually two core problems identified. The company lacks a comprehensive improvement plan that involves most of the other departments in the company and the company's attendance policy isn't followed. If we were to attack these two problems, there is a good chance that most of the UDEs identified could simply go away. The silos could be broken, specifications could be updated and be less vague, excessive rework could be reduced, problems could be solved, absenteeism could be reduced, and so on." Bob explained.

16. *Trim Non-Essential Graphic Blocks*

"Although I don't believe this step is critical, if you have rendered some branches of your Current Reality Tree neutral, Dettmer recommends that you, for housekeeping purposes, should eliminate any of these neutral branches," Bob explained.

17. *Choose the Root Cause to Attack*

"As just discussed, if there is a core problem to solve, then clearly you should attack it. But suppose there isn't one? Which root cause should you assail? Dettmer provides three 'rules-of-thumb' to guide us in this selection," and he flashed onto a new slide.

   a. The one with the highest probability of you being able to influence
   b. The one that accounts for the highest number of UDEs
   c. The one that accounts for the most precarious UDE

"In my opinion, it is always better to attack the problem that is causing the most serious UDE for several reasons. First, the positive impact on the organization will be felt and realized immediately. Second, by solving this problem, it could serve as a rallying point to achieve future buy-in for this approach to problem identification and resolution. Third, if you have chosen the root cause that has the largest financial impact on the organization, it may very well be used to fund other solutions to other more complex root causes that might require a capital expenditure. Finally, leaders want to see results as quickly as possible," Bob explained.

Bob continued, "As I said in our example, there are two key core problems to solve. The first one involves the lack of a comprehensive improvement plan that ties together all of the individual groups working to achieve the goals of the company. The real problem as it related to throughput was the excessively long cure times of the various adhesives used to produce the tanks. The second problem related to the specifications supplied by the engineering group. This problem wasn't so much that the specifications didn't exist, but rather a problem associated with updating the specifications to reflect better ways of producing products as these new ways were developed. If this company could solve both the specification clarity and update problem and discover ways to reduce the long cure times, then both should automatically result in significant throughput gains simply because rework and cycle times should be reduced. So, the question becomes one of coming up with simple solutions to these two core problems."

"This is what the Current Reality Tree is and how to construct one," Bob said. To quote Bill Dettmer [1], "It's been said that a well-defined problem is already half-solved. The Current Reality Tree is a problem identification tool. It helps us examine the cause-and-effect logic behind our current situation. The CRT begins with undesirable effects we see around us, which tell us that we have a problem. It helps us work back to identify a few root causes, or a single core problem, which generate all the undesirable effects we're experiencing. The core problem is usually the constraint we're trying to identify in the five focusing steps. The CRT tells us *what to change*—the one simplest change to make that will have the greatest positive effect on our system."

Bob continued, "The remaining Logical Thinking Process tools are the Conflict Resolution Diagram, the Future Reality Tree, the Prerequisite Tree, and the Transition Tree. I will discuss these tools, but not in the same level of detail that we did with the Current Reality Tree." And with that, Bob continued his presentation, "Now that we have a completed learning about the Current Reality Tree, and have identified and selected the root causes and/or core problems to attack, what's next? Just how do we go about attacking a system's problem or a policy constraint. We do so by developing simple breakthrough ideas and solutions. But with every problem there are conflicts that seem to get in the way of our ideas for problem resolution."

Bob explained, "There are three primary types of conflict that we must deal with as we work to resolve problems, or more specifically, system problems and policy constraints. The first conflict is one where one force is pulling us to do one thing, but an equal and opposite force pulls in the opposite direction. Dettmer [1] refers to this type of conflict as *Opposite Conditions*. The second type of conflict is one in which we are forced to choose between different alternatives which Dettmer calls, quite appropriately, *Different Alternatives*. The third type of conflict is what I refer to as *The Hidden Agenda* conflict. In a hidden agenda conflict, there is generally a personality involved that is typically manifested in a desire or inherent need to hold onto some kind of power." Bob scanned the room and it appeared that everyone understood what he had just explained, so he continued.

"In attempting to resolve conflicts, it is important to recognize that there are three types of resolutions that can be achieved; *win-win*; *win-lose*; or *compromise*. Of the three possibilities, we should always attempt to achieve a win-win solution, but sometimes it isn't practical. In a win-lose situation, one side typically gets just about everything it wanted while the other side gets very little. This type of solution serves to create antagonistic or hostile attitudes and your chances of success are diminished because the losing side might attempt to sabotage your solution. Not openly, mind you, but rather covertly or secretly," Bob explained.

"In the case of a compromise, generally, the solution ends up being sub-optimized because you are attempting to satisfy most of the requirements of both parties engaged in the conflict. But having said this, a compromise is better than a win-lose or imposed solution, but remember, it generally results in a sub-optimized solution. The solution for a hidden agenda conflict is much like what happens in a win-lose conflict in that someone works against you behind the scenes in hopes of holding on to their apparent power. So how do we resolve conflicts?" Bob explained.

"Goldratt developed a tool he refers to as a Conflict Resolution Diagram (CRD) or as it is also called, the Evaporating Cloud. The Conflict Resolution Diagram identifies and demonstrates the relationship between the key elements of a conflict and then suggests ways to resolve it. As I explained earlier, for a detailed description of how to create and use a Conflict Resolution Diagram, read Dettmer's, *Breaking the Constraints to World-Class Performance* [1]. The diagram includes the system

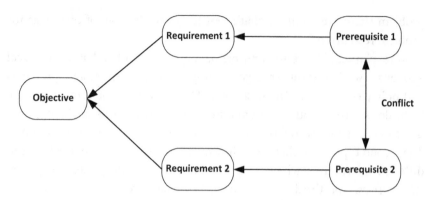

FIGURE 12.9
Conflict Resolution Diagram.

objective, necessary-but-not-sufficient requirements that lead to it, and the prerequisites needed to satisfy them. Figure 12.9 is the basic structure of the evaporating cloud," Bob explained.

Bob continued his CRD explanation, "The Conflict Resolution Diagram" was developed by Goldratt to achieve at least eight different purposes:

- To confirm that the conflict exists and that it is real
- To identify the conflict associated with the problem
- To identify all of the assumptions between the problem and conflict
- To provide a comprehensive answer as to why the problem is present
- To create solutions that could result in win-win situations
- To create innovative solutions to problems
- To provide a resolution of the conflict
- To avoid compromising situations

"Figure 12.10 is an example of a Conflict Resolution Diagram from our example company. In this example, the conflict was between the Manufacturing and Assembly (M & A) department and Engineering with the objective being minimal rework of products. On the one hand, Manufacturing and Assembly had a requirement for their operators to follow the shop floor specifications while at the same time Engineering had a requirement to focus more resources on new product development. M & A's prerequisite was to receive clear, unambiguous, and up-to-date specifications from Engineering while Engineering needed to reduce the time spent writing and updating shop floor specifications so that they

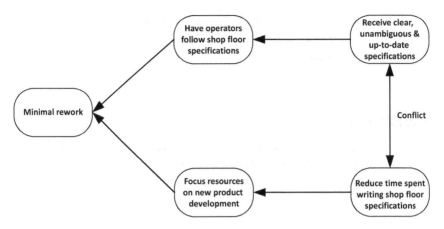

FIGURE 12.10
Conflict resolution example.

could focus more resources on new product development and herein was the conflict," Bob continued. "As you can see, the requirements are not in conflict with each other, but the prerequisites certainly are," Bob added.

Bob continued, "The key to breaking conflicts are the assumptions surrounding the conflict, so it's imperative that we understand what they are. The assumption of the M & A department was that Engineering didn't care about the quality of the specifications they were delivering to M & A, while the Engineering group's assumption was that M & A was asking for specifications that were just too specific. There was a third assumption that stated that additional manpower could not be hired by either group. Once the two departments came together and understood the other's requirements, prerequisites, and assumptions the conflict was resolved. The engineers had been writing the specifications, but because they had very little clerical help, it was difficult to keep them up-to-date as better methods were found. At the same time, there were new products on the horizon that needed to be engineered. The conflict was resolved when M & A offered to supply some existing clerical support to Engineering to relieve some of the burden of updating the specifications. The solution was simple, and the conflict was resolved."

"I understand that what you just heard might seem to be overwhelming. I know it was for me the first time I was introduced to the Logical Thinking Processes. But I do have hope for you and that hope is referred to as *The Goal Tree*. Mark and Tom, we need to schedule another off-site meeting to discuss this important tool. Mark called his secretary and asked her to schedule another off-site meeting for the next day. And with that, the training session ended.

REFERENCE

1. H. William Dettmer, 1998, *Breaking the Constraints to World-Class Performance*, American Society for Quality, Milwaukee, WI.

13

The Goal Tree Improvement Initiative

Like before, in previous sessions, the same group filed into Tires for All's off-site conference room at the same hotel they had used before. Bob welcomed everyone and began. "Many people who have gone through a TOC Jonah training session on the Logical Thinking Processes have come away kind of overwhelmed and sometimes feeling like they are unable to apply what they had supposedly just learned. Let's face it, the Theory of Constraints Logical Thinking Process tools are just not easy for some people to grasp and apply. As a result, many people kind of put them on the back burner, rather than taking a chance of doing something wrong. Well, for everyone who fits into this category, I have hope for you, and this hope is referred to as the Goal Tree. The Goal Tree is another logic diagram that is actually simple to construct, and unlike the Logical Thinking Processes, it is one that I think you would feel confident using. In the spirit of learning a tool and making it your own, I have changed the way the Goal Tree was first presented, but I'll get to that change later. So, let's review both the history and basics of the Goal Tree," Bob explained.

Bob began again, "Bill Dettmer [1], who is generally credited as being the man who developed the Goal Tree, tells us of his first exposure to the Goal Tree back in 1995. Bill had attended a management skills workshop conducted by Oded Cohen at the Goldratt Institute. Back then, the Goal Tree was referred to as an Intermediate Objectives (IO) Map, but in recent years, Dettmer has recommended that the IO Map should now be referred to as a Goal Tree. Bill now believes that it should be the first step in a full Logical Thinking Process analysis. He believes this because he believes that it defines the standard for goal attainment and its prerequisites in a much more efficient manner."

"I believe that the Goal Tree is a great focusing tool that will help everyone understand why an organization is not meeting its goal. Dettmer tells us that there is another advantage of using a Goal Tree and that is by including it in your system analysis, there is a better integration of the rest of the Logical Thinking Process tools. Bill believes that by using it first, it will ultimately accelerate the completion of Current Reality Trees, Conflict Clouds, and Future Reality Trees. While I agree with Bill in this regard, the thing I like most about the Goal Tree is that it can be used as a stand-alone tool, which results in a much faster analysis of the organization's weak points. In this session, we will discuss the Goal Tree as a stand-alone tool," Bob explained.

Bob continued, "When using the logic-based TOC Logical Thinking Process tools, there are two distinctly different types of logic at play, sufficiency type logic and necessity type logic. Sufficiency type logic is quite simply a series of if-then statements. If I have 'this,' then I have 'that.' On the other hand, necessity-based logic trees use the syntax, in order to have 'this' I must have 'that.' The Goal Tree falls into the necessity-based category. For example, in order to have a fire, I must have a fuel source, a spark, and air. If the goal is to have a fire, it must have all three components. The fuel source, spark and air are referred to as Critical Success Factors (CSFs). Take away even one of the CSFs and you won't have a fire," Bob explained.

Bob began, "Our first deliverable today is that we must first define our *span of control* and our *sphere of influence*. Our span of control includes all of those things in our system over which we have unilateral change authority. In other words, we can decide to change those things on our own because they are within our control and don't require approval from someone outside our system. On the other hand, our sphere of influence are those things we may want to change, but we must get approval to do so." Mark then said, "I would think our span of control covers everything within our four walls, from the time we receive our raw materials until we ship our products to our customers." He then added, "Our sphere of influence, simply put, would be everything before receiving raw materials, as well as the receipt of our products at our customers. Do I have that right Bob?" he asked, and Bob indicated that was right.

Bob continued, "The distinction between what our span of control and sphere of influence is very important, simply because our sphere of influence is not a fixed entity. In your systems here at Tires for All, you can influence way more than you control and it's probably much more than you realize. Generally speaking, as Mark said, many things within the walls of your manufacturing facility represent you span of control. But having said that, not everything fits into this category. For example, things like governmental regulations under which your business is regulated are not considered within your span of control. You might be able to influence them, but you certainly don't have control over them. So, for now, let's go with your definitions, but we must exercise caution." With Tires for All's span of control and sphere of influence defined in limited terms, the creation of their Goal Tree began.

Bob continued and inserted a new slide onto the screen, "This figure (Figure 13.1) demonstrates the hierarchical structure of the Goal Tree. The Goal Tree consists of a single Goal, several CSFs, which must be in place to achieve the goal, and a series of Necessary Conditions (NCs), which must be in place to achieve each of the CSFs. The Goal and CSFs are written as terminal outcomes, as though they are already in place. The NCs are, more or less, written as activities that must be completed in order to achieve each of the CSFs. We'll be completing our own Goal Tree, but a completed Goal Tree's basic structure looks like this," Bob explained.

Bob continued, "Suppose that your organization is profitable, but you want to become a highly profitable one, just like Tires for All. You assemble the General Manager and key members of his staff to develop an

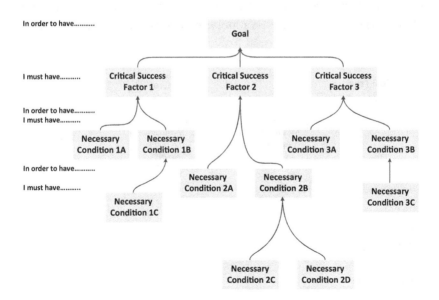

FIGURE 13.1
Goal Tree basic structure.

effective plan to achieve this goal. In the Goal Tree drawing on the screen (Figure 13.2), after much discussion, you agree on your Goal as 'Maximum Profitability,' and place it inside the Goal box. This goal statement, which is the desired end state, is written as a terminal outcome as though it's already been achieved. You think to yourself, 'What must I have in place for our goal to be realized?' You think, 'I know that we must have Maximum Throughput, Minimum Operating Expenses, and Minimum Inventory,' so you place each of these in separate CSF boxes. One by one, you continue listing those things that must be in place to achieve your goal and place them into separate CSF boxes like Figure 13.2. In a Goal Tree, you should have no more than three to five CSFs."

Bob then explained, "Because the Goal Tree uses necessity-based logic, it is read in the following way: 'In order to have a highly profitable company, I must have maximum throughput, minimum operating expenses, and minimum inventory. Directly beneath the CSFs are the NCs that must also be in place to achieve each of the CSFs.' So, continuing to read downward, 'In order to have maximum throughput, I must have two NCs, high on-time delivery rates, and excellent quality.' Remember, the CSFs are written as terminal outcomes, as though they're already in place."

"You continue reading downward, in order to have, for example, maximum throughput, I must have maximum revenue and minimum totally variable costs. The NCs represent actions that must be completed

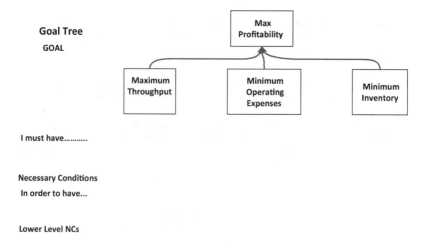

FIGURE 13.2
The Goal Tree with goal and critical success factors.

to achieve each individual CSF, so they form the basis for your company's improvement plan. In like manner, your team completes all of the NCs until you are satisfied that what you have in place on the Goal Tree will ultimately deliver the goal of the organization. The completed Goal Tree might look something like this figure (Figure 13.3)," and he flashed it on the screen. Bob pointed out the existence and direction of the connecting arrows for each entity which are used to tie each entity together.

Bob asked if there were any questions or comments so far and Tom said, "I can see how this tool can be used by Tires for All to create our improvement plan. But my question is, how detailed should you make the wording in each of the boxes?" "Good question Tom," Bob replied. "Typically, the wording is intended to be a sort of shorthand note so that your team can look at it and know the details of what you are saying. If you look at the wording in this figure, you'll see that in each box they are, in effect, short statements of your intended results and actions you plan to take to achieve each one," Bob explained and continued on with his presentation.

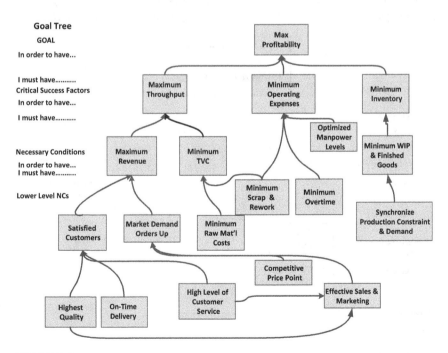

FIGURE 13.3
Completed Goal Tree.

"So, let's work on creating your Goal Tree," Bob said. "The Goal that we start with is the responsibility of the owner or owners, but since they are not here with us, Mark, it is your responsibility to state the Goal." Mark responded and said, "Well, since I have had meetings with our Board of Directors, and they made their desires very clear, I would say our Goal would be 'Optimum Profit Margins.'" "I know they told me at least 20 percent, but I'm sure they would like our margins to be higher," he added. Bob agreed and on a previously prepared flip chart page, he recorded the Goal statement (Figure 13.4).

Immediately, Tom raised his hand and asked, "Bob, what does the '100' you have in our Goal box mean?" Bob explained that in each entity box, "I will add a number which is simply a shorthand location marker. I find it easier, if someone has a question about one of the boxes, to just call out the location marker."

Bob then continued, "With this Goal in mind, what do you believe we must have in place to achieve this Goal?" Cliff Hasting was the first to respond and said, "Well, based upon all of the problems we've had with our production schedule, I think one of the things we must have is work scheduled to meet demand." Bob recorded his response on the flip chart (Figure 13.5) and asked, "What else do we need to satisfy our Goal?"

```
┌─────────────────────────┐
│           100           │
│  Optimize Profit Margins │
└─────────────────────────┘
```

FIGURE 13.4
Goal Box.

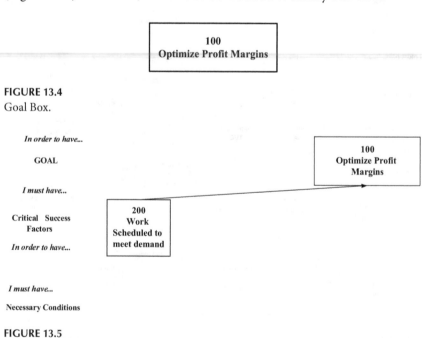

FIGURE 13.5
Goal Tree with first CSF.

Again, Cliff spoke up and said, "We need all of our tools and equipment available when we need them." Bob recorded Cliff's new response on the flip chart (Figure 13.6) and asked what else they needed.

The group continued adding Critical Success Factors until they were satisfied that they had included all of them. Bob carefully worded each response and recorded each one on the flip chart (Figure 13.7).

With the Goal and Critical Success Factors in place, it was now time to select the Necessary Conditions that must be in place to satisfy each of the CSFs. "Okay everyone, let's start with our first Necessary Condition and remember our logical statements take the form of, 'In order to have a CSF, we must have the NC or NCs,'" Bob explained. Mark was the first to respond and said, "In order to have work schedule to meet demand (CSF 200), I would say that we must have an enhanced scheduling system and a schedule that based on our demand." Bob shortened the wording a bit and recorded them on the flip chart with the entity numbers included (Figure 13.8).

Bob then said, "So, let's stay with these two entities and explain what we need in order to satisfy the requirements for both of them." Mark then said, "Well I think scheduling our facilities to meet demand, doesn't need anything because we just do it. As far as what we need for an enhanced scheduling system, it needs to be an automated one that includes an effective priority system." Mark then asked, "Bob, may I continue with the

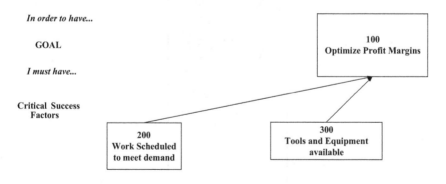

FIGURE 13.6
Goal Tree with first two CSFs.

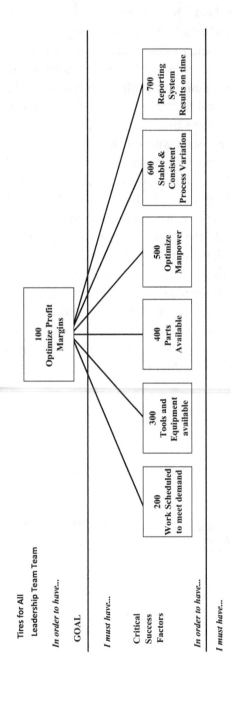

FIGURE 13.7

Goal Tree with all CSFs.

additional Necessary Conditions required to satisfy these two conditions?" "Of course, Mark," Bob replied. "I think in conjunction with these two NCs, we need both of these requirements to be defined," Mark added. "Okay, got it Mark," and Bob carefully summarized Mark's comments and added them to the Goal Tree under construction (Figure 13.9).

One by one, the group continued the creation of their Goal Tree by recommending and discussing each of the Necessary Conditions required to be in place in order to deliver each level above. There were numerous discussions and disagreements as they progressed, but in the end, they were all able to agree on the completed structure. Bob was very happy with the final Goal Tree they had created and worked hard to turn their suggestions for Necessary Conditions into understandable shortened versions for each one.

Bob then took the time to change what they had created on a flip chart to an electronic version. Bob then made copies of the completed Goal Tree (Figure 13.10) and handed out a copy to each member of the team. He then said, "I want to take a short break, but while you're on this break, review our Goal Tree and let me know if there are any changes you want to make."

When everyone returned from their break, Bob asked the group if they had any changes they wanted to make or if they had any questions or comments about the Goal Tree exercise? Tom was the first one to respond to Mark's question and said, "Bob, I've been part of Tires for All's improvement planning, and I have never experienced creating a logic-based plan like this one. I'm confident that this completed Goal Tree will lead us to improved profitability, so thanks for leading us through this effort. And to think we completed this effort in a little over two hours just blows my mind!"

Bob thanked him for his comments, but then explained that we weren't done yet. He then explained, "What we have created this morning is just the beginning of our effort to create our improvement plan." Mark then asked, "What's the next step Bob?" Bob replied, "We will now take this Goal Tree, make some subtle changes to it, and then use it to create our long-term improvement plan." "Is everyone ready to get started?" Bob asked and when everyone indicated that they were, Bob began.

"Earlier, I said that I have changed the way the Goal Tree was first introduced. This change has to do with how the Goal and Critical Success Factors are worded (and some of the NCs). One of the key learnings in the book, *The 4 Disciplines of Execution: Achieving Your Wildly Important*

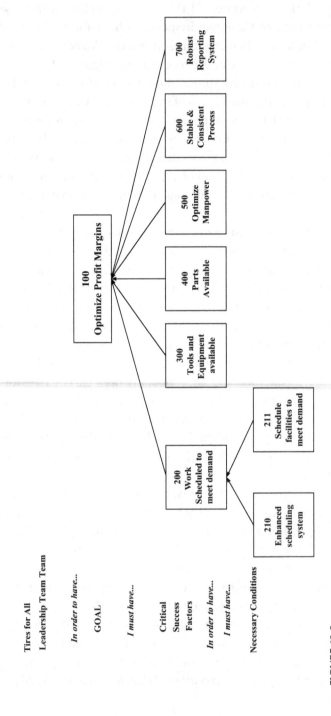

FIGURE 13.8

Goal Tree with all CSF and first two NCs.

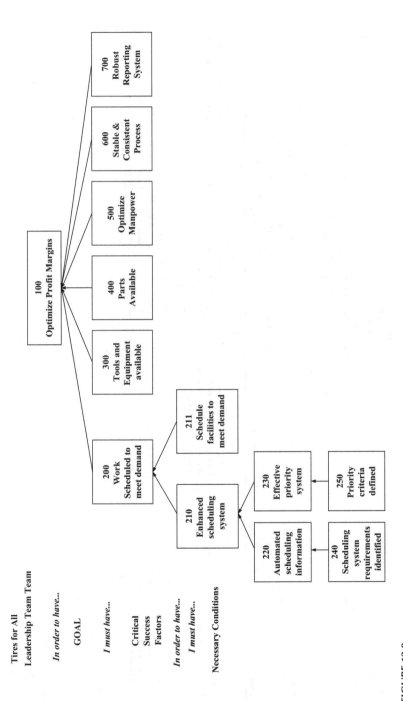

FIGURE 13.9

Goal Tree with lower level NCs.

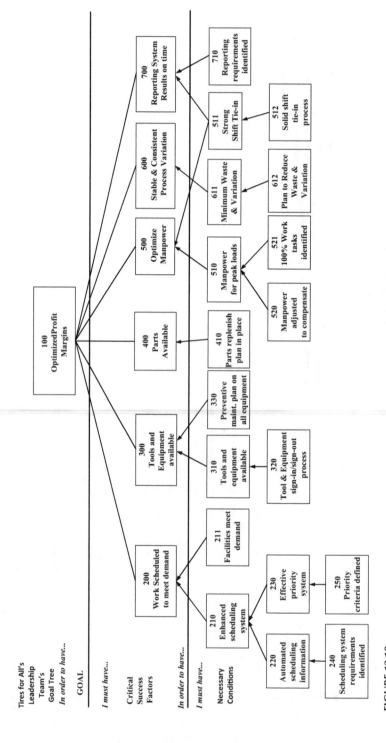

FIGURE 13.10
Completed Goal Tree.

Goals [2], was the concept of Lead and Lag Measures. The lag measure has to do with Goal achievement and should be written in such a way that there is a clear measurement of Goal units with a well-defined target. So, for example, instead of the Goal being written as 'Optimized Profit Margins' like we have in our Goal Tree, let's word it as though it was a performance measure with a target. Let's say that your company's current profit margins are around 19 percent. What if we re-wrote the Goal as follows: Profit Margins above 25%? Written this way, we can measure it and it has a clear target, just like a finish line in a race. In this way, everyone knows what the company wants to achieve and how to measure success," Bob explained. "Any questions so far?" Bob asked, but when there weren't any, he continued.

Bob began again, "Now let's look at the CSFs. The first CSF in our Goal Tree is written as Work Scheduled to Meet Demand. What if we added something like 'Greater Than 20%' to our original CSF? Can you now see how vague this CSF was as it was originally written? Written in this manner, it is neither measurable nor does it have a target for the improvement team to shoot for. By including our target, it becomes measurable and has a clear target or measure of success to attain."

Bob continued, "What I'm suggesting is that the CSFs should be written as Lead Measures that tie directly to the Lag Measures. In other words, if we were able to move the Lead Measures in a positive direction, then the Lag Measure would eventually improve as well. Let's look at the original Goal Tree with the remaining CSFs that I have changed using these simple guidelines." Bob loaded a new slide for everyone to see (Figure 13.11).

Bob continued, "As you can see, many of the CSFs are now measurable and display a clear success target. For example, CSF number 400 is now written as '400: Parts Available > 99%.' Clearly, this CSF is measurable and the target to reach has been set. Now let's look at the NCs. As written in the original Goal Tree, the NCs are written with the same clarity as the CSFs," Bob stated.

"I chose to do so because, when they are measurable and have a target, as many of them do, it becomes much easier for the improvement team to define activities that will move these Lead Measures. And if these lower level Lead Measures move in a positive direction, they will move the upper level Lead Measures in like manner. For example, one of the lower level NCs is stated as '410: Parts replenish plan in place > 99% on time %.' If this is achieved, then the assumption is that '400: Parts Available > 99%' will

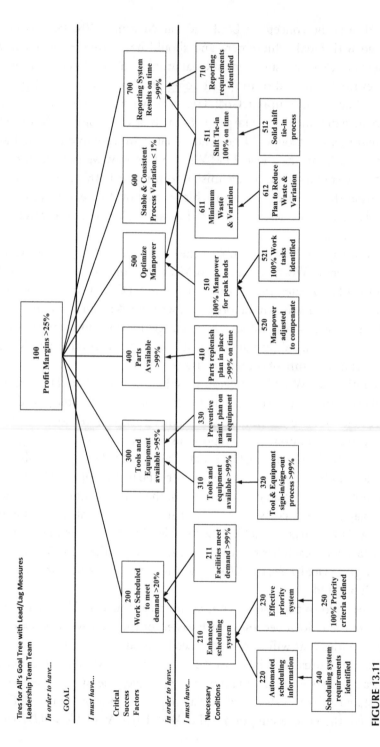

FIGURE 13.11

Original Goal Tree with Lead and Lag Measure Targets.

also be met. And if this CSF is met, then it should move the Goal closer to its hoped-for level of 25 percent. As we know, each CSF contributes to achievement of the Goal, but all of them must be achieved to meet the final Goal target." Bob added, "So, review this new version of your Goal Tree and let me know what you think of it." There were no objections, so they moved on.

Bob began, "Here's another area where I've departed from the traditional Logical Thinking Process methodology. Bill Dettmer recommends the next step would be to use the Goal Tree to construct a Current Reality Tree. And although I totally support Bill Dettmer's approach, when time is not a factor, I would continue on with the Goal Tree in the way that Bill recommends. But, when time is a factor, which it is at Tires for All, my immediate next step is to facilitate a critical discussion with the improvement team on the real-time status or current state of the Goal, CSFs, and NCs." "I use a simple Green, Yellow, and Red coding system to describe how each of the Goal Tree entities exists in our current reality. With this new approach, the status of each entity becomes much easier. I might add that the coding system I will now describe is a departure from the way I had been using the Goal Tree in the past," Bob explained.

Bob explained and inserted a new slide of the new Goal Tree onto the screen. Bob then said, "Notice the key on the bottom right hand side of the Goal Tree and you'll see that a box shaded in green indicates that the measure is at or above the target level. Green can also be used to describe actions that we plan to take to drive the lead measures in a positive direction. In this case, the required action is in place and functioning, so no changes need to be made," Bob explained. Bob continued, "Likewise, a yellow box indicates that a lead measure is greater than 5 percent, but less than 25 percent away from the defined target. Or if it's a required action, then it means that there is something in place, but that it needs improvement."

"A box shaded in red means that the lead measure is greater than 25 percent from its target or if it's a required action, then the entity is either not in place or that something is in place, but it isn't functioning adequately. So, here is our Goal Tree with instructions for each entity listed at the bottom. We will now go through an exercise where we assess each entity and color-code it according to the instructions at the bottom of this figure (Figure 13.12). But here's the catch, I want you to do it as a group, without me present," he added and left the conference room. And

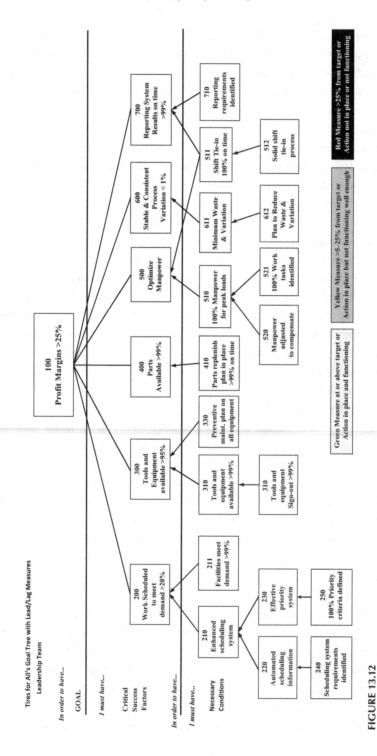

FIGURE 13.12

Goal Tree with color coded instructions.

Green Measure at or above target or Action in place and functioning	Yellow Measure >5–25% from target or Action in place but not functioning well enough	Red Measure >25% from target or Action not in place or not functioning

FIGURE 13.13
Instructions for assessing Goal Tree entities.

with these instructions, the team began. Before Bob left the conference room, he had suggested that Tom lead this effort, since Bob believed that Tom was totally grasping this new Goal Tree concept used to assess the organization (Figure 13.13).

Tom began, "So, just to review what we're going to be doing, we will use the instructions at the base of our Goal Tree to assess how we're doing with our Goal, Critical Success Factors, and Necessary Conditions," and with that he posted the three instructions on the screen. Basically, if what we have in place is at or above our target, or the action is in place and functioning well, we color it green. If we are between 5 to 25 percent from our target or we have an action in place, but it isn't functioning well enough, then we color it yellow. And finally, if our measure is greater than 25 percent away from our target or we don't have an action in place or what we have in place is not functioning, then we color it red. Does everyone understand what we're doing?" he asked.

Everyone seemed to understand the instructions as laid out by Tom and the discussions began. One by one, the team discussed each of the entities, and although they had disagreements at times, they were able to work their way through them and come up with a final product. When they were finished, they called Bob back into the room to show him their results. Tom flashed their completed Goal Tree assessment on the screen (Figure 13.14).

Tom began, "Bob, we have completed the assessment of our Goal, Critical Success Factors, and Necessary Conditions and we'd like you to take some time to review our final product." Bob thanked them for their work and began studying what they had put together. He had questions, but in each case, they were answered to his satisfaction. He then began discussing more on this new tool. "It should be obvious that any entity shaded in red has a higher priority than one shaded in yellow. Please understand that these guidelines that I've established are mine, so they are not hard and fast rules taken from some textbook. I encourage you that when you use the Goal Tree in this manner to develop your own guidelines going forward," Bob stated.

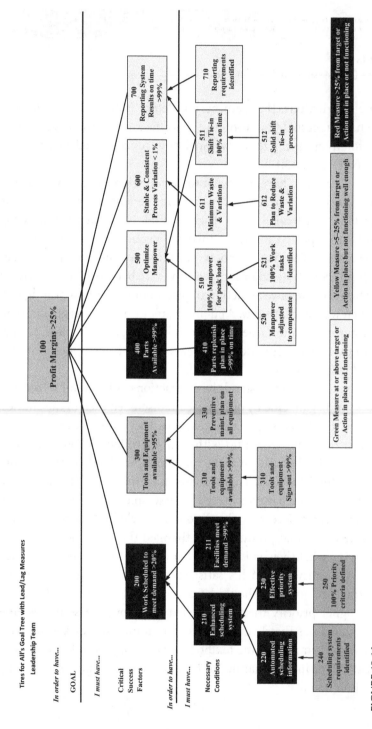

FIGURE 13.14

Assessed Goal Tree.

"As I previously stated, where we observe red boxes, it should be apparent that these are the areas we must focus on first, because they offer the greatest potential source for improved results. As we improve the Lead Measures in these areas, improvement in upper level Lead Measures will take place until ultimately, the Lag Measure, the Goal of Profit Margins Above 25%, should also be achieved. The key then for creating a focused improvement plan, using the Goal Tree, is to first develop the required Lag and Lead Measures and then set realistic targets to achieve each one of them. The key though is to make sure there is a relationship that correlates between the Lead and Lag Measures," Bob explained.

Bob continued, "So here it is, a different way to utilize a Goal Tree which is both easy to understand and construct and which permits the development of a very focused improvement plan. In my experience using this approach, the team that develops it will embrace it because it is their plan. And the good news is, from start to finish, it only takes less than a day, rather than days or weeks to develop."

REFERENCES

1. H. William Dettmer, 1998, *Breaking the Constraints to World-Class Performance*, Quality Press, Milwaukee, WI.
2. Jim Huling, Chris McChesney, and Sean Covey, 2012, *The 4 Disciplines of Execution: Achieving Your Wildly Important Goals*, Free Press, New York, NY.

14

The Strategic Plan

Now that the leadership team had completed their assessment of Tires for All's facility in Western Pennsylvania, it was now time to begin the development of their strategic improvement plan. They would use their Goal Tree with their assessment results to complete this task, and the good news was this effort would not take a lot of time. Bob had suggested that each member of the leadership team, over the next week, study their completed assessment Goal Tree and when they met again, present ideas on how to improve their system. Bob also stressed that they should be thinking about all they had learned in their sessions, which included the concept of the system constraint, as they developed their improvement ideas. Bob also recommended that they get together with their counterparts to form small teams to discuss their ideas. Bob had to leave Tires for All for two weeks to attend to some personal problems, but when he returned, he wanted to have another meeting with the leadership team.

Two of the first members of the leadership team to get together were Cliff Hastings, the Operation's Manager and Frank Dempsey, the Maintenance Director. Their discussion centered around Critical Success Factor 300, "Tools and Equipment available greater than 95 percent of the time." One of the problems that they had was in the area of equipment downtime, especially in the carcass-building area. The downtime levels, at times, were as high as 20 percent, so they both agreed to develop and implement an effective preventive maintenance plan. And since Tires for All did not have a third shift, they thought it would be a good idea to do their preventive maintenance on the third shift when no machines were running. Frank agreed to develop this plan and put it in place within two weeks.

Cliff also decided to meet with Jeffrey Cox, the Purchasing Manager, and Sally Hodges, the Industrial Engineering Manager, to look at solutions to their parts problems. One of the potential solutions was the Theory of Constraints Replenishment Solution, but they decided they would need Bob's help to better understand how to implement this solution. Based upon the description that Bob had given them in their training session, all three believed that this could be very beneficial for Tires for All.

Another meeting took place between Mark Roder, Sally Hodges, and Cliff Hastings to discuss the problems they were experiencing with their current scheduling system. They discussed at length what they knew about possibly implementing Drum Buffer Rope in conjunction with Buffer Management and their current ERP system. All three believed that this could be Tires for All's solution to their lack of synchronization which was evident throughout Tires for All. This was especially evident with the amount of work-in-process (WIP) inventory that seemed to pile up constantly. The three of them decided that, like the other TOC based tools, they would need Bob's help to implement this system. They all believed that implementing Goldratt's five focusing steps would be absolutely necessary if Drum Buffer Rope was to work.

Yet another meeting occurred between Tom Mahanan and Mark Roder to discuss how they would use Throughput Accounting to make all of their financial decisions. Tom was especially excited to get moving on this implementation. After all these years working in manufacturing, Tom was amazed at how backward his thinking was. For so many years, Tom and Mark had focused on saving money as a way to improve profitability instead of accelerating throughput to drive revenue higher. This approach to making money is clearly different than trying to improve their profits by saving money.

Sam Plankton, the Human Resources Manager, met with Mark Roder and Chris Samuels to discuss labor requirements. Prior to Bob Nelson coming to Tires for All, Mark and Sam had discussed the need for layoffs, but after hearing all that Bob had to say, Sam wanted to discuss future plans in this area. Mark was very clear from the beginning of the meeting that there would be no layoffs! Mark explained to Chris that since they would be using Throughput Accounting to make all of their financial decisions, layoffs were now off the table. When Sam asked why, Mark explained that Tires for All would need to take an "all-hands-on-deck" approach to manufacturing and that they may even need to hire additional help in the future. Needless to say, both Chris and Sam were very happy to hear these words.

After two weeks, Bob returned to Tires for All and immediately set up a meeting with the leadership team, plus several additions. He wanted to make sure that Chris Samuels, the Union Head, was also in the meeting. The meeting was again held off-site at the same hotel they had met in before. Bob greeted everyone as they entered the conference room and when everyone was seated, he began. "Good morning everyone, I'm very excited to hear what everyone has to say about their discussions on their Goal Tree. One by one, everyone presented the series of meeting they had held, and Bob was pleased to hear what everyone had to say. When everyone was finished with their reports, Bob began again.

"This morning I want to discuss the sequence of events going forward for our improvement effort," Bob explained. "We can't just rush off and begin implementing the various improvement ideas, it has to be done in a logical order," he added. He continued, "One thing to keep foremost in our minds is the overall goal of taking profit margins to over 25 percent! There is a logical order for implementing our various improvements, so we need to all agree on this order."

Bob continued, "I think we can all agree that one of the first things we need to put in place is Throughput Accounting for making financial decisions, simply because it will force us to focus on driving revenue higher. Think about it, if we drive revenue higher while maintaining the same level of operating expense, our bottom line will correspondingly improve. Does everyone agree with this?" Bob asked. It was clear that everyone did agree. "Remember, this doesn't mean that we abandon our current financial reporting, simply because we are required, by law, to report it this way," Bob added.

"OK, let's get started," Bob said. "Today we're going to plan on how to turn our problem areas, those we defined in red in our Goal Tree, into hopefully, strengths," he said. "Does anyone have any ideas on how we can turn our reds into either yellows or greens? In other words, what can we do that might positively impact delivery rates, customer service, and synchronize production to the constraint and demand?" he asked.

Cliff Hastings, the Operation's Manager, was the first to speak and said, "If we can come up with a way to schedule our production based upon the needs of the constraint, it seems to me that we could really have a positive result for on-time delivery rates and at the same time it would reduce our WIP and

Finished Goods (FG) levels?" he said more in the form of a question. Tom Mahanan then said, "Since you mentioned Drum Buffer Rope, I've been reading more about it and it seems that this scheduling method is supposed to do exactly what you just described," he said directly to Cliff.

Mark Roder responded by saying, "He's right, Drum Buffer Rope limits the rate of new product starts, because nothing enters the process until something exits the constraint." "So, let's look at what happens to the reds and yellows if we were to implement Drum Buffer Rope," he added and pointed at the Goal Tree. "The way I see it is, if we implement Drum Buffer Rope, we will minimize WIP. If we minimize WIP, we automatically minimize Finished Goods, which minimizes our investment dollars which positively impacts our profitability," he explained enthusiastically. "We should also see our on-time delivery rates jump up, which should result in much higher levels of customer satisfaction," he added. "This should also allow us to be more competitive in our pricing and stimulate more demand and with our ability to increase throughput, we will positively impact profitability," he explained.

Cliff then said, "Last night I read more about the Theory of Constraints, and it seems to me that one thing we must do is stop tracking efficiency in our non-constraints, and if we do that, we should also reduce our WIP." Jim Fredo, the Quality Director spoke up and said, "I'm thinking that if we effectively slowdown in our non-constraints, we should see our scrap and rework levels improve significantly because our operators will have more time to make their products. And I also believe that we should implement Bob's Ultimate Improvement Cycle. This improvement will reduce our scrap and rework levels, and in conjunction with Drum Buffer Rope, will reduce both our Operating Expenses and Totally Variable Costs. The combination of these improvements will both contribute to our profitability." Bob listened and just smiled as it was clear that this team was focused on making improvements at Tires for All. Before Bob could say anything, Tom said, "One other thing is that we should see our overtime levels drop which will also improve profitability." "I am just amazed that by making these basic changes, we could see a dramatic improvement to our financials!" Bob exclaimed.

After listening intently to what everyone was saying, Bob began. "In our training on Throughput Accounting, we defined Net Profit as Throughput minus Operating Expense or NP = T − OE. The lag metric of choice for our Goal Tree was correctly stated as Net Profit and we set our target for Net Profit to be greater than 25 percent." "Excuse me for interrupting you Bob, but Mark and I would like to present something we put together last night," Tom said. Bob, with a surprised look responded and said, "Not a problem Tom, both of you come up to the front of the room and speak away," Bob said with a smile.

With that being said, Tom and Mark moved to the front of the room. Tom began, "Mark and I met last night to chat about today's meeting. Mark wanted to get my opinion on something he had been thinking about. What Mark wanted to do was to create a Goal Tree that was focused on Throughput Accounting. He wanted to do this because he thought it would help us today and I agreed with him. So, what you're about to see is that Goal Tree and we welcome any comments and even corrections." With that said, Tom inserted his flash drive and a figure (Figure 14.1) appeared on the screen.

Needless to say, Bob was very surprised and impressed at what he saw on the screen! To think that Mark and Tom had taken it upon their own to develop this new Goal Tree just amazed Bob. Bob studied this new Goal

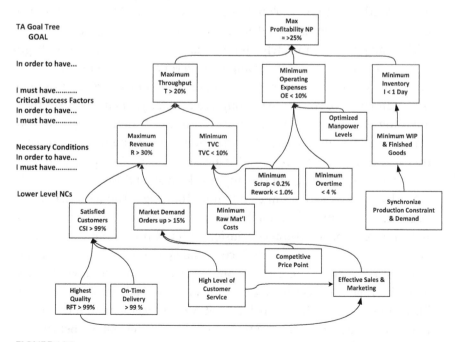

FIGURE 14.1
Tom and Mark's Goal Tree.

Tree, looking for anything that might be incorrect and to his amazement he could not find anything of concern. With this in mind he spoke up and said, "Well done guys!" In addition, he asked, "So tell me again, what prompted you to create this Goal Tree, obviously based upon what you learned on our session on Throughput Accounting?"

Mark looked at Tom and motioned for him to answer Bob's question. Tom stood up and began, "When we created our original Goal Tree, which I thought was well done by the way, we didn't have our financials with us. I thought long and hard about whether some of the assumptions we had made were correct or not. So, I called Mark and explained some of my concerns and he agreed to come to my office with our latest financials. We both reviewed our latest financial information and it was then that I suggested that we create a different Goal Tree centered around the teachings of Throughput Accounting."

Bob then said, "Well, for what it's worth, I think you had an excellent idea and I think we should go through it, step-by-step and develop a color-coded version of your TA Goal Tree." Mark looked at Tom and smiled. "Bob, as you will see shortly, Tom and I have already created an assessment of Tires for All using this newly created Throughput Accounting Goal Tree," Mark explained. "Would you like to see it?" Mark asked and of course everyone did, so Tom flashed it onto the screen (Figure 14.2).

This caught Bob completely off guard and all he could do was to begin a round of applause which prompted everyone else to applaud as well. "In all my years of consulting, I have never seen something like this done before and both of you are to be congratulated for your efforts! So, is there anything else you want to show us?" Bob asked. Both Mark and Tom smiled and told him that yes, they did and would be happy to review what they had come up with. Bob smiled again and said, "Yes, please do. And for the record, how long did you guys work on all of this?"

Mark answered with a smile and said, "Too long." And with that, Mark began again, "Tom and I thought about all that we had learned from you Bob and we came to several conclusions. First, Cost Accounting is full of holes, so Tom has set up a new accounting system that uses Throughput Accounting. It doesn't replace the one required by law, but it will be used to make financial decisions going forward. Second, if we look at the Throughput Accounting Goal Tree that we put together and focus on the red boxes needed to drive revenue up by at least 30 percent, we believe that if we implement Goldratt's Five Focusing Steps in conjunction with Drum

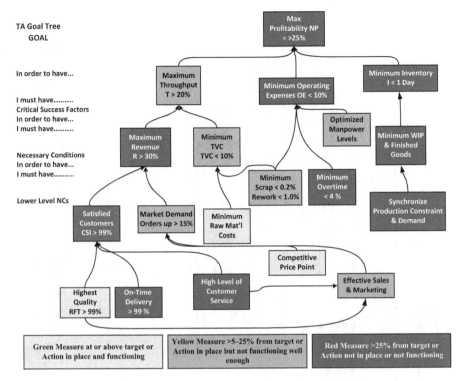

FIGURE 14.2
Throughput Accounting Goal Tree assessment.

Buffer Rope and Buffer Management, we can achieve our throughput gain of greater than 20 percent! In addition, our Totally Variable Costs should decrease because of the five focusing steps." "Very impressive!" Bob said. "What else?" Bob asked.

Tom answered, "We believe that if we successfully implement Drum Buffer Rope and Buffer Management, our on-time delivery will skyrocket, which will improve our level of customer satisfaction and market demand for our products will rise proportionally. Now, if we look at our Operating Expenses, how do we reduce that? We know that because of what we've done with our Six Sigma effort, our scrap and rework levels have decreased and will continue to do so. This effort will have a positive impact on our overtime levels, so the combined result of these two things will drive our Operating Expenses to less than 10 percent!" "Wow, you guys really thought this through!" Bob said. "Is there more?" Bob asked and with that said, a new slide appeared (Figure 14.3).

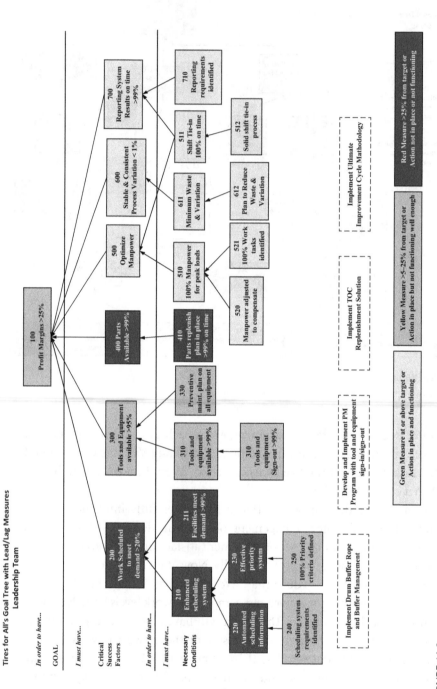

FIGURE 14.3

Goal Tree with action items.

And so, with this newfound sense for the future, Tires for All was ready to begin their journey to the improvement promised land. The leadership team, along with the shop floor workers, were all ready to begin. So, what was the next step in their journey? The next step is always the most important step in any journey.

15

The Next Step

Tires for All had developed their plan and had begun implementing much of it. Within three weeks, they had witnessed their work-in-process inventory shrink to levels they had never seen before! And while their work-in-process inventory was now at a manageable level, the important thing was their new levels of on-time delivery of finished product was now approaching 92 percent, which was a level that had never been achieved before. Things were progressing nicely in this facility, that is until Mark received a call from the Board of Directors that they wanted him to come to Chicago for an update the next day.

They made it crystal clear that he better come prepared to discuss his sudden drop in their manpower efficiency levels, which now stood at 72 percent! The previous values were in the neighborhood of 90 percent and they let Mark know that this new level was completely unacceptable! Mark knew that the reason for the decrease in efficiency levels was that they no longer managed efficiency in the non-constraints, since they successfully implemented the Theory of Constraints.

While Mark wasn't too worried about his corporate efficiency metric, he was very curious about what his new profit and on-time delivery metrics were, so he called Tom and told him about his trip to Chicago the next day. Tom arrived at Mark's office within minutes and sat down. When Tom arrived, he had a huge smile which Mark noticed right away. Mark asked Tom, "Why are you smiling so much Tom?" "You'll see shortly Mark, as I have come up with a way to monitor profitability on a weekly basis and just know that you'll be very happy with the results," Tom replied. "Really?" Mark replied. "Yes Mark, I have plotted our Profit Margins, our On-Time Delivery, and your favorite metric, Efficiencies. Which one would you like to see first Mark?" Tom asked. "Let me see your plot of our

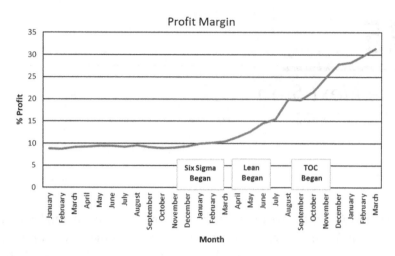

FIGURE 15.1
Profit Margins by month.

Profit Margins first, since that is really the key metric that we track!" Mark replied excitedly. And with that, Tom flashed the plot on the screen of his laptop (Figure 15.1).

When Mark saw the graph of Profit Margins versus time, he became very excited and was extremely happy! "Tom, our margins are up over 30 percent! That's incredible!" he shouted with excitement. Tom replied, "Yes, for our latest month our margins are actually 31.4 percent and I fully expect next month's to be a bit higher, but I'll let you know then." What would you like to see next?" Tom asked. "Since the other metric they always ask me about is our On-Time Delivery, so let me see that one next," Mark requested, and Tom flashed another graph on the screen (Figure 15.2).

Once again, Mark was very excited to see their results and said, "Holy crap Tom, our On-Time Delivery metric is over 95 percent!" Tom responded by saying, "It's actually almost 96 percent, at 95.7 percent! And like our margins, I would not be a bit surprised if next month it's up around 98 percent!" "Wow Tom, this will be my most enjoyable trip to Chicago, ever!" he said with glee. "Okay, let's see our plot of efficiencies and I assume this metric will be heading South?" Mark asked. Tom responded by smiling and shaking his head in the affirmative as he posted this graph on his screen (Figure 15.3).

"Oh my gosh!" Mark exclaimed. "I fully expected it to go down, but it took a nosedive!" he added. "Yes, it did but with the other two metrics,

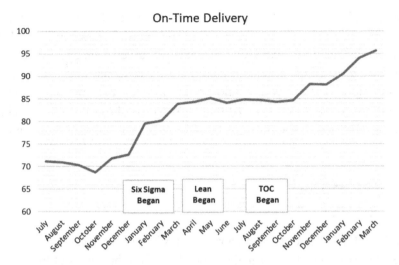

FIGURE 15.2
On-Time Delivery by month.

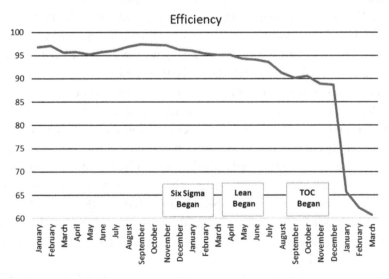

FIGURE 15.3
Plot of Efficiency by month.

it clearly shouldn't worry you at all in Chicago. The Board of Directors should be very happy with your results, but if I were you, I would take your PowerPoint presentation on the Theory of Constraints and enlighten them as to what it can do for their other companies," Tom suggested. Mark smiled and said, "I have a much better idea Tom." "And what is your idea Mark?" Tom asked. "I think the better approach would be for you to come with me and you present it to the board," Mark replied. "Me?" Tom said. "Yes Tom, you know I've told you several times how quickly you have grasped the teachings of the Theory of Constraints, so for that reason alone, I think you should be the one that presents our results," Mark replied. So, it was decided that both Tom and Mark would travel to Chicago and report the status of Tires for All to the Board of Directors.

THE BOARD MEETING

Mark and Tom met at the airport and both were very excited to make the trip. After they were seated on the plane, Tom brought out his laptop and loaded his presentation to review with Mark. They both reviewed the contents, made a few minor changes, and then put it away and just talked. "Tom, I've been thinking about our meeting today with the Board and I have an idea I want to bounce off of you," Mark said. "Sure Mark, what is it?" Tom asked. "Before you say anything, hear me out on what I have to say," Mark said. "I can do that Mark," Tom replied.

"Tom, I hope you understand how much I appreciate the work that you do. But even more, since Bob Nelson came to our plant, you have impressed me very much on how quickly you grasp new ideas, and this was especially true for the Theory of Constraints," Mark said. "Well thank you for your very kind words Mark," replied Tom with a proud look. Mark continued again, "I truly believe that your presentation will be very impressive, and when you're done, I believe that the Board of Directors will be impressed. So much so, that I'd like to recommend that you lead an enterprise-wide effort to do what we have done at Tires for All, to all of the Board's holdings." Bob explained.

"You want to recommend me?" Tom replied in disbelief. "Why me?" "Why not someone like Oscar Francis, our Master Black Belt?" he asked. "Tom, it takes a leader that understands the basic concepts of what Bob taught us?" Mark replied. "Well, speaking of Bob, why don't we just recommend him instead of me?" Tom asked. "Tom, you've earned the right to be the one that teaches others what Bob taught us." Mark replied. "Like I said, it takes a leader who understands what companies in our realm are up against. Think about it, if you are successful at convincing the Board that this methodology needs to be spread around, and I have no doubt that you will be, then convincing others of like persuasion to follow your lead, would be much easier," Mark explained. "Would you not want to do this Tom? Is that why you're pushing back?" Mark asked. "I would be honored to do this Mark, I'm just flabbergasted that you think I'm the right person, that's all," Tom replied. "Trust me Tom, you are the right person!" Mark added.

The plane landed and they took a cab to their hotel and checked in. They decided to meet in the lobby and have an early dinner, around 5:00 pm. Tom went to his room and was still amazed at what Mark had told him that he wanted to do. It was now time to meet Mark for dinner, so he went downstairs to the lobby. Mark was on the phone and when he was finished talking, Tom walked up and asked Mark if he was ready to go to dinner. Mark surprised him and said that the Chairman of the Board, Jonathan Briggs, had just called him and invited both of them to dinner with him. Mark said that the Chairman was sending a car to pick them up, so they went outside and waited for it to arrive. The car arrived and drove them to the restaurant.

THE DINNER

Mark and Tom walked inside the restaurant and, to their surprise, were quickly greeted by several of the Board members. They were led to a small room in the restaurant and were greeted by the Board Chairman, Jonathan Briggs. "Welcome to Chicago gentlemen," the Chairman said, and they all shook hands. "We're very happy you are here tonight, and we thought it might be a good idea if we discussed your performance metrics prior to our board meeting tomorrow." Jonathan explained. "So, tell us, why has your performance metric efficiency taken such a nosedive?" he asked. Fortunately, Tom had decided to bring his laptop with him to dinner, just to practice his presentation, so Mark said, "I'd like to have Tom answer your question." And with that, Tom got out his laptop and began.

"First, thank you for inviting us to have dinner with you tonight, it's much appreciated," Tom said. "I think the first thing we should do is show you the history of our metric efficiency," Tom explained and brought up the plot of efficiency onto his screen (Figure 15.4). Mark was surprised at how Tom had started answering their request.

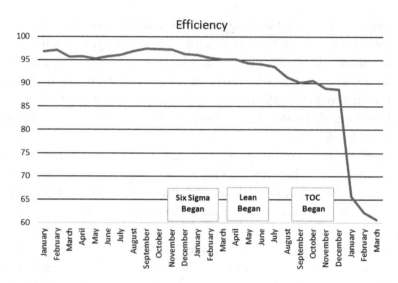

FIGURE 15.4
Efficiency by month.

The Board members were shocked to see this plot that demonstrated such a rapid decline in Tires for All's efficiency. Tom then explained, "At first glance, when you see this graphic image, you might be thinking that Tires for All is in serious trouble, but such is not the case." Jonathan responded and stated, "That's exactly what I am thinking, but why are you saying you're not in trouble?" Tom put his hand over his mouth to hide a smile, then put up his next graph onto his screen (Figure 15.5). "Contrary to what you might believe would be happening, here are our Profit Margins during the same time period," he explained. "How can that be?" Jonathan asked.

Tom answered Jonathan's question very abruptly and said, "Because the belief that efficiency is a good performance metric is a false belief!" "But, what about your metric for On-Time Delivery? How does it look?" asked Jonathan. And with that request, Tom flashed this graph (Figure 15.6) onto his laptop.

Jonathan then said, "I am totally confused by these graphs!" "You've got efficiencies nosediving, while at the same time, your profits and delivery metrics are skyrocketing upward?" "What's going on at Tires for All?" he asked. "Remember I told you that believing that efficiency is a good performance metric is a false belief?" Tom responded. "Yes, I remember," said Jonathan. "Would you like me to explain why I told you that?" Tom asked Jonathan. "Yes, absolutely I would!" Jonathan responded.

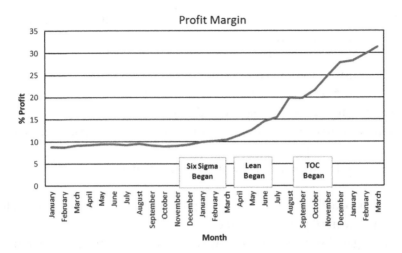

FIGURE 15.5
Profit Margins by month.

FIGURE 15.6
Tires for All's On-Time Delivery by month.

Tom began, "First, I need to explain something referred to as the Theory of Constraints. Have you ever heard of this?" he asked. Jonathan and the other board members told him no, so he continued on. "The Theory of Constraints was developed by a man named Eli Goldratt and made popular in his widely read and quoted book, *The Goal* [1]," Tom explained. "In this book, Goldratt developed what he referred to as the 'Five Focusing

Steps' for continuous improvement." Tom loaded a slide on his screen and said, "These five steps are:

1. Identify the system constraint.
2. Decide how to exploit the system constraint.
3. Subordinate everything else to the system constraint.
4. If necessary, elevate the constraint, but don't let inertia create a new system constraint.
5. When the current constraint is broken, return to Step 1."

Tom then loaded Bob's figure of the piping system used to transport water onto his screen (Figure 15.7) and continued.

Tom began, "What you see on my screen is a simple piping system used to transport water. Water, which is gravity fed, enters this piping system, flows into Section A, then flows to Section B and so forth until it collects in a receptacle at the base of the system. If the demand for water increased, tell me what you would do and why you would do it?" he asked Jonathan.

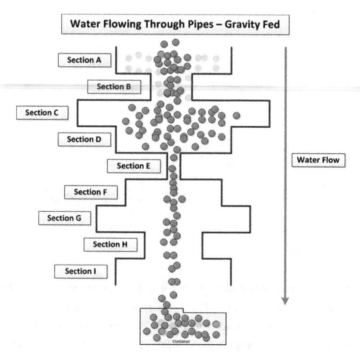

FIGURE 15.7
Piping Diagram with constraint at Section E.

Jonathan looked at the diagram and said, "Based upon the various diameters of the pipes, my guess is that you would need to modify the piping system by adding a larger diameter pipe in Section E." "Absolutely correct Jonathan! So, you just completed the first two steps of Goldratt's five focusing steps. You identified the system constraint and then decided how to exploit it," Tom said and continued. "The rest of the pipes were subordinated to the constraint, because they could only deliver water, based upon the output of the constraint."

"Suppose there is another increase in demand for water from this system? What would you do and why would you do it?" he asked Jonathan. Jonathan looked closely at the piping system and said, "In this case, once you opened up the diameter of Section E, the constraint moved to Section B of the piping system," he explained. "Basically, as you explained, you completed the first four steps of Goldratt's five focusing steps, namely, identify the constraint, decide how to exploit it, and then everything else will be at the mercy of the constraint. Since we opened up Section E's diameter, we have completed Steps 4 and 5, because we have elevated the current constraint. We now have to move back to Step 1," he explained. "The new constraint is Section B, so if we need more water, like Section E, we need to increase the diameter of Section B," Jonathan explained in detail. "The bottom line is, it's a continuous improvement process where new constraints pop-up and you have to be prepared to take action," he further explained.

"That was an excellent description of what has happened Jonathan," Tom said as he opened up and displayed a new figure (Figure 15.8) on his screen.

Jonathan then spoke up and asked, "So, Tom, what was the purpose of this exercise and how does it apply to what has happened at Tires for All?" "Great question Jonathan!" Tom responded, and with that posted a new figure (Figure 15.9) on his laptop's screen.

Tom began again, "What you see here is a simple four-step process with raw materials entering Step 1, are processed for five minutes, and are then passed on to Step 2, and so on, until the product exits Step 4 as finished product." "Thinking back to the piping diagram, what is the total processing time of the very first part through this process?" he asked Jonathan. "The total time of the first part would just be the sum of the individual cycle times, for a total of 105 minutes," he responded. "Correct, now assuming this process has been up and running for a while, what is

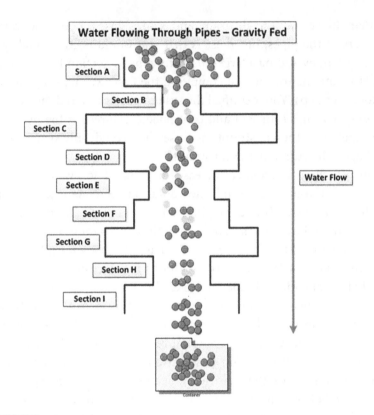

FIGURE 15.8
Piping system with a new constraint.

FIGURE 15.9
Simple four-step process.

the output rate of this process?" Tom asked. Jonathan studied the drawing and said, "Since Step 3, at sixty minutes, is the longest cycle time, it seems to me that it would control the rate that products are made?" he asked in a question format. "You're right again Jonathan, Step 3 is this system's constraint," said Tom.

Jonathan looked at Tom and said, "I know what you're going to ask me Tom, and the answer is, if we wanted to produce at a faster rate, we would need to reduce Step 3's cycle time because it is the system constraint." "Very good Jonathan, you're correct again," Tom said. "So, here's a new question for you Jonathan. Assuming this company is measured by manpower efficiency, like Tires for All is, what happens to this process if every step is run to its full capacity?" he asked. Jonathan studied the drawing of this simple process and simply said, "Holy crap! Why didn't I learn this sooner?" he said openly. The rest of the board members were confused by what Jonathan had just said and one of them finally spoke up and said, "What do you mean Jonathan?"

As Tom smiled, Jonathan turned to the group and said, "Think about it everyone. If you run every step to its capacity, there's only one thing that will happen. The process simply becomes full of work-in-process inventory!" he exclaimed. "Does your next figure demonstrate this Tom?" he asked. "It most certainly does Jonathan," he replied and posted the figure (Figure 15.10) onto his laptop's screen.

Jonathan, without hesitation began speaking, "What you have explained to us today is mind boggling Tom! To think that all of the holdings in our portfolio are being run according to a metric-like efficiency is simply wrong!" he stated emphatically. "Wow, to think that in less than thirty minutes, you have changed my thinking just blows me away Tom! And I want to thank you for sharing this very simple, but very valuable lesson with us!" he said. "Could you present this same material tomorrow to our Board of Directors Tom?" he asked. "Yes, of course, it's what I had planned to do anyway," Tom replied.

"Think about what you did this evening Tom," said Jonathan. "With eight simple slides, you've essentially changed the course of history for our portfolio of companies!" "What do you mean, Jonathan?" Tom asked. "What I mean is that I'd like all of the companies that exist within our portfolio to hear the same message from you Tom," he explained. And with that said, Mark covered his mouth to hide his smile. "I knew Tom

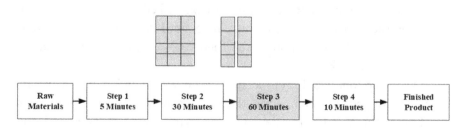

FIGURE 15.10
Effects of running each step to capacity.

would impress these guys," he thought to himself. Jonathan then spoke up and asked, "Okay, who's hungry?" And with that, dinner was served.

The next morning, Tom and Mark left to go to Corporate Headquarters. Along the way, Mark said to Tom, "Tom, you did such a fantastic job presenting the material to Jonathan and the two other board members who were there, I'd like you to present everything today, rather than me." Mark thought about the impact that Tom would make if he presented, rather than himself. Tom looked at Mark and simply said, "I'd be honored to present today Mark and thank you for this opportunity. I'm humbled Mark, simply humbled," he replied.

Tom and Mark arrived at Corporate Headquarters and proceeded to the conference room. When everyone was seated, Jonathan, the Chairman of the Board, was the first one to speak. He welcomed Tom and Mark and then told the Board of Directors that this meeting today is going to be different than what we had planned it to be. He then explained that dinner with Tom and Mark was a game changer for him and that he thought it would be for everyone else in attendance today. He then introduced Tom to the group and asked him to present the three slides on performance metrics that he had seen the night before, and with that he turned it over to Tom.

Tom followed the same format that he had done the night before, first presenting the graphs of Tires for All's performance metrics, then Goldratt's Five Focusing Steps, followed by the piping diagram and process slides. Not surprisingly, he received the same reaction to his presentation that he did the previous night. There were many questions from the Board members and Tom answered them all brilliantly. When he was finished, Jonathan began speaking again. The bottom line was that he proposed that all of the companies in their portfolio should be invited to hear what Tom has to say, and without exception, the Board members all agreed. Jonathan then turned to Tom and Mark and asked them, "Gentlemen, we are on the verge of something huge here, but I do have one question for you," he said. "Is there more to the Theory of Constraints that we haven't heard yet?" he asked.

Mark motioned to Tom to answer this question and Tom began, "The answer to your question is yes, there's a lot more." "Give us an example of other things it has to offer," Jonathan said. Tom responded and said, "What if I told you there was a parts replenishment methodology that will reduce your parts inventory by nearly 50 percent, while virtually eliminating stock-outs? Would that be of interest to you?" he asked and could see heads nodding up and down as a yes. "How about a very different accounting system that will provide real time information to financial decisions? Would that be of interest to you?" he asked and again, everyone motioned that they would be interested in hearing about that.

Tom continued on about what the Theory of Constraints could do for companies until Jonathan stopped him and said, "Tom, although I haven't spoken to the other members of the board, I would like to propose that your role should change in the future," he said. Hearing that, Mark just smiled, knowing what was coming next. "My proposal is that, going forward, your new role would be to work directly for the Board of Directors. Your new role would be to teach other companies in our portfolio what you've done at Tires for All," Jonathan said. Tom responded immediately and simply said, "I would be honored to accept your offer, assuming the compensation is acceptable?" he answered with a smile.

Jonathan responded and asked, "What would be an acceptable compensation for you Tom?" Tom wasted no time answering his question and said, "I would be willing to do this for the same salary that I receive now, but with one caveat. In addition to my salary, I would want 1 percent of the profit margins of each company," he explained. Jonathan looked at the other board members and said, "You sound just like Kevin O'Leary on *Shark Tank*, negotiating a royalty deal, but I do think that will work for us." The other Board members agreed, but Jonathan added one contingency which was that the 1 percent would be paid on an annual basis and would have a limit of two years maximum. Tom thought about his offer and agreed to it. Tom then said that he wanted another month at Tires for All before he started his new role with the Board. Jonathan then said, "We'll schedule another meeting with you Tom, so that we can hear more about the other facets to the Theory of Constraints."

And so just as Mark had predicted, Tom's new role would come to fruition. Mark and Tom packed their belongings and were driven to the airport. On their flight home, both of them just relaxed and even fell asleep, but this time, both of them had sweet dreams.

16

The New Direction

On Monday, Tom arrived at Tires for All very early, anxious to discuss his new role with Mark, who would fill his position as Director of Finance, and what he'd like to do to prepare himself for this new role. He called Mark and asked him, "Mark, do you have some time today that we could sit and talk about several things?" Mark replied, "Why yes, of course Tom. What is it that you want to talk about?" he asked. "I want to talk about my last month at Tires for All and my replacement," Tom replied. "And by the way, when will Bob Nelson be back on site?" Mark replied, "He should be back here tomorrow, why do you ask?" "I want to talk to him about how I can get training to become a Lean Six Sigma Master Black Belt and a Theory of Constraints Jonah," Tom replied. "Okay, well we can talk now if you like?" Mark said and with that they hung up.

Minutes later Tom arrived at Mark's office. He walked in, shut the door, sat down, and said, "What did you think of our Board meeting on Friday Mark?" Tom asked. "I think it went very well and I have to tell you, I loved the deal you made with Jonathan. He was right when he said you sounded just like Kevin O'Leary from *Shark Tank*, the way you made that deal for a royalty payment," Mark said. "Well, after you and I talked before we went to Chicago, I thought long and hard about what I would say in the event they did offer me something and it just so happens that *Shark Tank* was on that night. And you guessed it, Mr. Wonderful made a royalty deal, so I decided to try the same thing with Corporate if they offered me something," Tom explained. Mark smiled and said, "It worked, Tom. So, what did you want to talk about today?"

"During my last month here at Tires for All, I'd like to spend as much time on the shop floor that I can, just so I can become intimately familiar with all of the things we've done here to improve our tire processes," Tom explained. "But in order to do that, we have to get my replacement in place quickly," he added. "Did you have someone in mind Tom?" Mark asked. "Yes, I do," Tom said. "And who might that be Tom?" Mark asked. "Jerry Lindholm, my Finance Manager, is a very talented guy and I think he would make a valuable addition to our team," Tom suggested. "He knows our system very well, plus he now completely understands Throughput Accounting, I really like Jerry and he seems like he's very talented," Mark responded. "So, with your permission, I'd like to see if he's interested, and if he is, I'd like to offer the job to him right away," Tom suggested. "It's fine with me Tom, so go ahead and talk with him. And if you need me to be involved, just call me," Mark said. "Thanks Mark, I'll take care of this right away," and with that said, Tom left to talk to Jerry.

Tom met with Jerry and it didn't take long for Jerry to accept Tom's offer. Once Jerry agreed, Tom called in the rest of his team to let them know first, that he would be leaving Tires for All, and second, that Jerry would be the new leader of the Finance Department. Jerry was very popular and well-liked, so everyone was happy with Jerry's selection. Everyone was sad to see Tom leave the company, but they were also very happy about his new association with the Board of Directors. Tom thanked them all for their hard work and support over the years and the briefing came to a close. Tom called Mark and let him know the good news about Jerry accepting his offer.

The next morning, Tom arrived very early for work because he wanted to watch the start-ups on the production lines, especially in the Assembly and Finishing lines. Maintenance, who now performed their preventive maintenance after second shift ended, had just finished their work and machine operators were arriving to begin their day. Because of the high demand for one of their tire sizes, five of the machines in Assembly, and their corresponding Finishing machines, were now dedicated to this tire type.

Tom watched as the machines all began running, while paying particular attention to the Drum Buffer Rope system they had implemented. One of the things he noticed was that the rate that each of the Assembly machine operators produced carcasses was somewhat different, probably due to the experience level of the different operators. Some were relatively fast at making carcasses, while others were much slower. He noticed that some of the finishing operators had to wait for carcasses from the slower assembly operators. He also saw the same difference in production rate on the finishing machines, in that when a faster finishing operator was coupled with a slower assembly operator, they had to wait until the carcass was available before he or she could do their job.

Because of these production rate differences between Assembly and Finishing operators, he had an idea that might make these wait times decrease. He thought to himself, "What if we were to match the faster Assembly operators with their corresponding faster Finishing operators?" He decided to speak with Cliff Hastings, the Operations Manager, about running a quick study, matching the faster Assembly operators with the faster Finishing operators. They would also match a slower Assembly operator with a slower Finishing operator. Cliff followed his logic and agreed to try it. The results came swiftly as the machine they tried it on with the faster operators, produced a total of three additional green tires on one shift, while their slower counterparts produced one less green tire, for a net gain of two green tires.

Both Cliff and Tom were somewhat surprised with the results and decided to have Sally Hodges, the Industrial Engineering Manager, do time studies on each Assembly and Finishing operator and then use the results to best match the operators. They were confident that this matching method would work, simply because the operator speed of either the Assembly or Finishing operators controlled the output. So, if there was a mix of slow and fast operators, the slower of the two would determine the build pace. In effect, the slower of the two operators was the constraint. Tom felt good about what they had done and let Mark know about it. It was estimated that within a week, the time studies would be completed, and they would then balance the speed of the Assembly and Finishing operators across the shop.

Tom saw that Bob had now returned to Tires for All's plant and he let him know what they had done with the speed matching. Needless to say, Bob was very impressed with what they had done. Tom also let him know about his new role with Corporate and that he would probably be calling on him at the various companies in the portfolio. Bob congratulated Tom and let him know that he could call him any time he needed help.

The next thing Tom wanted to check on was the Theory of Constraints Replenishment System they had implemented. If they had done it correctly, the number of stock-outs should have decreased significantly while the overall amount of cash tied up in inventory should have been nearly cut in half. When they implemented this new system, they had also implemented a tracking system so they could see the impact of this method on the

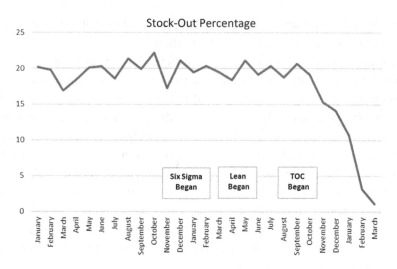

FIGURE 16.1

Tires for All stock-out percentage.

parts replenishment. Tom went to purchasing, retrieved the data they had collected and then developed a Run Chart to see the impact of TOC's Replenishment System (Figure 16.1). The clear impact of this improvement effort was very profound. They had been averaging around a 20 percent stock-out rate before the change, and now it was approaching zero! He would now try to estimate the dollar value of the on-hand inventory, but he was confident that it would decrease by nearly 50 percent. He was able to find enough data on inventory value to "guesstimate" it, and sure enough, it had decreased by approximately 46 percent.

Tom showed Bob the Run Chart he had created on stock-outs and Bob explained that he had seen this impact many times before, so he wasn't surprised by the results they had achieved by implementing the Theory of Constraints Replenishment Solution. Tom also showed Bob the other graphs he had prepared for the Board of Directors and Bob was very much impressed. The final bit of information he shared with Bob was his royalty idea that the board agreed to pay. Bob just laughed and said, "That was similar to the offer I made to Mark, but I wish I had offered you guys that good of a deal. I probably could have retired."

Later that afternoon, Tom received a call from Jonathan, the Chairman of the Board, who told Tom he had arranged a meeting for Monday so the Board could hear more about the Theory of Constraints and all it had to offer. Jonathan told Tom that he had also invited the CEOs and General

Managers of the various portfolio companies they owned. He told Tom that he wanted Tom to put together a presentation that demonstrated Tires for All's accomplishments over the past year. He was also instructed to present the basics of TOC, plus Throughput Accounting, plus anything else Tom thought would add value to this meeting. Tom agreed to attend and went back to his office to think about his upcoming presentation. Needless to say, Tom was very excited to make this trip, so he spent the remainder of the week reviewing Tires for All's achievements and preparing his presentation.

Tom thought long and hard about what the presentation should include and decided that he would start the presentation with a slide that simply said, Focus and Leverage. He would then present a slide that summarized the before and after performance metrics for Tires for All. His reasoning was that if they could see the end results first, it would stimulate interest to hear about how they had achieved such a remarkable turnaround in a relatively short amount of time. Kind of a tease, so to speak.

Tom looked at this slide and excitedly thought to himself, "Wow! We really did achieve a turnaround at Tires for All!" Tom then decided that he would ask the audience if they would be interested in hearing about how they had achieved these results. Continuing, Tom thought that he would present Tires for All's improvement journey, explaining how they had first implemented Six Sigma and then Lean Manufacturing, and that they did see improvements using these two methodologies, but something was missing.

He then reasoned that it would make sense to present the piping system, so that the audience could understand the basics of the Theory of Constraints and especially the concept of a system constraint. He would then present the slides of the simple manufacturing process to demonstrate what happens to the process if they run each step to maximum capacity to achieve higher levels of efficiency. He reasoned that everyone would then realize that efficiency is not a good metric, at least not in non-constraints. This would also give them an idea of why focus and leverage are so critical to success in any improvement initiative.

He would then present Goldratt's five focusing steps so that the audience could see the right sequence of events in their improvement effort. At this point, Tom believed that it would be a good time to present the concept of Throughput Accounting and explain why the profitability focus should not be on how much money could be saved, but rather it should be on how much money could be made. The difference, of course, being that the real key to improving profitability, according to Throughput Accounting, is to focus on increasing Throughput or revenue and not on how much money you can save! Tom then thought it might be prudent to present a series of slides on one of his favorite tools, the Goal Tree, so he put together a series of slides on this tool. He decided that he would use the Goal Tree that he and Mark had prepared because it would tie into the final performance metrics and provide a good explanation on how they got there.

He reasoned that his next series of slides should be on the Theory of Constraints Replenishment Solution and what it can do to reduce the amount of money tied up in excess inventory and how it can be used to significantly reduce part stock-outs as well as the dollar amount tied up needlessly. He would also present how all of this can significantly improve on-time delivery of products to customers. But the most significant improvement of all, the one that should be of utmost interest to all in attendance, is the final impact on the profit margins. He decided he would end his presentation with the Run Charts he had prepared on efficiency, on-time delivery, stock-out percentage, and finally, the chart on profitability. Tom worked the rest of the week refining the slides for his presentation at the Corporate Headquarters in Chicago.

On Sunday afternoon, Tom drove to the airport, parked his car, and headed into the terminal. He was amazed at how long the security line was and he thought, "These guys could use a lesson on the Theory of Constraints." He finally boarded the plane and to his surprise, he was immediately upgraded to first class. The flight to Chicago took about an hour and a half and when they landed and exited the plane, he was surprised to see a man with a sign with his name on it. Apparently, the Board had arranged to have a limo drive him to his hotel and he felt very important that they would do that for him.

The next morning, a driver arrived to take Tom to the Corporate Headquarters building and he was escorted to the main conference room. Jonathan was there to welcome him along with the entire Board of Directors and the various CEOs and General Managers from the portfolio companies. Jonathan was the first to speak and he welcomed everyone. He explained that what they were about to hear could be the most important information they might ever hear, and he encouraged them to take notes. Tom had sent a copy of his presentation to Jonathan, so that he could give each attendee a copy to follow. With that, he introduced Tom to the group.

TABLE 16.1

Before and After Performance Metrics for Tires for All

Metric	Before	After
% Efficiency	97%	62%
On-Time Delivery	70%	95%
Stock-Out %	20%	1%
Profit Margin	10%	32%

As planned, Tom started the presentation with his table of performance metrics (Table 16.1). He went through each one of the metrics which created a murmur through the audience. He then asked the audience if they might be interested in hearing how they went from where they were, the before in the table, to their new levels, the after. Without exception, all of the Board Members, the CEOs, and the General Managers were excited to hear the details.

So, with that introduction, Tom began his presentation with his first slide that simply said, Focus and Leverage. He asked the group, focusing on the CEOs and General Managers, "With a show of hands, how many of you have used Six Sigma to improve your processes?" About half of those in attendance raised their hands. And then he asked, "And how many of you have implemented Lean Manufacturing at your facilities?" and about the same number raised their hands. "How about a combination of Lean and Six Sigma?" he asked and several of the CEOs raised their hands. "At Tires for All, that's the route we took, first with Six Sigma and then with Lean, and although we did see improvements, the level of improvement was not what we had hoped for," he explained.

Tom continued, "But then we had an awakening, so to speak." "By accident, we heard about something referred to as the Theory of Constraints and it changed our entire approach to improvement. Has anyone here today heard of the Theory of Constraints?" Two of the CEOs raised their hand, but when asked if they were using it, they indicated that they were not. When Tom asked them why, they didn't really have an answer. "Well today, I'm going to show you why you should be using it, not as a stand-alone tool, but rather combining it with Six Sigma and Lean Manufacturing," he explained. "But before I explain this integrated methodology, I want to first explain the Theory of Constraints," he said and posted a slide of the piping system (Figure 16.2).

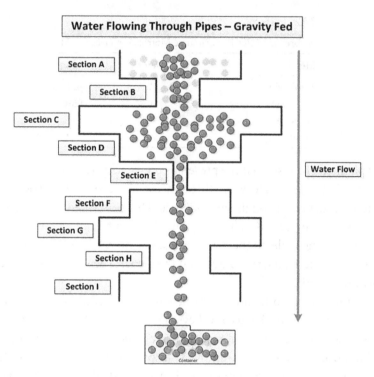

FIGURE 16.2
Piping system used to transport water.

"What you see on the screen is a very simple piping system used to transport water. Water enters Section A, then flows into Section B, then Section C, and so forth until the water collects in the receptacle at the system's base. If you were told that a faster rate of water is needed to enter the receptacle, think about what you would do and why you would do it. And remember, the water flows via gravity, meaning that you could not just increase the water pressure to deliver more water," he explained.

"So, based upon what you just heard, what would you do to increase the output of this system?" he asked, and several hands went up. They all answered by saying they would increase the diameter of Section E. Tom continued, "In the Theory of Constraints jargon, Section E is referred to as the system constraint. System constraints control the output of any system and unless and until they are first, identified and then acted upon, the throughput of the system will not improve." Tom then added a figure of the same piping system with Section E's diameter enlarged (Figure 16.3).

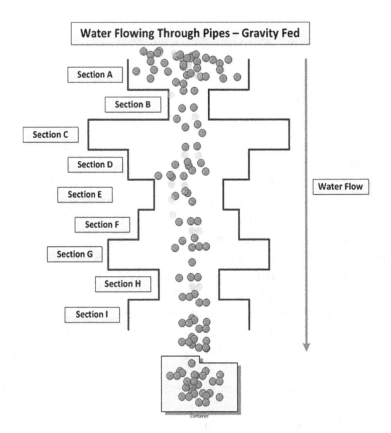

FIGURE 16.3
Piping system with Section E's diameter enlarged.

Tom continued his explanation of the Theory of Constraint and said, "This is the same piping system, but Section E's diameter has been enlarged. So, when you addressed and improved Section E, another constraint appeared immediately at Section B. So, if more water flow is needed, then you would have to focus improvements on Section B. How does this apply to your manufacturing processes?" he asked rhetorically and then posted a new slide (Figure 16.4).

"What you see here is a simple, four-step manufacturing process used to produce some kind of finished product. Raw materials are introduced into Step 1, are processed for five minutes, and are then passed on to Step 2, and so forth until the finished product exits Step 4. The very first part through this system would be the sum of the individual processing times or 5 + 30 + 60 + 10 minutes or a total of 105 minutes. So, here's a question for you.

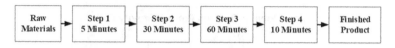

FIGURE 16.4
Simple manufacturing process.

Once this process is full, what is the output rate of this process?" he asked. One of the General Managers raised his hand and said, "Based upon what we learned from the piping system, you would produce one part every sixty minutes." "And why do you think that is true?" Tom asked. "Well, you told us that the constraint controls the output rate of any system and Step 3, at sixty minutes, is clearly the constraint," he responded.

"Very well said," Tom responded. "And if you wanted to increase the output of this process, what would you need to do?" Tom asked. The same General Manager responded and said, "You would have to reduce the processing time of Step 3." "Would reducing the time of any other step improve the output rate of this process?" Tom asked and the same General Manager responded and said, "No, again because the constraint is what controls the throughput of any process." "Correct!" Tom responded.

"Okay, so here is another question for everyone," Tom said. "Based upon what you just heard, how fast should Steps 1 and 2 be running?" Tom asked. One of the CEOs raised his hand and said, "They should be running at their maximum speed so that efficiencies can be maximized." "So, let me get this straight," Tom responded. "You believe that maximizing efficiencies is a good thing?" The CEO responded and said, "Well of course I do, it's one of our key performance measures." "In fact, when you posted your first Run Chart, I noticed how your company's efficiencies had deteriorated," the CEO said. And with that, Tom posted a new slide (Figure 16.5).

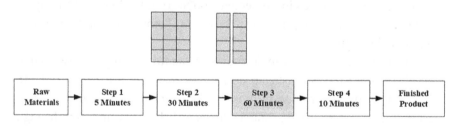

FIGURE 16.5
With excess work-in-process.

"In our process we have just been discussing, this is what happens when Steps 1 and 2 continue running at their maximum capacity. As you can see, the process will have excessive amounts of work-in-process inventory," Tom explained. "And the longer you run, the more excess work-in-process will accumulate," he added. "So, again, I ask how fast should both Steps 1 and 2 be running to avoid this excessive inventory build-up?" Tom asked. "Another CEO raised his hand and said, "My guess is that Steps 1 and 2 should be running at the same speed as the system constraint?" he asked. "You are absolutely correct!" Tom exclaimed.

A hush came over the audience probably because every one of their companies was using the performance metric efficiency and they all knew that in order to drive it higher, all process steps needed to run as fast as they can. One of the CEOs raised his hand and asked, "If this metric is so bad, then why are we measuring it at all?" Tom responded, "I didn't say it was a bad metric, but only if it's used to measure the performance of the system constraint." Tom then turned to Jonathan and asked him if he had anything he wanted to add to this conversation and Jonathan responded. "Effective immediately, we will no longer use efficiency to measure the full process, but we will measure and report it on the system constraint!" he stated emphatically and then turned the meeting back over to Tom who immediately flashed a new slide on the screen (Figure 16.6).

"Now that you've all heard about the Theory of Constraints, I want to give you some history of it and a simple way to remember the key points. Dr. Eli Goldratt and his co-author, Jeff Cox, published a very special book entitled *The Goal* which I highly recommend that you purchase and read. In this book, the authors outlined what they refer to as their Five Focusing Steps which are what you see on the screen now," Tom explained.

"These five steps form the foundation of the Theory of Constraints and if you think about what we just went through with our simple four-step

1. Identify the system constraint.

2. Decide how to exploit the system constraint.

3. Subordinate everything else to the system constraint.

4. If necessary, elevate the system constraint.

5. When the constraint is broken, return to Step 1.

FIGURE 16.6
TOC's five focusing steps.

process and the piping system, you'll be able to relate what we did to these five steps," Tom explained. "In both examples, we clearly identified our system constraint. We then decided how to exploit, or increase the capacity, of our constraints. And in order to avoid an explosion or work-in-process inventory, we subordinated the other steps to the speed of the system constraint. We then had to figure out a way to 'break' the current constraint and when we did, we had to start all over with Step 1 of this five-step process," Tom explained to the group. Upon finishing this brief summary, Tom recommended that the group break for lunch. Jonathan then announced that lunch was to be served in their adjoining conference room and that they should all be back in thirty minutes.

As the group left the room for lunch, Jonathan approached Tom, shook his hand and said, "Very well done, Tom! I think it was a real eye-opener for everyone here today and I think you made some excellent points." "What do you plan on discussing when everyone returns from lunch Tom?" he asked. "Remember I told you that the Theory of Constraints uses a different form of Accounting?" he asked Jonathan. "Yes, and I'm very excited to hear about that," he replied. "Well, after lunch, I will be presenting Throughput Accounting and I think everyone will find it to be very interesting and informative," he replied. "Let's go get some lunch Tom," said Jonathan.

When everyone was back in the room and seated, Tom began his afternoon session. "As you just heard, the efficiency model, when measured and implemented at the wrong system location, can have disturbing effects on your system results. Actually, the end results were probably the opposite of what you expected to happen. In this afternoon's session, one of the things I want to talk about is the Theory of Constraints' version of accounting known as Throughput Accounting. I want to briefly compare Throughput Accounting with the version you all use called Cost Accounting," he explained. "So, let's begin with Cost Accounting," Tom said. "This presentation will take a while, and it will be full of new information, so please feel free to stop me and ask questions if you need clarifications," Tom said.

Tom began, "Before I begin, I want you all to know that I have been a Director of Finance for quite a few years and a strong advocate for the principles of Cost Accounting. I had never been exposed to the Theory of Constraints or Throughput Accounting, but after I heard about both, it absolutely changed my approach to financial decisions as soon as I learned what it had to offer. So, if any of you were or are involved in financial decisions, I want you to pay close attention to what I have to say today. I truly believe that if you listen to what I have to say, with an open mind, it will absolutely change your approach to making money for your company."

Tom began again, "The primary focus of Cost Accounting, as many of you know, is per part or per unit cost reductions. Because perceived cost reductions are viewed so favorably, is it any wonder why there is so much emphasis on the performance metric efficiency? And yet cost reductions don't seem to be the answer for most companies. There have been very many highly efficient companies that have come close to going out of business or have actually gone out of business. Have you ever heard of a company that has saved themselves into prosperity?" he asked rhetorically, and he noticed heads nodding up and down in agreement.

"Many companies will categorically state that the primary goal of their company is to make money, and yet they spend the largest portion of their time trying to save money. It would almost appear as if they've forgotten what their goal really is. I'm here to tell you that the strategy you use to make money is infinitely different than the strategy you would use to save money," he explained. He continued, "For most companies, the assumption is that the actions required to save money are the same actions required to make money. That is, if you somehow save enough money, it's believed in many cases to be the same as making money, but believe me this is absolutely not true," he explained. "Any questions so far?" he asked, but there weren't any, so he continued.

"These two approaches to making a profit are opposite in their thinking, and each one takes you in a distinctly different direction with absolutely different results. If the factual goal of your company is to save money, then probably the best way to accomplish your goal might be to just go out of business. Think about it, wouldn't this action save you the maximum amount of money! However, if the goal of your company is to make money, then a much different strategy must be used and that is by maximizing throughput through the system," Tom explained. One of the CEOs raised her hand and said, "I'm confused Tom. If you save enough money, won't you end up making money?" Tom responded and said, "I used to think along those same lines, but what I learned changed my approach completely. Stay with me and I'll show you why," he said.

"Maybe it's possible that some of these Cost Accounting rules and methods might be wrong and might mislead you into thinking some results are better than they really are. Is it possible that there might be another way to look logically at the practice of Accounting that will truly get us closer to our goal of making money? What if there was another way? A way that provides an alternative accounting method that allows us to remove, abandon, or even ignore the Cost Accounting rules that are causing so much trouble? Let's now have a look at Throughput Accounting, but before I do, I want everyone to understand that we can't totally abandon Cost Accounting, simply because it's required by law when we report our results. What I'm about to explain is a better way to make real-time financial decisions," he explained to a very captive audience, especially Jonathan.

"As I mentioned, Throughput Accounting is not an attack on Cost Accounting, but rather a different way to view the accounting measures, solve issues, and manage the company at a much higher success and profitability level. In its basic form, Throughput Accounting uses primarily three performance metrics which are Throughput (T), Investment/Inventory (I), and Operating Expense (OE). These metrics are a simplified methodology that removes all of the mystery of accounting and rolls it into three simple measures. So, let's look at the definition of these three, primary metrics," he said and posted a new slide (Figure 16.7).

Tom then said, "When you read and understand these definitions, it seems likely that all the money within your company can be categorized to fit within one of these three measures." He then asked if there were any

1. Throughput is the rate at which inventory is converted into sales. If you make lots of products and put them in a warehouse, that is not throughput, it's just inventory. The products or services only count as Throughput if they are sold to the customer and fresh money comes back into the business system.

2. Investment/Inventory is the money an organization invests in items that it intends to sell. This category would primarily include inventory, both raw materials and finished goods. It also includes things like buildings, machines and other equipment used to make products for sale, knowing that any, or all of these investments, could at some point in time, be sold for cash.

3. Operating Expense is all of the money spent generating the Throughput. This includes things like, rent, utilities, phone, benefits, wages, etc. It is any money spent that does not fit within one of the first two Throughput Accounting categories.

FIGURE 16.7
Definitions of T, I, and OE.

questions or comments, but there were none. This audience was captivated by what Tom was saying.

Tom then explained, "In thinking about Throughput Accounting, it's important to consider the following thoughts. Throughput Accounting is neither costing nor Cost Accounting. Instead, Throughput Accounting is focused on cash without the need for allocation to a specific product, which is very different than Cost Accounting." He continued, "This concept includes the variable and fixed expenses for a product. The only slight variation would be the calculation for Total Variable Cost (TVC). In this case, the TVC is a cost that is truly variable to a product or service, such as raw materials, paying a sales commission, or shipping charges."

Tom continued, "The sum total of these costs becomes the product Totally Variable Costs or TVC. TVC is only the cost associated with each product. Some would argue that labor should also be added as a variable cost per product, but this is simply not true! Labor is no longer a variable cost, it's a fixed cost. Think about that! In terms of hourly labor measures, you pay employees for vacation, holidays, and sick leave. You even pay them while they are making nothing! The employees cost you exactly the same amount of money, whether they are at work or not. Using this example, labor is an Operating Expense and not a variable cost associated with products, which is a vastly different concept than how Cost Accounting treats labor," Tom explained and then inserted a new slide (Figure 16.8).

"Are there any questions about what I've presented so far? he asked. Another of the CEOs raised his hand and asked, "Where did all of this come from Tom?" Tom responded, "Throughput Accounting was proposed by Eliyahu M. Goldratt as an alternative to traditional Cost Accounting in his and Jeff Cox's classic book, *The Goal* [1]. "Okay, thank you," the CEO responded.

He continued his explanation, "Some would argue that Throughput Accounting falls short because it is not able to pigeon-hole all of the categories of Cost Accounting into Throughput Accounting categories. Things like interest payments on loans, or payment of stock-holder dividends, or even depreciation of machines or facilities. However, this argument is not valid. Ask yourself, which one of those specific categories can't be placed into one of the Throughput Accounting categories?"

"The baseline Throughput Accounting concept is really very simple. Think of it this way. If you have to write a check to somebody else, it's either

The following definitions apply to Throughput Accounting:

1. Throughput (T) = Product Selling Price (SP) – the Total Variable Cost (TVC).
Or simply $T = SP - TVC$

2. Net Profit (NP) = Throughput (T) minus Operational Expense (OE).
Or $NP = T - OE$

3. Return on Investment (ROI) = Net Profit (NP) divided by Inventory (I).
Or $ROI = NP/I$

4. Productivity (P) = Throughput (T) divided by Operating Expense (OE).
Or $P = T/OE$

5. Inventory Turns (IT) = Throughput (T) divided by Inventory Value (IV).
Or $IT = T/I$

FIGURE 16.8
Throughput Accounting definitions.

an Investment (I) or it's an Operating Expense (OE). It's an Investment if it is something you can sell for money at some point in time. It's an Operating Expense if you can't. Just put this debt in the category that makes the most sense. On the other hand, if somebody is writing a check to you, then it's probably Throughput (T). Cost Accounting rules have made it much more complicated than it needs to be. And when you make it that complex and difficult, the stranglehold that Cost Accounting has on your thinking becomes even more obvious," Tom explained.

"Throughput Accounting is really focused on providing the necessary information that allows your decision makers to make better decisions in real time. If the goal of the company is truly to make more money now, or make more money in the future, then any decisions being considered should get the company closer to the goal and not further away. Effective decision-making is well suited for an effective Throughput, Inventory, and Operating Expense analysis. This analysis can show the impact of any local decisions on the bottom line of the company," Tom explained. Jonathan then asked, "Why has this form of accounting not been made more well-known? I mean, based on what you've explained so far, why isn't it taught more in graduate schools?" "I wish I had a good answer for you Jonathan, but I don't. All I know is that when I learned about it, it changed my whole approach to how companies should go about making better profits," he responded.

He then said, "Ideally, good business decisions should cause these three things to happen." First, Throughput (T) should increase, while, at the same time, Investment/Inventory will either decrease or stay the same. It is possible that Investment/Inventory can go up as long as the effect on Throughput is exponential. In other words, sometimes a very well-placed investment can cause the Throughput to skyrocket. The third thing that will happen when a good decision is made is that Operating Expenses will either decrease or stay the same. It is not always necessary to decrease Operating Expenses in order to have a dramatic effect on Throughput and ultimately profits. Consider the situation where the Throughput actually doubles and you didn't have to hire anyone new to do it, nor did you have to lay anyone off."

"The decision-making process becomes much easier when these factors are considered. The movement either up or down of these three measures should provide sufficient information for good strategy and much better decisions. Any good decision should be based on global impacts to the company, and not just a single unit or process in isolation. If your thinking is limited to the lowest level of the organization, and you are focused on the wrong area, then the positive impact will never be seen or felt by the entire organization," Tom explained.

And again, Tom continued, "If we compare these two concepts at the highest level, then Cost Accounting is all about the actions you take to try and save money, while Throughput Accounting is all about the actions you take to make money. Once you've made the cost reductions and you still need more, what do you do next? Where else can you reduce costs? On the other hand, making money, at least in theory, is infinite. What is the limit on how much money your company can make now?" Tom asked rhetorically.

"In conclusion, the Throughput Accounting cost model contains only Total Variable Cost (TVC) and Throughput (T). The calculation is simple: T = Selling Price – Totally Variable Costs. Throughput, in essence, equals the dollars remaining from selling the product after you have subtracted the Totally Variable Cost. Nothing is allocated, nothing is assumed, it's just a simple cash calculation from the sale," he explained. "The bottom line is this, if you have sales that you can't meet, it's time to focus on your constraint and drive Throughput higher and higher. When Throughput increases and Operating Expenses decrease or remain the same, your profit margins will increase proportionally," Tom stated.

Tom continued and explained, "This is what we did at Tires for All and our margins increased. Before I conclude, I want to show you several run charts of our key performance metrics," and with that said, he posted the run charts (Figures 16.9 through 16.12). "Here are our run charts for Profit Margins, Efficiency, On-Time Delivery, and Stock-Out Percentage, and as you can see, everything improved over time except for our Efficiency. In fact, if you compare our profit margins with our efficiency numbers, they

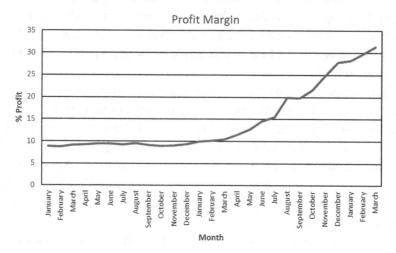

FIGURE 16.9
Profits versus time.

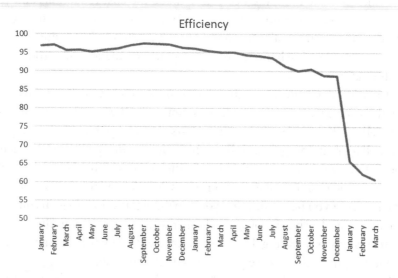

FIGURE 16.10
Efficiency versus time.

FIGURE 16.11
On-Time Delivery versus time.

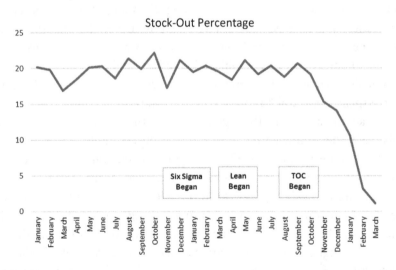

FIGURE 16.12
Stock-out percentages versus time.

are polar opposites. That is, as our efficiency decreased, our profit margins increased at the same time. What conclusions can you draw?"

With all this being said about the accounting method comparison, Tom recommended that everyone take another break, but to be back in fifteen minutes. Before they left, he asked if there were any questions and one of the Board members raised his hand. "In your last graph, you show stock-outs decreasing dramatically. Why did this happen?" "Hold that question until we come back," Tom said.

Once again Jonathan stayed behind to speak with Tom. "Tom, I have to tell you, that was one of the finest presentations I have ever heard!" "Well, thank you Jonathan, can I ask what you liked about it?" Tom asked. "So many things Tom. You took a very difficult subject and made it seem so easy, but what I really liked is that you have convinced me that all of our portfolio companies need to implement Throughput Accounting!" Jonathan replied. "It's as though we have been tripping over dollars to pick up pennies!" he added.

"Like I told this group, throughout my career, I have been working in the financial world in some capacity, but once I heard about Throughput Accounting, and what it can do for a company, I was convinced immediately that Tires for All needed to apply this method to our financial decision-making process!" Tom explained. "And the good news is, once we focused on increasing Throughput, our profitability dramatically improved to the level we now have," he added. "When everyone comes back from break, I want to say a few words to everyone, before you begin your next subject," Jonathan said.

When everyone was back in the conference room and seated, Jonathan began speaking. "I don't know about everyone else, but once I heard what Tom had to say about Throughput Accounting, I was convinced that this has to be embraced by all of our holdings. I say this, not because I want everyone to abandon Cost Accounting, but rather because I am convinced that in terms of real-time financial decisions, Throughput Accounting is much superior to it. So, with this in mind, I want all of our portfolio companies to begin using Throughput Accounting to this end. I truly believe that by coupling our decision to eliminate driving efficiencies higher in non-constraints with driving Throughput higher, the profitability of your companies will skyrocket!" And with that, he turned the podium back over to Tom.

REFERENCE

Eliyahu Goldratt and Jeff Cox, 1992, *The Goal: A Process of Ongoing Improvement*, North River Press, Barrington, MA.

17

TOC Replenishment Solution

Tom continued his presentation, "In the spirit of making more money now and in the future, I want ask everyone a question," Tom began. "How many of you here today have a problem with stock-outs at your factories?" At least five different hands went up, so Tom asked them all a question, but pointed to one of the General Managers who had his hand up. "Why do you think you have this problem?" he asked. The General Manager replied, "I'm pretty sure that we're not very good at predicting what we need in the future." "Why do you think that's the reason?" Tom asked. "I think it's just hard to predict our future needs," he replied. "You know, customers will make an order and then right in the middle of fulfilling it, they'll change their mind on how many parts they need. And when this happens, we end up over-ordering on some parts, while we're running out of parts for another order," he added. Tom could see others in the room agreeing with the General Manager.

Tom then said, "What if I could show you a method that would cut your stock inventory by half, while, at the same time, reducing your frequency of stock-out to nearly zero? Would that be of interest to you?" he asked and without exception, everyone indicated that they would love to hear about this method. Tom began, "The cost of inventory management is swiftly increasing in today's comprehensive marketplace. And while improvements to supply-chain management have been noted in certain industries, there are three very common factors that typically affect the success of any improvement initiative along these lines. These three factors are complexity, unpredictability or volatility, and risk."

Tom continued, "There are linkages between critical business systems such as operations, materials management, and supply chains that are very often disjointed and inadequate, if they exist at all. Estimating uncertainty with absolute confidence is not possible in any system, leading to potentially negative consequences. Replenishment was originally invented to manage the distribution of goods, but it can also be used by service providers and direct sales businesses," he explained.

He continued, "Replenishment is also called the Theory of Constraints supply-chain solution, because one business's distribution chain is often another's supply chain. Replenishment gets its name from the specific way in which goods are distributed or supplied. The figure in the next slide is a simplified distribution chain. Many businesses have far more factories, warehouses, and retail outlets in its distribution chain," and then Tom posted a new slide (Figure 17.1).

Tom continued, "The figure you see on the screen was taken from a book by John Ricketts, entitled *Reaching the Goal* [1], and it depicts a simplified distribution chain. Many businesses have far more factories, warehouses, and retail outlets in its distribution chain. In traditional distribution, products produced by the factories are immediately shipped in large batches to regional warehouses. Each regional warehouse in turn periodically ships smaller, but still sizeable batches, to retail locations. So, as a result, most inventory is pushed through the chain to retail locations on the assumption that it will eventually be sold to the end consumer." "So far, are you with me? Have I gotten your replenishment systems correct?" Tom added and

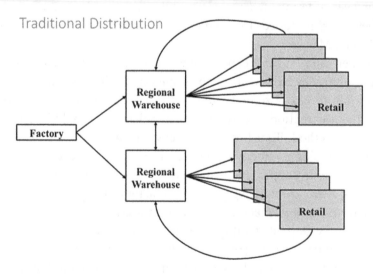

FIGURE 17.1
Traditional Parts Distribution Chain.

1. Some retailers might have lots of products, while at the same time others have none.

2. There's no easy way to ship inventory from one retail locations to another to both reduce overstocks and stock-outs.

3. When stock-outs occur, if the time required to restock a retailer from the warehouse is longer than customers are willing to wait, stock-outs turn into lost sales rather than backorders.

FIGURE 17.2
Undesirable effects.

everyone motioned that he had. "I'm going to present an example that comes from retail providers like department stores," Bob added.

Continuing, Tom loaded a new slide (Figure 17.2) and said, "Unfortunately, because variability is highest at retail locations, several undesirable effects occur."

Continuing, Tom then explained, "As a result of these undesirable effects, retailers that have excess inventory, will return it to the warehouse, while those with no inventory lose sales while waiting for shipments. When cross-shipments between warehouses are needed to cover shortages, those shipments may be delayed by the desire to ship large batches in order to save shipping costs."

"Add to this that whenever new products are introduced, retail locations and the entire distribution chain are filled with obsolete products. So, as these new products are pushed through the chain, the obsolete products must be discounted to be able to clear them from the retailer's inventory which reduce the sales of the new products. Traditional manufacturing is driven by sales forecasts which are notoriously inaccurate. The bigger the batches and the less frequently they are distributed, the longer the horizon on sales forecasts, which in turn makes forecasts even less accurate, which calls for bigger batches," he explained, and again, heads were nodding up and down indicating that they agreed with what he said so far.

Tom continued, "The net result of these inaccurate forecasts, and pushing large batches through the distribution chain, is low reliability even though the supply chain is filled with excess inventory. So, where is the constraint now?" he asked rhetorically. "You might be tempted to conclude that shipping or the warehouse capacity is the constraint, but because inventory tends to pile up ahead of the true constraint, it's the consumer. The amount of product that should be distributed is ultimately by sales to customers, so the constraint is now external in the market."

"The best way to break a market constraint is to sell customers what they want, when and where they want it, at a price that corresponds with perceived value better than your competition. Most, if not all, businesses are linked one way or another to some kind of supply chain. They need stock keeping units (SKUs) or raw materials from somebody else, in order to do what they do and pass it on to the next system in line until it finally arrives at the end consumer. For many organizations, the supply chain/ inventory system of choice is one often referred to as the Minimum/ Maximum or (MIN/MAX) system. SKUs, or inventory, are evaluated based on need and usage, and some type of maximum and minimum levels are established for each item. So, to get the right products, in the right amounts, to the right locations, at the right time, the solution has to be an alternative to sales forecasts, big batches, and infrequent shipments. Before we look at TOC's Solution, let's look at the 'why' of this problem," Tom explained.

There was a clear interest in the audience on what Tom was explaining and he began again by posting a new slide (Figure 17.3) and said, "The traditional basic rules and measures for these systems are usually quite simple."

Tom continued, "The foundational assumptions behind these rules and measures are primarily based on the belief that, in order to save money and minimize your expenditures for supply inventory, you must minimize the amount of money you spend for these items," Tom explained. "There's that 'save money' effect again," he added. He continued, "The assumption here is that the purchase price per SKU could be driven to the lowest possible level by buying in bulk, and the company would save the maximum amount of money on their purchase. In reality though, there always seems to be situations of excess inventory for some items and stock-out situations

- Rule 1: Determine the maximum and minimum levels for each item.

- Rule 2: Don't exceed the maximum level.

- Rule 3: Don't reorder until you meet or go below the minimum level.

FIGURE 17.3
Traditional rules of the Min/Max system.

for others. Why is it that even though we have plenty of inventory, these stock-outs continue to happen? Let's look at the typical rules for managing the Min/Max system again."

"Is everybody with me so far?" he asked, and it seemed as though everyone was, so he continued. "The system reorder amount is the maximum amount, no matter how many SKUs are currently in the point-of-use storage bin. Many supply systems only allow for one order at a time to be present for a specific SKU. Orders for SKUs are triggered only after the minimum amount has been reached or exceeded. Total SKU inventory is held at the lowest possible level of the distribution chain, the point-of-use (POU) storage location, and SKUs are inventoried once or twice a month and orders are placed, as required," Tom explained as he posted a new slide (Figure 17.4). "This is a graphic depiction of what happens in the Min/Max system in terms of stocks-outs and holding excess inventory," Tom explained.

"Here's another way of looking at parts and inventory flow from a central distribution location to point-of-use locations," as he posted a new slide on the screen (Figure 17.5).

"Parts are ordered, received, and distributed directly to the point-of-use location, the lowest level of the supply chain," Tom explained. "When the minimum level is reached or surpassed, a reorder is sent back up through this system, but unfortunately, many times there are stock-outs

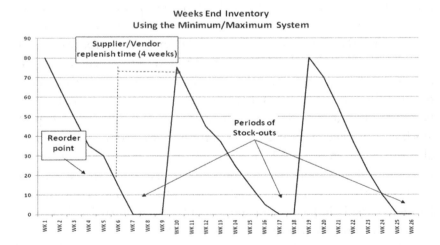

FIGURE 17.4
Impact of the Min/Max system over time.

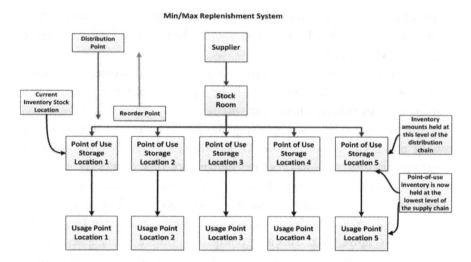

FIGURE 17.5
Min/Max replenishment system.

that permeate this system," he explained. "So, what's the answer to this dilemma?" he asked rhetorically.

"The TOC Distribution and Replenishment Model is a robust SKU replenishment system that allows the user to be proactive in managing the supply-chain system. It's also a system based on usage, either daily or weekly, and not some minimum amount. The TOC Distribution and Replenishment Model argues that the majority of the inventory should be held at a higher level in the supply chain and not at the lowest level. For example, in a direct sales business, not all of the inventory should be on shelves, but rather, some should remain in the stock room," Tom explained.

Tom continued, "The TOC Distribution and Replenishment Model also argues that the use of min/max amounts should be abolished. And instead of using the minimum amount to trigger the reorder process, it should be triggered by daily usage and vendor lead time to replenish the part. Stock is positioned at the highest level in the distribution system so that all available inventory can be used to satisfy demand at multiple points of use. In addition, more frequent ordering can be completed because the central warehouse sums the demand usage of the various consumption locations. Finally, larger order quantities can be accumulated at the central warehouse sooner than at each separate location."

"Buffers are positioned at points of potential high demand variation and stocked and restocked at levels determined by stock on hand, demand rate, and replenishment lead time. Order frequency is increased, and order quantity is decreased, in order to maintain buffers at optimum levels and avoid stock-out conditions which obviously cause interruptions to the flow of parts. Ordering is determined by depletion of the buffer, and how much to order and where to distribute available stock are determined by buffer status. Buffer size is managed dynamically, whereby buffer depletion data provides signals to determine when and by how much to modify buffer size," Tom explained. "Surely there are questions about this method?" but there were none, so he continued.

"Order urgency is based on buffer depletion and is used to set ordering priorities," he explained in detail. "The bottom line is that TOC's replenishment method accounts for buffer depletion and local demand information, so that the right mix of SKUs are ordered and distributed to the priority locations. In a direct sales business, the buffer is what remains in the stock room and when it is used up, it's time to reorder." Tom explained and then posted a new slide (Figure 17.6).

"The next slide is what the TOC replenishment system looks like and points out the basic buffers needed for this system to work (Figure 17.7)," Tom stated and then explained how it works.

Criteria for the TOC Distribution and Replenishment Model:

✓ The system reorder amount needs to be based on daily or weekly usage and SKU lead time to replenish.

✓ The system needs to allow for multiple replenish orders, if required.

✓ Orders are triggered based on buffer requirements, with possible daily actions, as required.

✓ All SKUs/inventory must be available when needed.

✓ SKU inventory is held at a higher level, preferably at central supply locations or comes directly from the supplier/vendor.

✓ SKU buffer determined by usage rate and replenish supplier lead time. Baseline buffer should be equal to 1.5. If lead time is 1 week, buffer is set at 1.5 weeks. Adjust as required, based on historical data.

FIGURE 17.6
Criteria for TOC's Model.

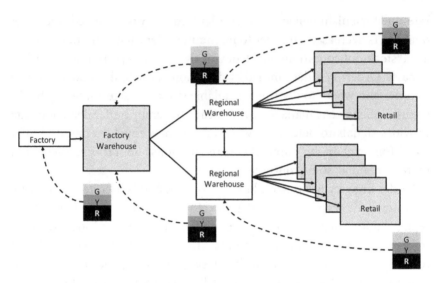

FIGURE 17.7
TOC's Distribution and Replenishment Solution with buffers.

"Buffers are placed at better leverage points in the supply chain. That is, most inventory is held in the factory warehouse. Likewise, regional warehouses and retail locations have buffers for each product. Buffers, which are typically physical products, are divided into green, yellow, and red zones, and this replenishment system relies on aggregation to smooth demand. Demand at regional warehouses is smoother than demand at retail locations, simply because higher-than-normal demand at some retail locations is offset by lower demand at other ones. Demand at the factory warehouse is even smoother than demand at the regional warehouses. Goods produced by the factory are then stored in a nearby warehouse until they are needed to replenish goods consumed by sales," Tom explained.

Tom continued, "Because sales occur daily, shipments also occur daily, and the quantities shipped are just sufficient to replace the goods that were sold. You might be thinking that this method would increase your shipping costs over what could be achieved by shipping large batches, less frequently, but the truth is, the net effect on total shipping costs is that they actually decrease. The fact is, by stopping the shipment of obsolete goods, and the reshipment of misdirected goods, more than compensates for increased costs created by smaller shipments of saleable goods." Jonathan then said, "Does everyone understand the impact we could see when we convert everyone to this system? And we will be doing this going forward," he added as everyone indicated that they did understand.

Tom continued, "The bottom line is the ability to capture sales that would otherwise be lost due to insufficient inventory makes the TOC solution a better alternative. In this system, replenishment is driven by actual consumption, and not a sales forecast. As sales are made, the buffer levels at retail locations drop, eventually triggering replenishment from the factory warehouse, which, in turn, triggers a manufacturing order to resupply the appropriate buffer before it runs out."

"So, how do you know how large to make these buffers?" Tom asked. "Buffer sizing is based on both variability and the time it takes to resupply. The more variable the consumption is, the larger the buffer must be to cover the variability. Also, the longer it takes to resupply, the bigger the buffer needs to be to be able to cover the demand during the resupply waiting times.

The benefits of TOC's replenishment solution can be very striking. A traditional distributor that is 85 percent reliable can reasonably expect to increase its reliability to 99 percent, while reducing its inventory by at least 50 percent! Think about what that alone would do for your available cash on hand?" he stated. "Instead of having cash tied up in excess inventory, you could reduce that amount by 50 percent, thus freeing it up to spend on other things," he added.

Continuing, Tom then said, "The average time to resupply retail locations typically drops from weeks or months to about one day. A central benefit of TOC's replenishment solution is to change the distribution from push to pull. That is, nothing gets distributed unless there is a market for it. Market pull, the external constraint, then optimizes distribution while minimizing inventory." "So, let's review what I have presented here today," Tom said as he posted another slide (Figure 17.8).

"The graphical representation of the outcome of TOC's Replenishment Model is very profound," and he loaded a new slide (Figure 17.9). "What you end up with is an inventory reduction of roughly 40 to 60 percent that is maintained within a very stable range. In addition, stock-outs are usually totally avoided," he explained.

"I want to finish this subject with a very simple example that I think everyone will relate to," Tom explained. "Consider a simple soda vending machine. When the supplier, the soda vendor, opens the door on a vending machine, it's very easy to see what products have been sold and which ones

Criteria for the TOC Distribution and Replenishment Model:

✓ The system reorder amount needs to be based on daily or weekly usage and SKU lead time to replenish.

✓ The system needs to allow for multiple replenish orders, if required.

✓ Orders are triggered based on buffer requirements, with possible daily actions, as required.

✓ All SKUs/inventory must be available when needed.

✓ SKU inventory is held at a higher level, preferably at central supply locations or comes directly from the supplier/vendor.

✓ SKU buffer determined by usage rate and replenish supplier lead time. Baseline buffer should be equal to 1.5. If lead time is 1 week, buffer is set at 1.5 weeks. Adjust as required, based on historical data.

FIGURE 17.8
The Dynamic Replenishment System review.

needs to be replaced and to what level to replace it. The soda person is holding the inventory at the next highest level, which is on his soda truck, so it's easy to make the required distribution when needed. He doesn't leave six cases of soda when only twenty cans are needed.

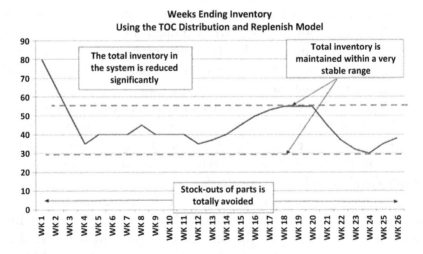

FIGURE 17.9
Graphical representation of TOC's Replenishment Solution.

If he were to do that, when he got to the next vending machine he might have run out of the necessary soda because he made distribution too early at the last stop," Tom explained.

He continued with his simple example, "After completing the daily refill of the vending machines, the soda person returns to the warehouse or the distribution point to replenish the supply on the soda truck and get ready for the next day's distribution. When the warehouse makes distribution to the soda truck, they move up one level in the chain and replenish what's been used from their supplier. Replenishing in this way significantly reduces the on-hand inventory while significantly reducing stock-outs. If a type of soda always runs out, then more should be added to the vending machine, which would, in this case be the safety buffer."

"So, to complete this presentation, let's review the benefits of TOC's Distribution and Replenishment Solution. One of the first things you get is the reduction of total inventory required to manage and maintain the total supply-chain system. In fact, this inventory reduction is typically on the order of 40 to 60 percent while at the same time you end up with the virtual elimination of SKU stock-out situations and distribution of SKUs is made at the right time to the right location. And as a result, the frustration caused by stock-out situations disappears.

Not only in being able to complete the work, but also the elimination in the time spent looking for and waiting for SKUs to become available. And

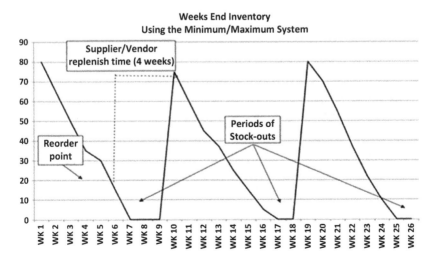

FIGURE 17.10
TOC Distribution and Replenishment Model.

because waiting due to stock-outs virtually disappears, parts flow and synchronization improves dramatically which improves the throughput of parts through the entire supply chain. And finally, because throughput improves, profitability increases proportionally to the level of sales," Tom explained and then posted his final slide (Figure 17.10) and asked the group which system they wanted.

He finished by simply saying, "The choice is yours!" and his session ended. Tom then suggested that they take one last break before he presented his final presentation, "The Goal Tree."

REFERENCE

1. John Ricketts, 2008, *Reaching the Goal*, IBM Press.

18

The Goal Tree

When everyone was back in the conference room and seated, Tom began a new presentation. "Throughout the day, we have discussed many different tools associated with the Theory of Constraints, but there are other tools, referred to as the Logical Thinking Process tools that we haven't discussed. And while these are very important tools, we don't have enough time left today to discuss these tools. But having said this, there is one tool that I do want to discuss in depth and that is the Goal Tree."

"When using the logic-based TOC Logical Thinking Process tools, there are two distinctly different types of logic at play which are sufficiency type logic and necessity type logic. Sufficiency type logic is quite simply a series of if-then statements. If I have 'this,' then I have 'that.' On the other hand, necessity-based logic trees use the syntax, 'In order to have "this" I must have "that."' The Goal Tree falls into the necessity-based category. For example, in order to have a fire, I must have a fuel source, a spark, and air. If the goal is to have a fire, then all three components must be available. The fuel source, spark and air are referred to as Critical Success Factors (CSFs). Take away even one of the CSFs and you won't have a fire," Tom explained. "So, with this in mind, I want to share Tires for All's Goal Tree experience and demonstrate how we used it to develop our strategic improvement plan. And please stop me along the way if you have any questions," Tom said.

Tom began, "The first two deliverables that we had to achieve was a definition of our span of control and our sphere of influence. Our span of control included all of those things in our system over which we would have unilateral change authority. In other words, our company could decide to change those things on our own because they are within our control and don't require approval from someone outside our system. On the other hand, our sphere of influence were those things we may have wanted to change, but we had to get approval from someone else to do so. We decided that our span of control covered everything within our four walls from the time we receive our raw materials until we ship our products to our customers." He then added, "We defined our sphere of influence as everything before receiving raw materials, as well as the receipt of our products at our customers. So, with these two things clearly defined, we could now begin," he added. Bob added an instruction for the group, "As I walk you through what we did at Tires for All to develop our Goal Tree, I want you to do two things, take prolific notes and stop me with any questions you have along the way."

Tom then began again, "The distinction between what our span of control and sphere of influence was very important, simply because our sphere of influence is not a fixed entity. In your systems, you can influence way more than you control and it's probably much more than you realize. Generally speaking, many things within the walls of your manufacturing facility represent your span of control. But having said that, not everything fits into this category. For example, things like governmental regulations, under which your business is regulated, are not considered within your span of control. You might be able to influence them, but you certainly don't have control over them," he explained.

Tom continued and inserted a slide onto the screen, "This figure (Figure 18.1) demonstrates the hierarchical structure of the Goal Tree. The Goal Tree consists of a single Goal, several CSFs, which must be in place to achieve the goal, and a series of Necessary Conditions (NCs), which must be in place to achieve each of the CSFs. The Goal and CSFs are written as terminal outcomes, as though they are already in place. The NCs are, more or less, written as activities that must be completed in order to achieve each of the CSFs. I will show you the Goal Tree we completed, but a completed Goal Tree's basic structure looks like this," Tom explained.

"With this description of the Goal Tree, we began creating our own Goal Tree by next deciding on an appropriate Goal. It's important to remember that the Goal we started with was the responsibility of the owner or owners to define. But since the owners were not there with us, our General Manager, Mark Roder had the responsibility to state the Goal. Mark responded and told us that since he had meetings with our Board of Directors, and that they had made their desires very clear, we would say our Goal would be 'Optimum Profit Margins.' Mark knew they wanted margins of at least 20 percent, but he was sure they would like our margins

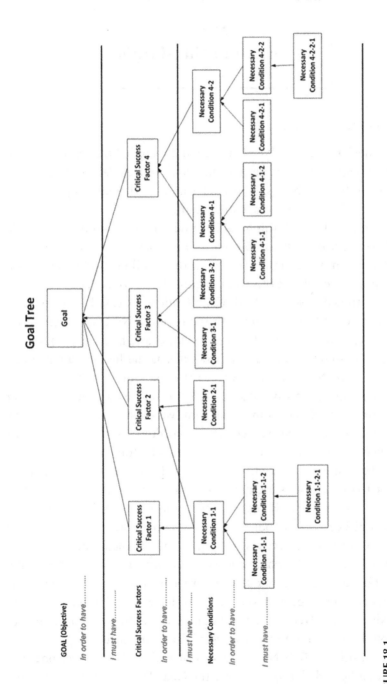

FIGURE 18.1
Goal Tree basic structure.

```
┌─────────────────────────────────────┐
│                                      │
│               100                    │
│    Optimized Profit Margins          │
│                                      │
└─────────────────────────────────────┘
```

FIGURE 18.2
Tires for All's Goal statement.

to be higher," he added. "We all agreed and recorded the following Goal statement (Figure 18.2) and placed it in a box," Tom explained. Tom added, "The 100 in the Goal box is there as a location marker and as you will see going forward, each box has a distinct marker."

Tom continued, "With this Goal in mind, we asked ourselves, what do we believe must be in place to achieve this Goal? After much back and forth discussion, as a team we came up with the following Critical Success Factors needed to achieve this Goal (Figure 18.3)," Tom added.

Tom continued, "Now that all of the Critical Success Factors were in place, we now had to come up with the required Necessary Conditions to achieve each of the Critical Success Factors," and he posted a new slide (Figure 18.4). Tom explained, "For example, as the figure demonstrates, our first Critical Success Factor was written as 'Work scheduled to meet demand,' so using necessity-based logic we said as a group, 'In order to have work scheduled to meet demand, we must have two Necessary Conditions.' We must have an enhanced scheduling system and we must then schedule our facilities to meet our demand," Tom explained.

"In a like manner, we continued creating Necessary Conditions until all of the Critical Success Factors were in place as is demonstrated in this next slide (Figure 18.5)," Bob explained to the group. "While we thought we were finished creating our Goal Tree, the consultant we had hired to help us, told us that we weren't done yet," Tom explained. "Our consultant then explained, 'What we have created this morning is just the beginning of our effort to create our strategic improvement plan.' Mark Roder, our General Manager asked him what our next step was, and he told us we will now take our Goal Tree, make some subtle changes to it, and then use it to create our long-term improvement plan," Tom explained.

"Our consultant, Bob Nelson, who you will probably meet one day, told us that he had changed the way the Goal Tree was first introduced. He explained that the change he made has to do with how the Goal and

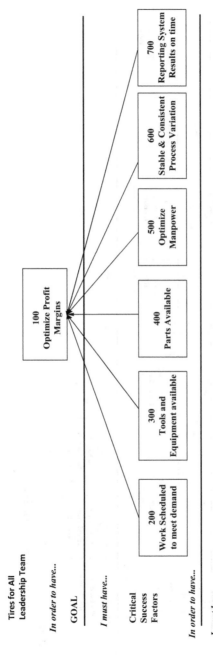

FIGURE 18.3

Tires for All's Goal and Critical Success Factors.

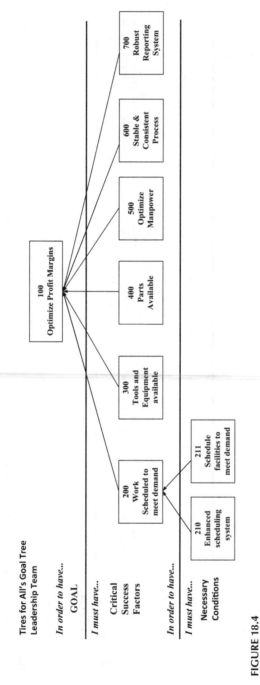

FIGURE 18.4

Goal Tree with first two NCs included.

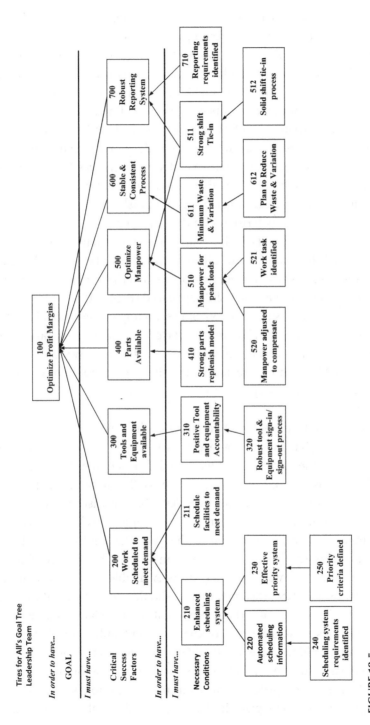

FIGURE 18.5
Completed Goal Tree.

Critical Success Factors are worded, as well as some of the NCs. He also explained that one of the key learnings in the book *The 4 Disciplines of Execution: Achieving Your Wildly Important Goals* [1] was the concept of Lead and Lag Measures. He explained that the lag measure has to do with Goal achievement and that it should be written in such a way that there is a clear measurement of Goal units with a well-defined target. So, instead of the Goal being written as 'Optimized Profit Margins' like we had in our Goal Tree, he re-worded it as though it was a performance measure with a target. The final Goal statement we ended up with, was Profit Margins Above 25%? He further explained that written this way, we could now measure it and it has a clear target, just like a finish line in a race. His logic was that if our Goal was written like this, everyone would know exactly what our company wanted to achieve and how we could measure success," Tom explained. Tom continued, "The next thing we did was to look at each of the Critical Success Factors, we rewrote each of them to be like our Goal statement," and with that a new slide appeared (Figure 18.6).

Tom continued and said, "As you can see, many of the Critical Success Factors were now measurable and displayed a clear success target. For example, CSF number 400 was now written as '400 Parts Available > 99%.' Clearly, this CSF was now measurable and the target to reach has been set. If you look at the new Necessary Conditions, they are also written in the same format."

"Our consultant said he chose to do so in this manner because, when they are measurable and have a target, as many of them do, it becomes much easier for the improvement team to define activities that will move these Lead Measures, and it made sense to us. The bottom line for us as we saw it, was if we could get the lower level Lead Measures moving in a positive direction, they would then move the upper level Lead Measures in like manner. For example, one of the lower level NCs was stated as '410: Parts replenish plan in place > 99% on time %.' If this was achieved, then the assumption was that '400: Parts Available > 99%,' would also be met. And if this CSF was met, then it should move the Goal closer to its hoped-for level of greater than 25 percent. As I explained earlier, each CSF contributes to achievement of the Goal, but unless all of them are achieved, we would not meet the final Goal target." Tom suggested.

"Our consultant, Bob Nelson, then explained that, although normally one would use the complete Logical Thinking Process tool kit to construct a strategic improvement plan, he had developed a different, and much

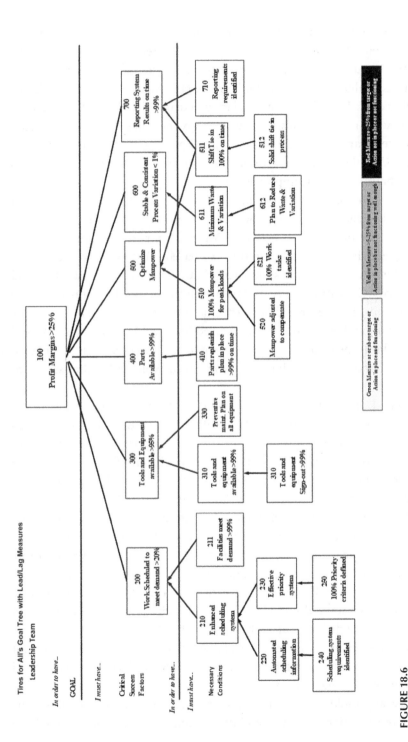

FIGURE 18.6
Goal Tree with re-written CSFs and NCs.

simpler way to accomplish this. He explained to us that he used a very simple color-coding system to assess the current state of each of the entities in our Goal Tree. He explained that if the measure is at or above the target value, we should color it green. He added that green can also be used to describe actions that we plan to take to drive the lead measures in a positive direction. Likewise, a yellow box indicates that a lead measure is greater than 5 percent, but less than 25 percent away from the defined target. Or if it's a required action, then it means that there is something in place, but that it needs improvement."

"Finally, our consultant explained that a box shaded in red means that the lead measure is greater than 25 percent from its target or if it's a required action, then the entity is either not in place or that something is in place, but it isn't functioning. So based on these instructions, we were instructed to fully assess each of our Critical Success Factors and Necessary Conditions in accordance with the instructions provided. He also told us that we should perform this activity as a group and take our time doing it. He told us that we needed to take one entity at a time and look at both the state of the measures and the potential actions we want to take to move it in the right direction," Tom explained to the assembled group.

"To make this activity easier for use to accomplish, our consultant had prepared our completed Goal Tree with our measures in place, as well as the targets we had discussed at length. This revised Goal Tree, with instructions included on the bottom, was very helpful for us as a group to be able to complete," Tom explained and with all this said, he posted a new slide, which included the finished Goal Tree (Figure 18.7).

"Before our consultant left the conference room, he had suggested that I lead this effort, since he believed that I was totally grasping this new Goal Tree concept used to assess the organization. I began this effort by reviewing what we're going to be doing," Tom explained. Tom continued, "I explained we will use the instructions at the base of our Goal Tree to assess how we're doing with our Goal, Critical Success Factors, and Necessary Conditions," and Tom posted the three instructions on the screen for everyone to review. "I explained that it was extremely important that everyone understand these basic instructions and with that, I reviewed them with the group," Tom explained.

"Basically, I told everyone that if what we have in place is at or above our target or the action is in place and functioning well, we color it green. If we

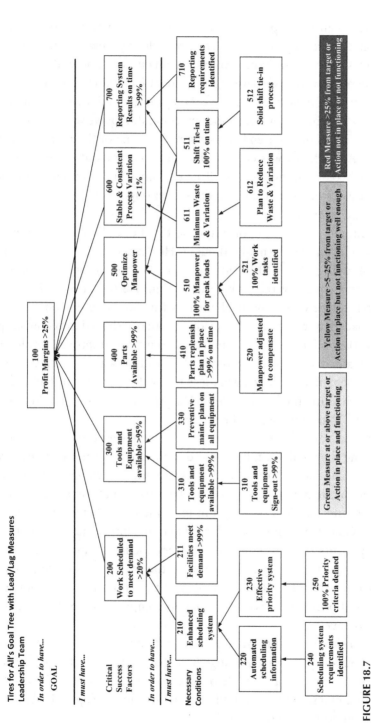

FIGURE 18.7
Completed Goal Tree with assessment instructions.

are greater than 5 to 25 percent from our target or we have an action in place, but it isn't functioning well enough, then we color it yellow. And finally, if our measure is greater than 25 percent away from our target or we don't have an action in place or what we have in place is not functioning well enough, then we color it red. I then asked everyone if they understood what we're doing."

"Just to be sure that everyone did understand what we were about to do. I asked a series of open-ended questions on some of the more nebulous entities. And when I was comfortable that everyone did understand, we began our color-coding exercise," Tom explained and inserted a new slide with the assessed Goal Tree onto the screen (Figure 18.8) for everyone to review and understand.

"I went and located our consultant so that he could take a look at our work and let us know what he thought. He thanked us for our work and began studying what we had put together. He had questions, but in each case, they were answered to his satisfaction. He then began discussing more on this new tool and explained that it should be obvious that any entity shaded in red has a higher priority than one shaded in yellow simply because they offer the greatest potential source for improved results. He also explained that as we improve the Lead Measures in these areas, improvement in upper level Lead Measures will take place until ultimately, the Lag Measure, the Goal of Profit Margins Above 25%, should also be achieved," Tom explained to the group.

Tom then said, "The key then, for creating a focused improvement plan using the Goal Tree, is to first develop the required Lag and Lead Measures and then set realistic targets to achieve each one of them. The key though is to make sure there is a relationship that correlates between the Lead and Lag Measures," Tom explained. "So here it is, a way to utilize a Goal Tree, which is both easy to understand and construct, and which permits the development of a very focused improvement plan. In my experience using this approach, the team that develops it will embrace it because it is their plan. And the good news is, from start to finish, it only takes less than a day to complete, rather than days or weeks to develop."

Tom finished by saying, "My suggestion is that when you go back to work tomorrow, you get your team together, create a Goal Tree and use it to create an improvement plan." Before everyone left, one of the CEOs asked him if he could see how they used the Goal Tree to develop their plan. Tom agreed and posted a new slide (Figure 18.9).

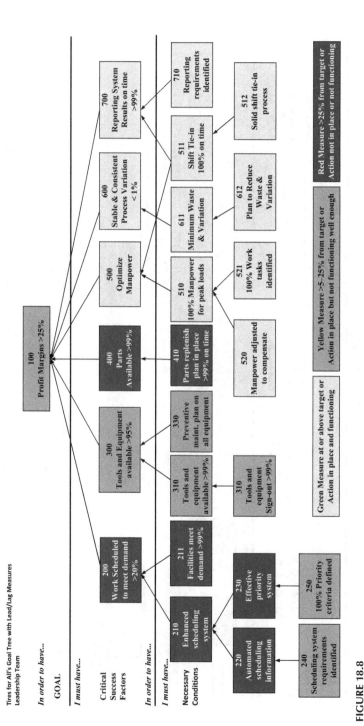

FIGURE 18.8

Fully assessed Goal Tree.

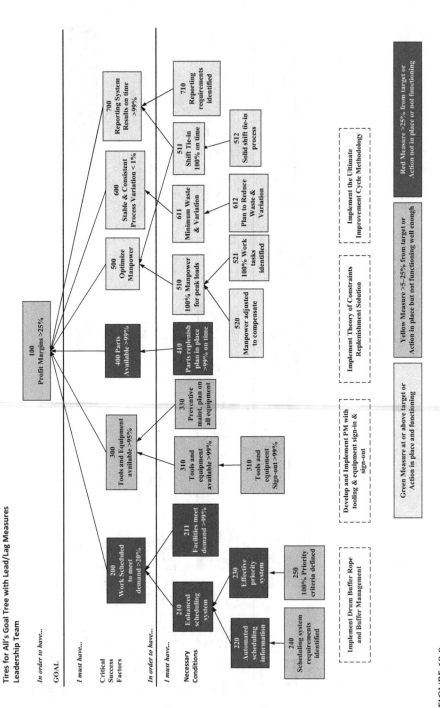

FIGURE 18.9

Goal Tree with improvements included.

Tom began his explanation, "Although I don't have a copy of our improvement plan with me today, there were four major activities that we implemented at Tires for All. In order to improve our scheduling system, we implemented TOC's scheduling system called Drum Buffer Rope along with Buffer Management. We used this in conjunction with our Enterprise Resource Planning (ERP) system by scheduling the system constraint. The outcome from doing this was a continuous stream of product ready for the system constraint to process," he explained. Tom continued, "We then moved to the second improvement activity which was to develop and implement both a Preventive Maintenance program plus a tool and equipment sign-in/sign-out procedure. The net effect of this was a major reduction in unplanned downtime which dramatically improved the capacity of our processes."

"We then moved to our third improvement activity, the implementation of TOC's Replenishment Solution with the net effect being a significant reduction in part stock-outs, and our overall cash amount tied up in excess inventory also was significantly reduced. The final action we took was the implementation of something referred to as The Ultimate Improvement Cycle or UIC," he explained. He continued, "UIC is an improvement methodology whereby the Theory of Constraints, Lean, and Six Sigma are blended into an improvement method that we think is much better than trying to generate improvements using each component in isolation." Three people put up their hands and all three wanted to hear more about this method.

Jonathan jumped into the conversation and explained that his plan was to have Tom come back to Corporate Headquarters to hear more about the Ultimate Improvement Cycle. In fact, Jonathan asked Tom if he could stay one more day and make the presentation. Tom agreed and the meeting came to an end.

REFERENCE

1. Jim Huling, Chris McChesney, and Sean Covey, 2012, *The 4 Disciplines of Execution: Achieving Your Wildly Important Goals*, Free Press, Milwaukee, WI.

19

The Ultimate Improvement Cycle

Tom, not expecting to stay an extra day, worked long into the night preparing his presentation for the next day at Corporate Headquarters. He had all of the slides he needed on his laptop, it was simply a question of putting them together to create a meaningful and informative flow of information. Tom worked until midnight and finally had his slide deck ready for their meeting in the morning. Even though Tom had worked so late, he still managed to wake up before his wake-up call, no doubt because he was excited about the day's presentation. Tom ate breakfast and went outside to wait for his ride to Corporate Headquarters.

He arrived at the Headquarters building and walked to the conference room to prepare for his day-long presentation. Jonathan was the first to arrive, followed by several of the CEOs and Board Members and each one greeted Tom and thanked him for what they had learned so far. When everyone was seated, Jonathan was the first to speak. "Ladies and gentlemen, I want to welcome everyone back today. I am very much looking forward to hearing what Tom will be presenting, especially because of the amazing results Tires for All has achieved over the past months. I encourage everyone to take prolific notes, simply because what you will be hearing today is something that I expect all companies in our portfolio to embrace and implement." With that introduction, Tom was asked to begin.

"Good morning everyone," Tom began. "What I want to present to you today lies at the heart of everything we have accomplished at Tires for All since we began our improvement efforts. This methodology has been dubbed The Ultimate Improvement Cycle and rightfully so, simply because we have achieved the ultimate improvement results. In front of you are three pages that contain the method, the tools, and the expected deliverables of this methodology. So, keep these three sheets in front of you as we progress through each one today," Tom suggested. "And as we go through my presentation, if you have questions or need clarification on any of the points I present, I want you to feel free to stop me," Tom added.

"When I first began my roles in various manufacturing environments, I really didn't know much about the inner workings of manufacturing facilities. I knew that you received customer orders, then you had to order raw materials, then create a production schedule, process them into a finished product, and then deliver them to a customer in a timely manner. I had no idea of the intricacies involved in doing all of this," Tom explained.

"In the years that followed, I began to better understand the different roles of other groups within a typical company and how they impacted the success of the company. I learned that processes don't always produce product according to plan because of things like downtime and quality problems. I also began to realize the impact and influence that we, as leadership, can have on any organization. Probably one of the most important things I learned was that the performance metrics we use to judge our performance have such an influence on the behaviors of the resources within our organizations. I've been at it for many years now and have come to some conclusions that I believe apply to all manufacturing companies, including Tires for All. Some of these conclusions directly contradicted what I had learned along the way from the various mentors and leaders that I worked for over the years," Tom explained.

"Before assuming my current role, I worked in Cost Accounting as a Director of Finance for Tires for All, and some of the things I learned in the past year absolutely shocked me! The first, and perhaps the most important conclusion of all, was my belief that Cost Accounting influences the behaviors of many manufacturing organizations in very negative ways. I had always been taught that if you were able to minimize the cost of each individual operation, then the total system would operate at minimal cost. I had also been taught that the total cost of each operation was directly proportional to the cost of direct labor for each operation, and that the total cost for the system, minus the raw material cost, would be proportional to the sum of direct labor costs," Tom continued. "But as you learned yesterday, when I presented the session on Throughput Accounting, what I had taken as being gospel, was pretty much bogus," he explained.

"Like most of you, I had also been taught that if I maximized efficiencies of each individual operation, I would have maximized the efficiencies of the entire system. I was taught that every operation was equal in value and that the key to increasing profits was to reduce the amount of money required to operate each individual process. In so doing, I was taught that manpower was expendable, so it was okay to lay off excess manpower," he explained. "Boy, how wrong I was!" he exclaimed. "Finally, I was taught that inventory was needed to protect all of the steps in the process, so that if we had downtime on the previous step, we could use inventory to continue running. In essence, I was taught that inventory was a good thing because it was impossible to avoid downtime and defects that resulted in rework and scrap. And besides, inventory was viewed by Cost Accounting as an asset, so how could it possibly be bad?" he explained with a chuckle. "Wrong again!" he said with a smile.

"Then Bob Nelson appeared on the stage and I realized that many of the things that I thought I understood, I didn't understand at all," he said. "Bob explained that maximizing the efficiency of each operation did not result in optimization of the total system at all. I learned that all it did was to create way too much work-in-process inventory. And speaking of inventory, I learned that Cost Accounting's belief that inventory was an asset was completely wrong! Why? Because it has a carrying cost associated with it. But even more important than this learning point was that excess inventory only works to increase the effective cycle time of processes, which decreases any manufacturing company's ability to ship product on time," Tom explained.

"There have been many other things I have learned since Bob came along. One of the most important learnings was that there is a better way to make the most of your precious resources. What I have to offer today is a way to make certain that your improvement effort is focused in the right place, at the right time, using the right methods and tools, and the right amount of resources to deliver the maximum amount of return on your improvement investment. This method, which Bob Nelson developed, addresses the problems associated with Cost Accounting, variation, waste, and performance measurements. But most of all, it focuses your organization on the right area which will optimize your Throughput, Operating Expense, Inventory, On-Time Delivery, Revenues, and Profit Margins," he explained in a passionate tone.

"I believe once you see the simplicity and logic behind what Bob Nelson refers to as the Ultimate Improvement Cycle, you will be motivated to move forward with it. The Ultimate Improvement Cycle is based upon the basic principles associated with Lean, Six Sigma, and the Theory of Constraints, but it's unique in that it capitalizes on a time-released formula for use of the key tools, techniques, principles, and actions of all three initiatives focused on the right area. Contrary to what you might think, it will not require any more resources than you currently have available. But having said this, it does provide the focus needed to achieve maximum resource utilization which translates into maximum return on investment," Tom explained. "If you follow the step-by-step method presented today, it will provide you with a self-funded improvement effort that will sustain itself," he stated emphatically.

Tom then explained, "One of the things that the Theory of Constraints tells us is that inter-dependencies exist within your operation and you should focus your efforts on the constraining operation. And while the Theory of Constraints provides this needed focus, Lean works to simplify and free your constraining operation of unnecessary waste. While Lean is doing this, Six Sigma removes excessive variation and defects within your system," Tom continued.

"Bob Nelson, our consultant, explained that the origin behind his Ultimate Improvement Cycle was based upon his many years of analysis of both failures and successes using Lean, Six Sigma, and the Theory of Constraints as stand-alone improvement initiatives. His analysis revealed a common thread between successful initiatives, no matter whether they were based on Lean, Six Sigma, or TOC models. He explained to us at Tires for All that the key to success is the leverage point, or where the improvement effort should be focused. While reducing or eliminating waste with Lean and reducing and controlling variation with Six Sigma are both critical components of all successful improvement initiatives, where these efforts are focused determines the ultimate impact on a company's bottom line. By integrating Lean, Six Sigma, and the Theory of Constraints into a single improvement cycle, you will have the needed recipe that will maximize your return on investment, cash flow, on-time delivery, and net profit," Tom stated emphatically.

Tom continued, "It's critical to remember that for-profit organizations exist for two purposes, which are to make money now and to make money in the future. Making money requires organizations to relentlessly remove excessive sources of waste and variation, so that their products and/or services are not only profitable but are consistently delivered on time and at the right price. What worked yesterday and today, probably won't work tomorrow or next year, so change is necessary. The good news is that it's much easier to manage change than it is to react to it. Because our products have such short half-lives these days, change must not only be expected, it should be pursued and embraced. Knowing what to change, what to change to, and how to implement change is usually the determining factor as to how successful an organization will be in the future."

"Many companies attempting either Lean or Six Sigma are having problems, but it's not at all because Lean and Six Sigma aren't good improvement initiatives. It's really a question of planning, execution, and focus and leverage. In more recent years, many companies have combined Lean and Six Sigma, but whether it's Lean, Six Sigma, or Lean Six Sigma, the hoped for bottom line improvements have simply not materialized to the extent many companies had anticipated, or at least were led to believe," Tom explained. "This was the case at Tires for All, but then we had an epiphany," he explained. "Our epiphany was that we were missing a key ingredient for our improvement effort to succeed," Tom explained. "So, with all this being said, let's get to the real reason we all came here today, how do we combine Lean, Six Sigma, and the Theory of Constraints."

And so, Tom began his explanation. "So just what would happen if we were to combine the best of all three improvement initiatives into a single improvement process? Just what might this amalgamation look like?" he asked rhetorically. "Logic would tell us that we would have an improvement process that reduces waste and variation, but primarily focuses effort in the operation that is constraining throughput." And with that, he loaded a new slide (Figure 19.1).

Tom then explained, "The figure you see on the screen is what is known to us at Tires for All as the Ultimate Improvement Cycle. The Ultimate Improvement Cycle combines the power of waste reduction from Lean, the variation reduction and control of Six Sigma, and the focusing power of the Theory of Constraints improvement cycles which forms the most powerful and profitable improvement strategy that exists today."

"This improvement cycle weaves together the DNA of Lean and Six Sigma with the focusing power of the Theory of Constraints to deliver a powerful and compelling improvement methodology. All of the strategies, principles, tools, techniques, and methods contained within each of the three improvement initiatives are synergistically blended and then time released to yield improvements that far exceed those obtained from doing these three initiatives in isolation from each other," Tom explained. "This

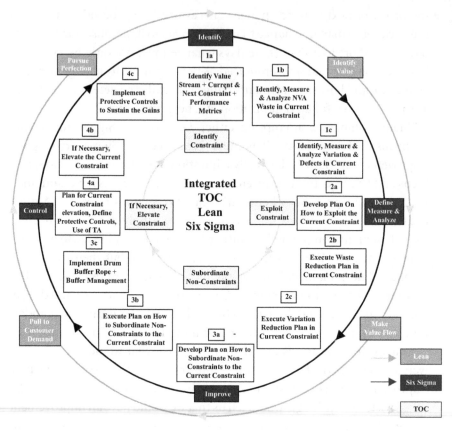

FIGURE 19.1
The Ultimate Improvement Cycle.

amalgamation of improvement initiatives was a turning point for Tires for All," Tom explained.

He continued, "Take a few minutes to digest the figure on the screen. You will notice that I used three different shades of gray to designate each of the components of each of the individual improvement methodologies. The actions in Steps 1a are aimed at describing the system we are attempting to improve by outlining the process value stream and identifying which step is limiting the full potential of the process, as well as the potential next constraint that would pop-up when we 'break' the current constraint. We are also interested in knowing what the performance metrics are in our system that drive the behaviors of the employees within our system."

Continuing, Tom explained, "In Step 1b, we are interested in locating the potential sources of waste that exist within our processes and system, but we do so only in the constraint. Although there will be a compelling urge to make changes during this phase, my advice to you is to wait. In this phase of the improvement cycle, we are only trying to define, analyze, and understand waste that currently exists in our process. By the same token, in Step 1c, we are looking for sources of variation within the process, again primarily in our system constraint. In other words, what are the things we see that are preventing our process from being consistent and stable? Keep in mind that the next phase deals with stabilizing the process by reducing both waste and variation in the constraining operation, so it's important, for now, to remember that we are simply trying to understand what is happening in our current process and more specifically our constraint operation." "Any questions so far?" he asked the group.

One question emerged from the group from one of the General Managers who asked, "Why are we only looking in our constraint?" Tom responded and said, "Although we will be focusing our attention primarily on the operation that is limiting our throughput, since the upstream and downstream process steps could be contributing to this limitation, they must be observed as well. For example, if an upstream process consistently stops the flow of product to the constraint, then we can't ignore it. Conversely, if a downstream operation is consistently losing constraint output to scrap or rework, then it can't be ignored either. In both cases, the result would be less than optimal throughput. But I want to emphasize, finding and eventually eliminating sources of excessive waste and variation in the system constraint is our ultimate objective. The reason I say this is because, if we want to maximize our Throughput, the constraint must become free of these sources of waste and variation," Tom explained.

With that explanation, Tom continued, "In the next series of steps, we are attempting to create stability. Before any process can be improved, there must be a focused plan developed or improvement efforts will become disjointed. In Steps 2a, 2b, and 2c, we are attempting to simultaneously both stabilize and improve our process. So, what does stabilize actually mean? Stabilizing means that we are attempting to make our process more predictable, reliable, and consistent. Steps 2a, 2b, and 2c serve primarily to reduce waste and variation within the constraint operation so that a new level of consistency and reliability are achieved," he explained.

Tom then explained further, "What we observed in the analysis phase at Tires for All formed the basis for our plan to achieve stability. It's important to remember that true and lasting improvement will never occur unless and until the process is consistent and stable over time. We will use a variety of tools and techniques during this phase of the Ultimate Improvement Cycle to accomplish this end. In order to achieve improved process flow, you must be patient and deliberate when reducing waste and variation," Bob explained. "Are there any questions about Steps 2a, 2b, and 2c?" he asked, but when there weren't any, he continued.

"In the next series of steps, we are trying to create both flow and pull. Specifically, the actions in Steps 3a, 3b, and 3c are intended to optimize the flow of products through the processes. Flow in this phase includes the flow of materials, information, and products through the process. Although we are seeking to create flow, creating it will also surface any problems that might inhibit it! So, in order to sustain flow, we must stop and solve these problems. Because of your past experiences, you might be tempted to fix these problems on the fly, but don't do it! You must begin to view problems as opportunities for long-term improvement, and not as a failure, so by stopping and fixing problems, it is actually a sign of strength in an organization," Tom explained.

"In this last series of steps, we want to take advantage of everything we've done so far by controlling the process in order to sustain the gains we've made. The actions taken in Steps 4a, 4b, and 4c serve to both increase constraint capacity, if we need to, and to assure that all of the changes made, and improvements realized, won't result in wasted effort. What a shame it would be to make big improvements that we can't sustain," he continued. "Remember, sustaining the gains is a hallmark of great organizations!" Tom emphasized. "So again, the four phases of the Ultimate Improvement Cycle are, analyze, stabilize, flow, and control, and each phase is critical to the optimization of revenue and profits."

Tom then explained, "The Ultimate Improvement Cycle accomplishes five primary objectives that serve as a springboard to maximizing revenue and profits. First, it guarantees that we are focusing on the correct area of the process or system, the constraint operation, to maximize Throughput and minimize Inventory and Operating Expense. Second, it provides a roadmap for improvement to ensure a systematic, structured, and orderly approach to assure the maximum utilization of resources to realize optimum revenue and profits. Third, it integrates the best of Lean, Six Sigma, and the Theory of Constraints strategies, tools, techniques, and philosophies to maximize your organization's full improvement potential. Fourth, it assures that the necessary, up-front planning is completed in advance of changes to the process or organization, so that your company will avoid the 'Fire, Ready, Aim!' mindset. And fifth, it provides the synergy and involvement of the total organization needed to maximize your return on investment."

Tom then turned to Jonathan and said he thought this might be a good time for the morning break. Jonathan agreed and told the group to be back in fifteen minutes. Tom then flashed a new slide on the screen (Figure 19.2), which would be used next in his explanation. Jonathan stepped up and told Tom that what he had explained so far was really informative, and that he could see all the companies in their portfolio using this methodology

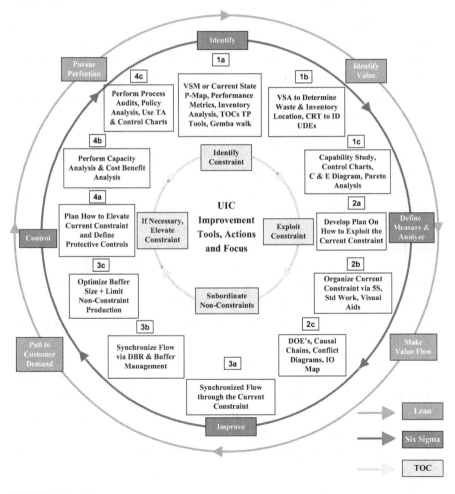

FIGURE 19.2
Tools, actions, and focus of the Ultimate Improvement Cycle.

going forward. Jonathan noticed the new slide and said, "This next section should really energize our audience today. While your first iteration of the Ultimate Improvement Cycle gave them an idea of what they should be doing in each of the steps, it looks like this section will define the actions they need to take and the tools they need to use to achieve the actions. I'm very much looking forward to the next section."

When everyone was back in the room, Tom began again. "So, now that you have heard what we're attempting to accomplish with each step of the Ultimate Improvement Cycle, you may be thinking, so just how do we accomplish each of the steps in the Ultimate Improvement Cycle? We do so by using all of the tools and actions that we would use if we were implementing Lean and Six Sigma as stand-alone improvement initiatives, but this time we focus most, if not all, of our efforts primarily on the constraint operation. The figure on the screen lays out the tools and actions we will use to perform at each step of the Ultimate Improvement Cycle. As you can see, there are no new or exotic tools that I am introducing. In creating the Ultimate Improvement Cycle one of Bob Nelson's objectives was to keep things simple, and I think you'll agree that he was successful in that the tools he's laid out to use are all of the basic and time-tested tools that have been around for years."

"As an example, in Step 1a, we will be creating a simple current state Value Stream Map to analyze things such as where the excess inventory is, what the individual processing times are, and the overall lead time within the process. We will use this tool to identify both the current and next constraint. We will also be looking at the current process and information flow and performance metrics to make certain that the metrics stimulate your company's workforce to exhibit the right behaviors and that they will, in fact, track the true impact of your improvement efforts," he explained.

Tom continued, "Likewise in Steps 1b and 1c, you will be analyzing your process by using simple tools like Pareto Charts, Run Charts, Spaghetti Diagrams, Time and Motion Studies, Cause and Effect Diagrams, and Causal Chains, as well as any other tools you think will give you the answers you need. In each phase of the Ultimate Improvement Cycle, Bob Nelson has recommended simple tools used to perform the tasks at hand."

"One last point we need to make is this. One of the primary reasons why companies have excess inventory on hand is to compensate for hidden problems, a kind of safety net if you will. Some people believe that there should be a radical inventory reduction to force the problems to the surface, but I adamantly disagree. As we discovered at Tires for All, most organizations aren't prepared to tackle these problems that have been covered up for so long. As inventory is reduced, these problems will surface and if the organization isn't prepared or capable of solving these problems, then improvements will not happen, and chaos will reign. There are many good books on problem solving, so my advice is to prepare yourselves now, rather than later. Now let's look more closely at each step in the Ultimate Improvement Cycle," Tom said.

One of the General Managers raised his hand and said, "In all my years in manufacturing, I have never heard improvement efforts explained in so much detail, and for sure, I have never been given a roadmap with such detail to follow. I am so very excited to use this methodology and can't wait to see the results we achieve at our company." One of the CEOs then raised his hand and said, "Tom, I too am excited about using this method, but I do have one question for you." "I'm sure there are expected deliverables we should be expected to deliver?" he asked. Tom responded and said, "It's ironic that you would ask that question, because in my next section, that's exactly what we will be discussing, the expected deliverables from the Ultimate Improvement Cycle," and with that said, he posted a new slide (Figure 19.3).

With the new figure on the screen, Bob then began his presentation on deliverables. "As I explained earlier, when Bob Nelson created this methodology, he wanted to keep everything simple, so as you can see, the wording is very descriptive, yet simple. In Step 1a, using things like Value Steam Maps, or simple Process Maps, or even Gemba Walks, you should come away with a complete picture of the system you're attempting to improve, in terms of flow, predicted people behaviors, and, of course, where your system constraint is located. In addition, you need to make sure that efficiency is now only measured in the step that is constraining system Throughput. This, of course, assumes that you have correctly identified the system constraint."

Tom continued, "In Step 1b, what you're attempting to gain is knowledge of both the location and type of waste within your system, plus the location of inventory, plus any potential core problems that might exist within the system you're attempting to improve. These problems could be a variety of different types of problems including things like high levels of work-in-process inventory, high levels of waste, or even excessive amounts of

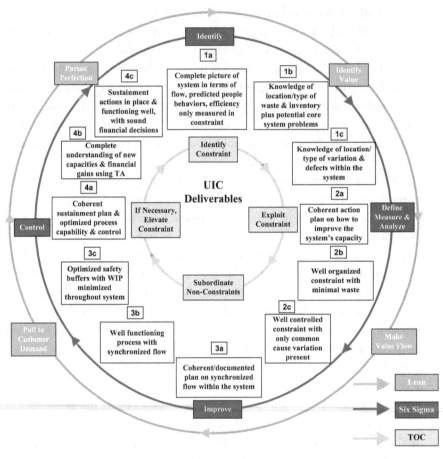

FIGURE 19.3
Deliverables for the Ultimate Improvement Cycle.

equipment downtime. Is this clear to everyone?" he asked, and everyone indicated that it was.

Tom continued his explanation of deliverables and said, "In Step 1c, we are interested in understanding both the location and type of variation we are experiencing, as well as any recurring defects that exist within the system being improved. In this step, you will be running Process Capability Studies, performing Pareto Analyses, creating Cause and Effect Diagrams, and maybe even creating some Control Charts on your key variables. This is a very important step, because recurring defects that result in either scrap or rework can seriously hinder the flow of products through your production system. It's important to remember that we are concerned with defects in the process directly feeding the constraint, because they might starve the constraint. Equally important are defects that occur after the constraint, because they would have a negative impact on the Throughput of your production system. In both cases, these defects could significantly reduce the Throughput of the total system, which could result in missed shipments and late deliveries of products to the end customer," Tom explained. "At Tires for All, this was a real awakening for us, because we had problems of this nature," Tom explained. "Any questions or comments on what you've heard so far?" Tom asked the group.

Once again, Jonathan raised his hand and said, "This makes perfect sense to me, but if I remember what you said earlier, we aren't supposed to take action on things just yet. Is that correct?" he asked. "Great question Jonathan," Tom responded. "The answer is, yes and no," Tom responded. "What we are attempting to do is only collect information so that we can develop a coherent strategic improvement plan. But having said that, the more sensible thing to do, if you found a problem that was fixable immediately, would be to fix it right away rather than waiting for a plan to be created before you took action," Tom explained. "Does that make sense to everyone?" Tom asked and everyone responded in a positive manner. "Are there any other questions?" he asked the group and when there weren't any, he continued his presentation on deliverables.

"In Step 2a, you will use the information you collected in Steps 1a, 1b, and 1c to produce an action plan on how you intend to improve the quality and capacity of the system you are trying to improve. You will, in effect, be using Goldratt's second step, 'exploiting' the system constraint. You should now know where the system constraint is located, the performance metrics that are in place, the location of excessive waste and variation, and you should no longer be measuring efficiencies in non-constraints. Here you are applying Goldratt's third step, subordination. My recommendation is that you should use your entire team to develop this plan and not just a single person. The plan itself should clearly identify specific actions to be taken," he explained. Tom continued, "In Steps 2b and 2c, your deliverable should be a well-organized constraint with minimal amounts of waste. In addition, after implementing your improvement plan, you should only have common cause variation present within the system being controlled and you will be using Control Charts to maintain control," Tom explained.

"Continuing, Step 4a's deliverable is a clear, well-documented plan on how you intend to synchronize flow throughout and within the system. Your plan should be focused on how to subordinate non-constraints to the current system constraint. And when you implement this plan, your result will be a well-functioning process with synchronized flow, using both Drum Buffer Rope and Buffer Management. In Step 3c you will have optimized your buffer size and you will have limited your non-constraint production by never outpacing the drum or system constraint. I can't emphasize enough how important this step is! Any questions here?" Tom asked.

Jonathan raised his hand and asked, "Just so everyone understands, how long do you estimate that should it have taken to get this far along on the Ultimate Improvement Cycle?" "Jonathan, while there isn't a specific amount of time expected to complete these first three steps, I would advise you not to apply a time limit. Obviously, if your process is already functioning well, then you might expect to complete this rotation fairly quickly. On the other hand, if your current system is delivering poor results, then it could take much longer to complete. The key point here is, I wouldn't rush through this process!" Tom explained.

With that question answered, Tom continued, "You want to make sure that all of the system improvements that you've made will remain in effect, so I advise you, at this point, to define some protective controls to guard against this happening. So, what I'm saying here is that your key deliverable in Step 3a is the development of a coherent sustainment plan which will include protective control devices and/or Control Charts. It would be a shame that after all of your plant's hard work to bring your process under control, that you could actually take actions that remove your control?"

Tom continued, "Having completed the first three major steps of the Ultimate Improvement Cycle, you should have significantly improved your production system. In fact, if you've done your work correctly, you may have already 'broken' your current constraint, but if you haven't, then you must develop a plan on how to 'elevate' the constraint. Remember back in Step 1a, I told you to identify both the current and next constraint? I said this in anticipation that the current constraint would eventually be broken and that a new one would immediately appear, so be ready to move to it," Tom explained.

Tom continued, "So, the deliverables for Steps 4a, 4b, and 4c would all be aimed at sustaining the gains you have already made. Your actions would include things like performing routine process audits and maintaining your process Control Charts. Another important deliverable in this step is at least a basic understanding of Throughput Accounting by everyone, including the shop floor employees. This is important because we want sound financial decisions to be made in real time. In addition, it is very important that the operators running the machines understand how Control Charts are maintained so that process control can be a way of life on the shop floor," Tom explained.

Tom continued, "So, this completes the first rotation of the Ultimate Improvement Cycle, but you're not finished yet. You must make sure that everyone is prepared to move to the next constraint immediately, which will appear when the current constraint is broken, and it will be broken if you follow these steps. By preparation, I mean that all of the sustainment tools we developed as we progressed around the Ultimate Improvement Cycle must be maintained if our improvements are to be sustained. This completes my presentation on the Ultimate Improvement Cycle, so I want to open the floor for questions, comments, and concerns," Tom stated.

Jonathan was the first one to comment and said, "I personally want to thank you Tom for your efforts this week at Corporate Headquarters. I have been to many training sessions on a variety of subjects, but I can honestly say that I have never been in a training session that was as complete and as informative as this one. So, Tom, I just want to say thank you again for the last two days. As I look into the future, I see very positive things happening at all of our portfolio companies! Why do I say that? I say that because I know that, if everyone follows the steps outlined in the Ultimate Improvement Cycle, we will have record profit margins across our entire portfolio. In addition to record margins, I see our on-time delivery becoming one of the best in the business!" he said.

Jonathan continued, "I want to make one thing perfectly clear to everyone here. I know I can speak for the rest of the Board of Directors, implementing what Tom has presented here today is not a request, it is a mandate!" he stated emphatically. "Tom will be available to all of your companies to assist you as you implement this miracle tool! I'm sure Tom will provide all of the necessary training needed in a timely manner for everyone in your facilities. But again, you don't have an option of whether or not to learn and apply this improvement methodology."

Jonathan then turned to Tom and asked if there was anything he wanted to say to the group. Tom stood up and said, "I think it's time to call it a day, so thank you again for taking the time to listen to what I had to say the past two days." And with that, the session ended.

20

The Portfolio Effort

Now that all of the training was completed for the CEOs and General Managers of the Board's portfolio of companies, it was time for Tom to begin his new role as the person responsible for driving profitability much higher. Tom was excited to begin his new role, but also concerned as to whether or not he would be successful. "The Ultimate Improvement Cycle (UIC) worked very well at Tires for All, but will it work equally well within the portfolio companies?" he thought.

Tom was waiting to receive an email back from Jonathan on the names and locations of all of the companies in their portfolio. He wanted contact names so that he could get copies of their most recent financial statements. Tom was interested in several primary performance metrics, which included on-time delivery, quality levels (scrap and rework), efficiencies, stock-out percent, and of course, profit margins. Like Tires for All, these would be his primary tracking metrics to understand how the improvement effort was coming along. The good news was that all but one of the companies in question were manufacturing facilities, so hopefully they would be able to share ideas and solutions. The one company that was not associated with manufacturing was strangely, a hospital.

Tom finally received an email from Jonathan with a listing of six of the portfolio companies (Table 20.1) that Jonathan wanted him to focus on first. In Jonathan's email, he stated that these six companies had the highest volumes of product and that if he could turn them around, the impact on total profitability would be huge. Tom smiled to himself and thought, "If I can correct most of these six companies, I can only imagine what my royalty dollars would be."

Tom spent much of the day reviewing the listing of companies plus what he could find out about them on the internet. He was not at all surprised

TABLE 20.1

Six Portfolio Companies

	Board of Directors Portfolio Companies						
Company Name	Primary Product	% On-Time Delivery	% Scrap	% Rework	Stock-Out %	% Efficiency	Profit Margins
Terox Automotive	Car bumpers	79.6%	4.1%	8.8%	10.7%	91.9%	4.9%
Sweeney Automotive	Auto parts	69.5%	3.8%	7.6%	11.7%	93.4%	6.1%
Johnson Electronics	Electronics	78.3%	7.2%	13.3%	10.9%	90.6%	7.7%
Westin Incorporated	Carbon powder	80.4%	9.5%	11.4%	8.8%	85.6%	8.8%
Watson Steel Products	Tire rims	77.8%	4.3%	8.8%	9.9%	90.4%	10.9%
Semena Rubber Products	Rubber raw mat'ls	80.2%	6.6%	6.7%	8.3%	86.2%	11.4%

to see that the performance metrics were not that different from Tires for All's before they began their improvement journey. One company on the list, Semena Rubber Products, was actually a supplier to Tires for All, in that they supplied the rubber raw materials needed to produce their tires. He also discovered that Westin Incorporated was a carbon powder supplier to Semena Rubber Products, who needed carbon powder to produce their rubber raw materials. "Sort of like a family," he thought. "If I could help Westin Incorporated improve their output, that would help Semena Rubber Products with their output, which would in turn, help Tires for All with their output," Tom imagined. So, with this family of products in mind, he decided that he would set up a meeting of these three companies to discuss potential improvement opportunities.

Tom arranged a meeting at the Corporate Headquarters in Chicago for the next day. The General Manager of Westin Incorporated, Bill Simpson, was the first to arrive, followed shortly thereafter by Jim Plankton, the CEO of Semena Rubber Products. And last, but not least, Mark Roder, the General Manager of Tires for All arrived. Tom had also invited Jonathan to be involved in this meeting as his time permitted. Once the introductions were completed, Tom began speaking, "I want to welcome you guys here and thank you for freeing up your schedule." He continued, "The reason

I called this meeting was because of the linkage your companies share together. My thinking was that if we can make improvements at Westin, that will help Semena, and ultimately, help Tires for All," he explained.

Bill Simpson was the first to comment, "After hearing what you had to say this past week on what's happened at Tires for All, I'm totally committed to making improvements at Westin." "Me too," said Jim Plankton from Semena. Mark then spoke up and said, "We have been very fortunate at Tires for All to have been involved in this effort. I never dreamed that we could improve our key metrics so quickly and so much. My advice to you is do whatever Tom tells you to do because it absolutely works! When we started with our consultant, Bob Nelson, I had my doubts, but when I saw the first set of results, I was convinced that what he had to offer was not only real, but it had lasting effects," Mark added. "I mean if you look at how our profit margins are now, which were around 10 percent when we started, they have grown to over 30 percent!" he explained.

"So, Tom, where do you plan on starting and when do you want to start?" Bill asked. "I'd like to start with your company Bill, and as far as when, just as soon as we can," Tom responded. "But having said that, Jim, I'd like to come to your plant as well so we can get some training done," Tom added. The three of them met for the remainder of the day and developed a schedule for Tom to come to each of their plants to start the effort. Just as they were about to end their meeting, Jonathan walked in and shook everyone's hand. "Sorry I couldn't get here sooner, but I had some important things to take care of," he said. Tom filled Jonathan in on their plans and then Jonathan said some compelling words. "I just want everyone to understand that whatever Tom wants you to do at your plant, do it!" he said emphatically. The meeting then ended, and everyone left to go home.

The next day, Tom flew to Boston, the home of Semena Rubber Products, to deliver two days-worth of training on the Theory of Constraints, but more importantly, the Ultimate Improvement Cycle. The training also included a session on Throughput Accounting to the members of the Finance Department and training on the Goal Tree. Tom used Tires for All as a baseline case study, demonstrating the before and after results that can be obtained if they just follow his lead. Teams were put together with specific actions that needed to occur over the next week. Some of these actions included determining where their system constraint was located, plus an analysis of waste and variation within it.

Before leaving, Tom led them through the creation of their own Goal Tree and demonstrated how to use it to assess the current state of each of the Goal Tree entities. And like Tires for All had done, they then used the assessment to create their strategic improvement plan. Tom indicated he would be in contact with Jim Plankton on a daily basis, but that he would return in two weeks.

Tom then traveled to Westin Incorporated, located in the southeastern corner of Alabama in the city of Dothan. Westin Incorporated is a producer of carbon powder, one of the ingredients needed to produce the rubber slabs that Tires for All receives from Semena Rubber Products and extrudes into various tire components, such as sidewall and tread rubber. Westin Incorporated produces large batches of carbon powder, and then ships it to Semena Rubber Products, who then turn it into the raw material slabs that are sent to Tires for All.

Westin Incorporated produces their carbon powder in large batches, and since their scrap rate of these large batches was relatively high at nearly 10 percent, Tom had an idea. He was thinking that they could significantly improve the flow of their products by reducing the number of batches that were scrapped. In effect, Tom was thinking that their scrap rate was their system constraint, and the best way to exploit the constraint in this case was to focus on the reasons the scrap rate was so high and reduce their incidence of scrap.

One of the major positive effects of reducing Westin's scrap rate on their batches of carbon powder would be a significant improvement in on-time delivery which stands at around 80 percent. The other positive impact of reducing their scrap rate would be that they would automatically increase the capacity of their plant, which could result in additional orders being fulfilled. This would increase their Throughput and add to their profit margins. Westin also has a relatively high amount of rework, at a little over 11 percent, so again, by identifying the major causes for such high rework, and then focusing improvements on those causes, they could again significantly improve the plant's capacity and on-time delivery. It's almost as if they have a dual constraint.

Tom spent the rest of the week providing training on the Theory of Constraints and the Ultimate Improvement Cycle to key members of Westin's staff and then walked them through the creation of their own Goal Tree. Like they had done at Semena Rubber Products and Tires for All, Westin Incorporated used their Goal Tree to first assess their organization's status and then create their strategic improvement plan. Before Tom left Westin, he and General Manager Bill Simpson developed a performance metric reporting system whereby Bill would report these metric results to Tom on a weekly telephone call.

During the next six months, Tom spent time traveling to the other portfolio companies and repeated what he had done at Westin, Semena, and Tires for All. In each location, he delivered the same training and led each of the companies through the creation of their Goal Trees and strategic improvement plans. And in each location, he established a performance metric reporting system with weekly conference calls to discuss their results. The results (Table 20.2) of everyone's efforts amazed the Board of Directors, not only because of the jump in profit margins, but because the results came so swiftly!

Things were going very well across many of the portfolio of companies and Tom was certainly building a name for himself as someone who could not only lead improvement efforts, but more importantly, he could deliver results. And while things were going well with the manufacturing companies, Tom received a call from Jonathan. Even though Jonathan was very happy with all of the results achieved so far with their manufacturing companies, they had one facility that he wanted Tom to look at improving. It was Saint Mary's Hospital located in Western Chicago.

Tom expressed some concerns simply because he had zero experience working in the healthcare field. But even though he had no experience, he was confident that the same tools, techniques, and methodologies would apply in the hospital. After a lengthy discussion with Jonathan, Tom agreed to travel to the hospital and see what he could do to improve things there. Jonathan agreed to call the hospital administrator, Cynthia Massey, to let her know that Tom would be coming the next day to begin an improvement effort. Because Tom lived in Western Pennsylvania, the trip to Saint Mary's Hospital would require a flight to Chicago. Tom called Cynthia to plan his first visit to the hospital and they agreed that Tom would arrive the next day.

Bright and early the next day, Tom arrived at Saint Mary's to begin his assessment of the hospital. Because of Tom's lack of experience in the healthcare field, Tom requested a tour of the major areas of the hospital. The tour included the surgical unit, the various hospital wards, the testing labs, and the emergency department. As they toured, Tom took prolific notes on what he had seen and when the tour was completed, he and

TABLE 20.2

Before and After Results

Company Name	Board of Directors Portfolio Companies											
	% On-Time Delivery		% Scrap		% Rework		Stock-Out %		Efficiency %		% Profit Margins	
	Before	After	Before	After	Before	After	Before	After	Before	After	Before	After
Terox Automotive	79.6	91.6	4.1	2.1	8.8	3.2	10.7	1.1	91.9	62.1	4.9	27.9
Sweeney Automotive	69.5	94.3	3.8	1.5	7.6	2.1	11.7	0.9	93.4	71.2	6.1	22.2
Johnson Electronics	78.3	92.2	7.2	2.2	13.3	4.2	10.9	1.8	90.6	65.7	7.7	30.4
Westin Incorporated	80.4	96.5	9.5	1.3	11.4	2.7	8.8	0.7	85.6	69.3	8.8	25.6
Watson Steel Products	77.8	95.5	4.3	2.2	8.8	3.2	9.9	1.6	90.4	70.5	10.9	30.8
Semena Rubber Products	80.2	97.7	6.6	3.0	6.7	1.8	8.3	0.2	86.2	71.1	11.4	28.8

Cynthia met in her office to discuss what Tom had observed and to get her take on how the hospital was performing.

Tom's first question revolved around the financial state of Saint Mary's and Cynthia's response was not a good one. It seemed as though this hospital vacillated between losing money and breaking even month after month. They also discussed the key performance metrics that they were required to track and report each month. This is where Tom wanted to focus his discussion with Cynthia, simply because if they could improve these key metrics, they could probably attract more patients which could add to their profitability. Tom recorded the list of key metrics and a brief explanation of each one, which included eight metrics (Table 20.3).

While all of these performance metrics are important, those metrics that interested Tom the most were those associated with time spent waiting. He believed that if the wait times could be reduced, then more patients could be seen and treated which could add to the hospital's bottom line. Tom was especially interested in the metric dealing with the Emergency Room. Tom asked Cynthia more specific questions about this metric and one of the areas that interested Tom the most was a sub-metric that involved patients in the process of having something referred to as a STEMI-type heart attack, with the actual metric being, Door to Balloon (D2B) time.

Tom didn't have a clue as to what D2B time actually was, so he asked Cynthia to explain it in more detail, but in simpler terms. Cynthia responded, "Door to Balloon is a time measurement in the Emergency Room/Cardiac Care Unit, specifically in the treatment of ST Segment Elevation Myocardial Infarction, or simply, a STEMI heart attack." Tom responded by saying, "What did you just say?" Cynthia chuckled and said, "The time interval starts with the patient's arrival in the Emergency Department and ends when a catheter guide-wire crosses the culprit lesion in the Cardiac Cath lab. In everyday language, this just means that a balloon is inflated inside one of the heart's primary blood vessels to allow unimpeded blood flow through the heart."

Cynthia continued, "The clock starts ticking either as a walk-in to the Emergency Department or in the field where a patient is being attended to by medical personnel. This metric is enormously important to patients simply because the longer this procedure is delayed, the more damage occurs to the heart muscle due to a lack of oxygen to the heart muscle. It's damaged because the cause of this problem is typically due to a blockage within the heart that prevents oxygen from being supplied to the heart,

TABLE 20.3

Key Hospital Performance Metrics

Metric	Metric Description
Average Hospital Stay	Appraise the amount of time your patients are staying in your hospital after admission?
Treatment Costs	Calculate what a patient costs your facility?
Hospital Readmission Rate	Calculate how many patients are coming back after they are discharged?
Patient Wait Time	Calculate your patient satisfaction score by assessing their average wait time.
Patient Satisfaction	How patients felt while being taken care of in your hospital?
Patient Safety	Identify any incidents happening in your hospital and reduce the patients' exposure to further risk?
ER Wait Time to See a Doctor	Evaluate the time patients spend from checking into the ER until they see a doctor.
Costs by Payer	Evaluate which type of health insurance they have and what it costs.

and without proper amounts of oxygen, muscle damage results. The inflated balloon 'unclogs' the blood vessel. Graphically, door to balloon might look like this (Figure 20.1)," as she loaded a picture on her laptop's screen.

Seeing this graphic image of what the procedure involved, made it much easier for Tom to understand. His conclusion was that this might be a good place to start the improvement effort within Saint Mary's. He then asked Cynthia if there was a specific metric value or standard that Saint

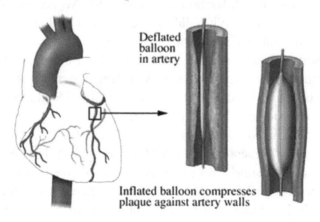

FIGURE 20.1
D2B Time graphic.

Mary's had to achieve. Cynthia replied and said, "Yes, the current median standard for D2B time is ninety minutes, and Saint Mary's was actually doing quite well against this standard." She continued, "We have a median score of sixty-six minutes, but we are anticipating that the standard will be changing to sixty minutes in the future." Tom then asked, "When you say median, do you actually mean that it's the average or mean time?" Cynthia responded and said, "No, for some reason this standard is tracked based on the median."

They continued discussing this standard and finally decided that this would be a good place to start the improvement effort at Saint Mary's. On further discussion with Cynthia, she explained that in addition to this new time benefitting the patient by experiencing much less heart muscle damage, there was also a financial incentive for the hospital. Apparently, reimbursement rates for Medicare and Medicaid patients are tied to completing the D2B time below the standard median time. They decided to put together a team of hospital subject matter experts to study the metric and look for ways to achieve this future target before it was mandated to do so.

The team was formed, and Tom conducted a training session for the team members focusing on how to use an integrated Theory of Constraints (TOC), Lean Six Sigma improvement methodology. Tom explained to the team that the Theory of Constraints and its Five Focusing Steps offers a much quicker solution to this type of project. When he described TOC's Five Focusing Steps, he used the hospital's jargon such as Figure 20.2 describes.

Tom also reviewed of the basics of both Lean and Six sigma and how to combine these three methodologies into a single methodology known as the Ultimate Improvement Cycle (Figure 20.3). Tom explained, "This a basic look at how these methods can be used together to generate improvements to any process or system being studied. Remember, the Theory of Constraints identifies the focal point for improvement, while Lean works to reduce waste and Six Sigma reduces and controls the variation within the process."

In addition, Tom displayed the UIC's tools and actions needed to implement the UIC as well as the expected deliverables. With this training in place, the team began their improvement effort by creating a simple Process Map (Figure 20.4) of another, lower level metric known as Door to Doctor process.

After completing the simple process map of Door to Doc time, the team was instructed to "Walk the Gemba" by going to both the Emergency

1. Identify the system constraint—In a physical process with numerous processing steps, like D2B Time, the constraint is the step with the smallest amount of capacity. Or another way of stating this is the step with the longest processing time.

2. Decide how to exploit the system constraint—Once the constraint has been identified, this step instructs you to focus your efforts on it and use the improvement tools of Lean and Six Sigma to reduce waste and variation but focus your efforts mostly on the constraint. This does not mean that you can ignore non-constraints, but your primary focus should be on the constraint.

3. Subordinate everything else to the constraint—In layman's terms, this simply means don't over-produce on non-constraints, and never let the constraint be starved. In a process like the Door to Balloon time, it would make no sense to push patients into this process, since they would be forced to wait excessively. But of course, the hospital cannot predict when patients with heart attacks will show up needing medical attention. But by constantly trying to reduce the constraint's time, the wait time should be continuously reduced.

4. If necessary, elevate the constraint—This simply means that if you have done everything you can to increase the capacity of the constraint in Step 2, and it's still not enough to satisfy the demand placed on it, then you might have to spend money by hiring additional people, purchasing additional equipment, etc. That is, anything that would reduce the time in the constraint. With a standard as important as D2B Time, this step would not be out of the question.

5. Return to Step 1, but don't let inertia create a new constraint—Once the constraint's required capacity has been achieved, the system constraint could move to a new location within the process. When this happens, it is necessary to move your improvement efforts to the new constraint if further improvement is needed. What is the thing about inertia? What this means is to make sure things you have put in place to break the original constraint (procedures, policies, etc.) are not limiting the throughput of the process. If necessary, you may need to remove them.

FIGURE 20.2
TOC's Five Focusing Steps.

Department and the Cardiology Department to observe what happened during the process and to have conversations with employees from both departments about problems they might have encountered. This was a fact-finding mission aimed at understanding how patients are managed through this treatment process. The team collected many observations during the walk, most of which would be used to construct their Current State Process Map for D2B Time.

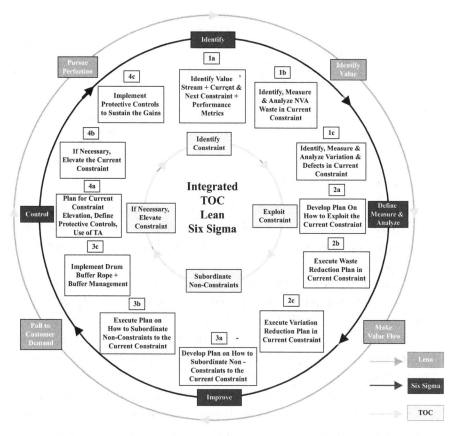

FIGURE 20.3
Ultimate Improvement Cycle.

The team then developed the following problem statement: *Hospital's current state cycle time is sixty-six minutes (median) for Door to Balloon Time when patients arrive at the Emergency Department and are classified as a STEMI candidate. The Hospital's goal is less than sixty minutes (median) 100 percent of the time.* In addition, the team set two primary performance goals as follow:

1. Hospital's median door to balloon time at sixty minutes or below.
2. Decreased door to balloon time will improve patient outcomes as measured by quality metrics. Additionally, these quality metrics are tied to the hospital's reimbursement based on the result of those outcomes.

The team then developed a business case for their efforts: *In addition to the quality and reimbursement benefits, this project will help in the marketing of*

**Door to Doctor Estimated Average Time:
88 Minutes**

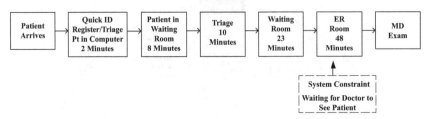

FIGURE 20.4
Current state Door to Doctor Time.

the hospital's cardiology services. Improved performance in quality metrics will lead to awards and preferred provider status. Examples include: Chest Pain Accreditation, Top 100 Heart Hospital, Blue Cross Distinction for Cardiac Care.

As a final step before their improvement work began, the team developed their performance metrics to be used to judge the final impact of their improvement efforts on D2B Time. These metrics were included in Table 20.4.

The team had access to D2B time data that had been collected on previous patients passing through this process. The team then analyzed the data to better understand what was happening on previous D2B events, and to determine the location of the constraint within this process. The team met with Tom and showed him what they had discovered (Figure 20.5) as a summary of this analysis before any improvements were initiated. They broke their analysis into three separate phases, which were Door to EKG, EKG to Table, and Table to Balloon.

Tom reviewed what they had done and then commented, "I really like the analysis you've put together as a team and how you've identified the system constraint in this system. Based upon your analysis, the first stage, Door to EKG, only takes an average of 4.75 minutes, while the second stage, EKG to Table, takes, on average, 36.7 minutes, while the third stage, Table to Balloon, takes 21.2 minutes. This clearly demonstrates where you must focus your improvement efforts and that is EKG to Table." Tom

TABLE 20.4

Performance Metrics for D2B Time

Metric/Unit: Complete cycle time in median minutes	Baseline: Median = 66 minutes	Goal: Future median = < 60 minutes	Future estimated median = 53 minutes

Door to Balloon Time after Improvements
Standard Threshold 90 minutes
Mean 52 minutes
Median 53 minutes

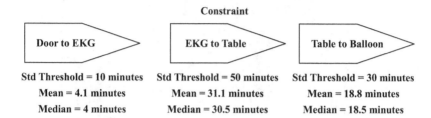

FIGURE 20.5
Door to Balloon Time Process.

continued, "I realize that you're measured on the median time to complete the full Door to Balloon Time, but my belief is that you should measure your progress using mean values, rather than median times. The reason I say this is because as you work to reduce variation in the system, the values for mean and median will come closer together and statistical tools and tests are all based on mean values. At any rate, this was a great first step," he concluded.

One of the tools Tom taught the team was an Interference Diagram, so he suggested that this would be a good tool to use to essentially dissect the process to develop improvement opportunities. Tom explained, "The purpose of the Interference Diagram, or ID for short, is to identify any barriers or obstacles or interferences that stand in the way of achieving a goal or objective." Tom then explained that the Interference Diagram can be used to develop an improvement plan on how to reduce the EKG to Table phase time. In the case for Phase 2, EKG to Table, the goal developed by the team was identified simply as "EKG to ED Exam Room Table Faster."

The team then reassembled and developed a list of "interferences" that stand in the way of achieving the goal they had set of reducing the EKG to ED exam room table time. One by one, the team recorded the interferences or obstacles that stand in the way of reaching their goal and created a slide to show Tom (Figure 20.6). They then called Tom and asked him to come to their meeting room so that they could have him see their completed Interference Diagram. Tom arrived minutes later, and they presented their finished product.

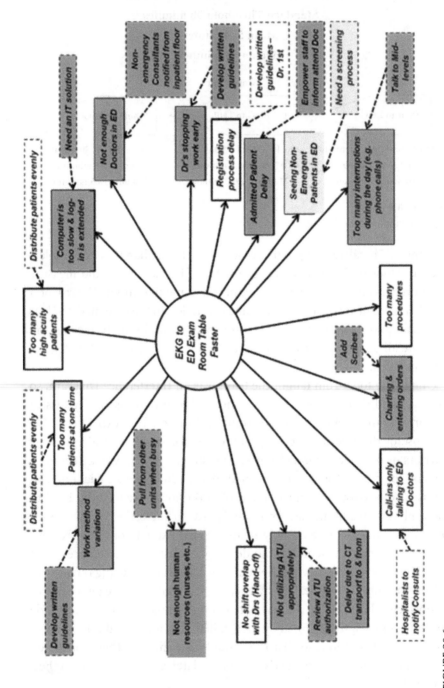

FIGURE 20.6
Completed Interference Diagram.

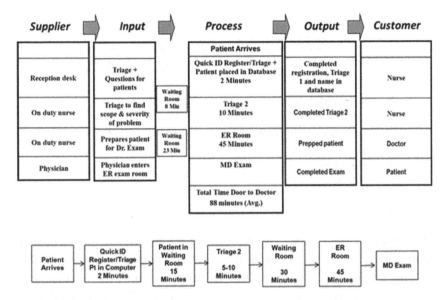

FIGURE 20.7
SIPOC Diagram.

Tom reviewed the work they had done, looked at the group and simply said, "Awesome work everyone!" The team leader walked Tom through the entire diagram, and he was very impressed to say the least. Tom had many questions about the writings within each box of the Interference Diagram, and without exception every question was answered to Tom's satisfaction.

Tom then spoke up and said, "I will be leaving Saint Mary's shortly, but the next thing I would recommend that you create is a SIPOC Diagram. In any process improvement activity, a SIPOC is a tool that summarizes the inputs and outputs of one or more processes in a table format." The acronym SIPOC stands for Suppliers, Inputs, Process, Outputs, and Customers, which form the columns of the table. Over the next week, the team worked hard to create the SIPOC Diagram.

They used their fact-finding "walks" (i.e., observations and conversations) and the Interference Diagrams to create it (Figure 20.7).

The team then created a series of process maps and did an excellent job of analyzing this important process and they were able to remove much of the waste contained within it. But the real improvement came in the overall potential time to complete the procedure, which had a significantly positive impact on damage to the patient's heart muscles when they implemented their solutions.

TABLE 20.5

Improvement Results Summary

Metric	Before	After	Improvement
Total # of Steps	69	42	−27
% of Value-Added Steps	38%	60%	31%
# of Swim Lanes	16	15	−1
Total Cycle Time	66 Minutes	53 Minutes	13 Minutes
# of Decisions	13	6	−7
# of Green Steps	26	29	3
# of Yellow Steps	16	10	−6
# of Red Steps	27	3	−24

When all of their actions were completed, the results they achieved impressed everyone at the hospital. The team decided to send an email to Tom, send him the results they had achieved, and then schedule a conference call with him. Tom received the email and immediately contacted the team at Saint Mary's to discuss their results (Table 20.5).

Tom was the first to speak and said, "I am amazed at how much progress your team has made on this very important metric, D2B Time! You were able to reduce the number of steps required from sixty-nine down to forty-two! That's a twenty-seven-step reduction, but another really important improvement is what has happened to the percentage of value-added steps which increased from 38 percent to 69 percent! But the most important improvement of all is the D2B cycle time which dropped from sixty-six minutes to fifty-three minutes! And after learning about how important this time is to a patient's heart muscle, this thirteen-minute reduction is a fantastic accomplishment!"

Tom knew that Jonathan would be interested in getting an update on Saint Mary's Hospital, so he scheduled a trip to Chicago for the next day. When he arrived, he drove his rental car to the hotel and decided to put together a brief presentation that he would deliver to Jonathan. In addition to the amazing work the team had done on D2B Time, there had also been other teams working on improving the other metrics, so he included some of them in his presentation to Jonathan. Tom put together a before and after review of some of the more important metrics that the hospital tracks (Table 20.6).

Tom was excited to meet with Jonathan and woke up early to review his brief presentation scheduled for 9:00 am. Tom drove his rental car to

TABLE 20.6

Metrics Review

Metric	Metric Description	Before	After
Average Hospital Stay	Time patients spend in hospital	4 days	2 days
Patient Wait Time	Average wait time for services	2 hours	1 hour
Patient Satisfaction	How patients feel about services	77%	95%
ER Wait Time	Time patients wait to see doctor	1.5 hours	45 minutes
Readmission Rates	Patient return after discharge	22%	8%

Corporate Headquarters and checked in. As he was waiting in the lobby, an emergency vehicle pulled up in front of the building, and several emergency workers came rushing in and took the elevator to an upper floor. It was now 9:30 am and he hadn't heard from Jonathan and he was getting anxious. He tried Jonathan's number several times, but there was no answer. He thought to himself, "Maybe I have the wrong day?"

As he was waiting in the lobby, the emergency workers exited the elevator pushing a stretcher very quickly. To Tom's surprise, it was Jonathan that they were rushing to the ambulance. Tom rushed to his side and he could see he was in pain. Jonathan recognized Tom and told the emergency personnel to wait and he motioned for Tom to come to him. "What's wrong with you Jonathan?" Tom asked. Jonathan replied, "I think I'm having a heart attack!" Jonathan replied. Tom looked at the driver and said, "Take him to Saint Mary's Hospital!" The driver agreed to do so and off they went. Tom jumped into his rental car and drove to Saint Mary's hospital and ran to the emergency room. Since he was not a close relative of Jonathan's, he was not permitted to speak to Jonathan and had to wait in the waiting room.

Tom noticed one of the members of the team, Janice Potts, that had worked on the Door to Balloon Time and motioned for Janice to come over to him. Tom explained that his immediate boss was one of their patients, apparently experiencing chest pains, and that he would appreciate and update on his condition. Janice agreed and said she would go find out and come back and let him know. He thanked her and patiently waited for her update, pacing back and forth. Tom knew the method they used to treat heart attack patients, or at least he did, if it was a STEMI-type one.

Five minutes later, Janice arrived back at the waiting room and told him that they had finished the first stage of treatment, otherwise known as Door to EKG in right around three minutes and that she would be back later to give him another update. She also confirmed that it was a STEMI-type heart attack. He thanked her and pulled up the data the team had given him on D2B. He saw that their new average time was around five minutes, but they had done it in three minutes. He was very happy with that!

He was waiting as patiently as he could be for Janice to come back with another update. It had been forty-five minutes since she last updated him and the data said that their new average time was right around thirty minutes for EKG to Table, so he was a bit worried that she hadn't updated him. Janice finally arrived and told him she was sorry she hadn't come sooner, but she got tied up with another patient. The EKG to Table time for Jonathan was an amazing twenty minutes, almost ten minutes below their average, so Tom was ecstatic and thanked her. Again, she told him she would be back when they finished the last stage, Table to Balloon.

Twenty minutes later, Janice returned and told him that they had finished inserting the balloon and that it only took them fourteen minutes to do so. Tom knew that their new median time was eighteen and a half minutes to complete so he did the math and discovered that the total time for Jonathan's procedure was not their new median of fifty-three minutes, but rather it only took thirty-seven minutes to complete the D2B Time. That meant that it was completed sixteen minutes below their new median time! Tom was so excited! Tom then checked to see which room he was admitted to and found out he was in the Intensive Care Unit and that he would be able to go visit him in about thirty minutes.

It seemed like thirty minutes was an eternity, but he was finally able to go visit Jonathan. He walked into the ICU unit and saw Jonathan talking to his doctor and his wife, Marie. Marie recognized Tom and invited him over. Tom hurriedly walked to Jonathan's bed and asked him how he was doing, and Jonathan said he was much better now. He also explained to Tom that the procedure he had just gone through was specific for a STEMI-type heart attack. Jonathan smiled and said he knew a lot about this type of heart attack. When Jonathan asked him how he knew about it, Tom just smiled and said that this was the first project the Saint Mary's team had worked on and that they had done a miraculous job of reducing the time from patient entry until the balloon is inflated and showed him his latest data on D2B Time (Figure 20.8) that he had planned to show him earlier at the Corporate Office.

Door to Balloon Time after Improvements
Standard Threshold 90 minutes
Mean 52 minutes
Median 53 minutes

Constraint

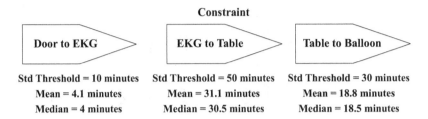

Door to EKG	EKG to Table	Table to Balloon
Std Threshold = 10 minutes	Std Threshold = 50 minutes	Std Threshold = 30 minutes
Mean = 4.1 minutes	Mean = 31.1 minutes	Mean = 18.8 minutes
Median = 4 minutes	Median = 30.5 minutes	Median = 18.5 minutes

FIGURE 20.8
D2B Time after improvements.

Jonathan and his wife Marie were totally surprised, but even more surprised when Tom explained how much time they had reduced the metric. But they were even more surprised when Tom shared the actual time it took to complete the procedure on Jonathan. Marie hugged Tom and thanked him for helping to save Jonathan's life. Jonathan shook hands with Tom and said, "I am so thankful that we made the decision to hire you to improve our portfolio companies. I never dreamed it would be a life-saving decision for me." Jonathan then asked to see the other results, but Tom declined and told him they would discuss them when he returned to work. He finished the conversation by saying, "Just so you don't worry, everything looks fantastic!"

In several weeks, Jonathan returned to work and immediately called Tom to schedule a meeting in Chicago. Tom was happy to hear from Jonathan and asked him how he felt, and Jonathan said, "Better than I have in years!" They chatted for a while and decided that later that week, Tom would come to Chicago and give him an update on all that was happening within their portfolio companies. Tom was so happy to be going to meet with Jonathan just to give him the good news about all of their portfolio companies. Tom decided that he would update the performance metric table of the portfolio companies and show it to Jonathan and the other board members, assuming they wanted to see it. Tom was very excited to be making the trip to Chicago, simply because of the current state of the performance metrics (Table 20.7).

TABLE 20.7

Portfolio Metrics Update

Board of Directors Portfolio Companies

Company Name	% On-Time Delivery		% Scrap		% Rework		Stock-Out %		Efficiency %		% Profit Margins	
	Before	After	Before	After	Before	After	Before	After	Before	After	Before	After
Terox Automotive	79.6	91.6	4.1	2.1	8.8	3.2	10.7	1.1	91.9	62.1	4.9	27.9
Sweeney Automotive	69.5	94.3	3.8	1.5	7.6	2.1	11.7	0.9	93.4	71.2	6.1	22.2
Johnson Electronics	78.3	92.2	7.2	2.2	13.3	4.2	10.9	1.8	90.6	65.7	7.7	30.4
Westin Incorporated	80.4	96.5	9.5	1.3	11.4	2.7	8.8	0.7	85.6	69.3	8.8	25.6
Watson Steel Products	77.8	95.5	4.3	2.2	8.8	3.2	9.9	1.6	90.4	70.5	10.9	30.8
Semena Rubber Products	80.2	97.7	6.6	3.0	6.7	1.8	8.3	0.2	86.2	71.1	11.4	28.8

Tom arrived at the Corporate Office, anxious to deliver the latest results to the Board of Directors. He arrived just in time for the 9:00 am meeting with the room full of board members. He walked them through the latest performance metrics (Figure 20.6) and he noticed that the room was full of smiles and side conversations. There were numerous questions until Jonathan stopped him and began speaking. "Tom, when we took you on in your current role, we expected big things from you. But I must say, we never expected the kind of results we are seeing today. So, congratulations on a job well done!" he said with enthusiasm.

The room, which had been relatively quiet, suddenly erupted in applause and then a standing ovation. Jonathan continued, "One of the things we agreed on was that you would receive a salary plus a percentage of profit margins and the percentage we agreed on was 1 percent of earnings improvement. Actually, at the time we referred to it as a royalty payment," he said with a smile and continued. "The board members and I had a long conversation last Friday and because the earnings have increased so much, we decided that we could not give you the 1 percent, but we did agree on a different amount. Just so you know, the combined profit margins for all of our holding, over the past year, have increased by $20,000,000. Jonathan handed Tom a sealed envelope and told him to go ahead and open it.

Tom was very concerned about the amount he was going to receive for the work he had done and was surprised that they would no longer agree to pay him 1 percent. Slowly, Tom opened the sealed envelope, looked at the cashier's check amount total. He looked at Jonathan with his eyes wide open and said, "Is this for real Jonathan?" Jonathan replied, "Yes, it is yours to keep! And as I said, as a token of our appreciation for the job you have done for us, we decided to double the amount of your royalty amount to 2 percent. Tom looked as his check again and couldn't believe that he was holding a check for $400,000! He was absolutely speechless! And then Jonathan said, "And one more thing Tom, I know we agreed that you would only receive this royalty amount for two years max, but we have decided to extend the payment to five years. Again, we just want to thank you for the amazing job you have done over the past year!"

Tom thanked Jonathan and the rest of the board members for giving him this amazing opportunity and again, applause filled the room. But Jonathan wasn't finished speaking. "I personally want to thank you for breathing new life into our portfolio companies, but more importantly, I want to thank you for breathing new life into me with the work you did at

Saint Mary's. I've had long conversations with the workers at Saint Mary's and they told me that they could never have done what they did for STEMI heart attack patients without what you taught them. So, the other thing we want to present to you is a lifetime seat on our Board of Directors, but with one caveat. You will continue in your present role of leading the improvement effort at all of our portfolio companies. And with that being said, this meeting is over."

The End

Index